Girls and Education 3–16
Con ... s,
New Agen ...

Girls and Education 3–16

Continuing Concerns, New Agendas

Edited by

Carolyn Jackson
Carrie Paechter
Emma Renold

McGraw Hill

Open University Press

Open University Press
McGraw-Hill Education
McGraw-Hill House
Shoppenhangers Road
Maidenhead
Berkshire
England
SL6 2QL

email: enquiries@openup.co.uk
world wide web: www.openup.co.uk

and Two Penn Plaza, New York, NY 10121-2289, USA

First published 2010

A catalogue record of this book is available from the British Library

ISBN 10: 033523562X (pb)   ISBN 13: 9780335235629 (pb)
ISBN 10: 0335235611 (hb)   ISBN 13: 9780335235612 (hb)

Library of Congress Cataloging-in-Publication Data
CIP data has been applied for

Fictitous names of companies, products, people, characters and/or data that
may be used herein (in case studies or in examples) are not intended to
represent any real individual, company, product or event.

Typeset by Aptara Inc., India
Printed in the UK by Bell & Bain Ltd, Glasgow.

Mixed Sources
Product group from well-managed
forests and other controlled sources
www.fsc.org Cert no. TT-COC-002769
© 1996 Forest Stewardship Council
FSC

The **McGraw·Hill** Companies

We dedicate this book to Diana Leonard

Contents

Part 2: Girls' experiences in the schooling system

Part 3: Relationships between girls' out-of-school experiences and school life

Contributors

Alexandra Allan is a lecturer in Education Studies in the School of Education and Lifelong Learning at the University of Exeter. Her research interests include gender, sexuality, childhood, social class, private education and single-sex schooling. Her publications include 'The Importance of Being a Lady: Hyper-femininity and Heterosexuality in the Private, Single-sex Primary School' (*Gender and Education*, 2009) and 'Bright and Beautiful: High Achieving Girls, Ambivalent Femininities and the Feminization of Success in the Primary School' (with Emma Renold, *Discourse*, 2006). Her current empirical research focuses on young middle-class girls' experiences of the private education system and their perceptions of risk.

Sheryl Clark is a PhD Candidate in Educational Studies at Goldsmiths, University of London. Her PhD explores the construction of girls' gender identities in the context of their involvement in sports and physical activities. She has published 'A Good Education: Girls' Extracurricular Pursuits and School Choice' in *Gender and Education* (2009) and 'Why Can't Girls Play Football? Gender Dynamics and the Playground' in *Sport, Education and Society* (2007, with Carrie Paechter). Sheryl's interests in sports and physical activities among girls have developed in conjunction with her own running pursuits; in April 2009 she ran the London Marathon for the first time.

Fin Cullen grew up in Lancashire and spent many of her teenage years drinking cider with friends in parks. She has worked as a youth worker, drugs educator, trainer and academic researcher. In 2007 Fin received her PhD from Goldsmiths, University of London for a study of young women's smoking and drinking cultures, and she is currently a lecturer at the Centre for Youth Work Studies, Brunel University. Her academic work to date has centred on children and young people's cultures and issues of gender and sexuality. She continues to manage and develop UK-based youth and community projects.

Jannette Elwood is Professor of Education at Queen's University Belfast. Her research expertise is in the field of examinations and assessment. She has published on the social consequences of assessment and examinations; gender and its interaction with assessment techniques and practices; the relationship between theories of mind and assessment. Research interests include sociocultural approaches to research in assessment; the impact of assessment on students' lives; theoretical and methodological issues in educational assessment research and practice. She is currently working on a 5-year longitudinal study of the impact of 14–19 qualifications on students, teachers and schools, funded by The Qualification and Curriculum Development Agency, England.

Becky Francis is Professor of Education at Roehampton University, UK. Her expertise and extensive publications centre on the production of subjectivities in educational contexts, social identity and educational achievement, and feminist theory. Her recently co-authored books include *Feminism and 'The Schooling Scandal'* (2009), *Reassessing Gender and Achievement* (2005) (with Christine Skelton), and *Understanding Minority Ethnic Achievement: Race, Gender, Class and 'Success'* (2007, with Louise Archer). She has also co-edited several readers on theory and practice in gender and education, including the *Sage Handbook of Gender and Education* (2006).

Rosalyn George was formerly a middle-school teacher and advisor for equal opportunities in an inner-city area. She is now Professor of Education at Goldsmiths, University of London. Her teaching and research are located in the areas social justice and education. Her current research is concerned with recent forms of migration and the impact this has for the promotion of non-colour-coded racism in schools. Her recent book, *Girls in a Goldfish Bowl: Moral Regulation and the Use of Power amongst Inner City Girls*, was published by Sense Publishers in 2007.

Valerie Hey is Professor of Education at the Sussex School of Education, Sussex University. She has recently been awarded an ESRC Seminar Series on 'Re-imagining the University' (with Louise Morley). She has a long-standing interdisciplinary interest in the cultural politics of education, especially in the production of intersectional forms of gendered and classed identities and in devising methodologies able to deconstruct them. She has published widely in the fields of gender and education, cultural studies, policy sociology, feminist theory and methodology, including recent publications in the journals *Higher Education Policy, British Journal of Sociology of Education, Journal of Education Policy* and *Gender and Education.*

Laura Hills is a lecturer in Sociology of Sport in the School of Sport and Education at Brunel University. Her research and teaching interests include gender, physicality and identity in the context of in/formal participation in sport. She is currently working on a project with the Football Association, on mixed-gender sport. Recent publications have focused on social and embodied aspects of girls' physical education experiences and intersections of gender, class and ethnicity in mediated sport. She is co-author of *Sport, Media and Society* (with Eileen Kennedy; Berg).

Carolyn Jackson is a senior lecturer in the Department of Educational Research at Lancaster University. She has published widely on aspects of gender and education, including on single-sex and co-educational environments, educational transitions, and the construction of 'lad' and 'ladette' identities. Her most recent book, *Lads and Ladettes in School: Gender and a Fear of Failure*, was published by Open University Press in 2006. Carolyn is now researching fear in education. As a 'sideline' she has also conducted research on the doctoral examination, and her book with Penny Tinkler – *The Doctoral Examination Process: A Handbook for Students, Examiners and Supervisors* – was published by Open University Press in 2004.

Jean Kane is a senior lecturer in the Faculty of Education, University of Glasgow. She works in the field of inclusive education with particular interests in social class and gender in education. Jane has been involved in a number of national and locally sponsored research projects in this area and has provided consultancy to local authorities seeking to develop more inclusive school provision.

Gwynedd Lloyd is an independent researcher and consultant. She has written widely about young people in trouble, gender and ethnicity in relation to inclusion/exclusion, and the medicalization of behaviour.

Gillean McCluskey is a lecturer in the School of Education at the University of Edinburgh. She has researched and published on issues surrounding exclusion from school. Her interests also include discipline and behaviour management in schools, pupil voice, and education for marginalized groups in general, and for Gyspy/Travellers in particular. Gillean previously worked in housing and in both mainstream schools and more specialized educational settings for young people with social, emotional and behavioural difficulties.

Jackie Marsh is Professor of Education at the University of Sheffield, where she is involved in research relating to the role and nature of popular culture, media and new technologies in young children's literacy development. Jackie's most recent publication is *Play, Creativity and Digital Cultures* (Routledge, 2008), co-edited with R.Willet and M. Robinson. She is a co-editor of the *Journal of Early Childhood Literacy*.

Barbara Martin recently gained her PhD in Educational Studies at Goldsmiths, University of London. She was a teacher in inner London primary schools for 20 years. Her research interests developed from her experience as a teacher and volunteer in early years settings. They include young children's gender identity development in the early years of schooling, the construction of young masculinities and femininities, and issues of social justice and equality.

Carrie Paechter is Professor of Education and Dean of the Graduate School at Goldsmiths, University of London. Her research interests, which have been developed out of her previous experience as a mathematics teacher in London secondary schools, include the intersection of gender, power and knowledge, the construction of identity, especially with regard to gender, space and embodiment in and outside schooling, and the processes of curriculum negotiation. She regards herself as a Foucaultian post-structuralist feminist in orientation and writes regularly on issues of research methodology in this context. Her most recent books are *Changing School Subjects: Power, Gender and Curriculum* (2000, Open University Press) and *Being Boys, Being Girls: Learning Masculinities and Femininities* (2007, Open University Press).

Emma Renold is a reader in Childhood Studies at the School of Social Sciences, Cardiff University, Wales. She is the author of *Girls, Boys and Junior Sexualities* (2005, Routledge) and co-editor of the international journal *Gender and Education* (with Debbie Epstein and Mary Jane Kehily). Working at the intersection of queer and feminist post-structuralist theory she has published widely on the gendering and sexualization of children and childhood across diverse institutional sites and spaces. Her current research project foregrounds locality, bodies, femininity and movement in a participative multi-modal ethnography of girls' negotiations of urban and semi-rural public space.

Sheila Riddell is currently Director of the Centre for Research in Education Inclusion and Diversity at the University of Edinburgh, and was previously Director of the Strathclyde Centre for Disability Research at the University of Glasgow. After seven years teaching English in a secondary school in the south west of England, she undertook a PhD at the University of Bristol on the topic of gender and subject option choice. Sheila moved to Scotland in 1988 and since then has researched and written extensively in the field of education, employment and social care policy, disability studies and gender and education.

Jessica Ringrose is Senior Lecturer at the London Institute of Education. Her research on intersectional femininities and competitive, heterosexualized aggression and bullying appears in *Feminism and Psychology*, *Feminist Theory*, *Girlhood Studies*, and *British Journal of Sociology of Education*. Her writing on post-feminism, neo-liberalism, class, and feminine 'success' can be found in *Gender and Education* and *Feminist Media Studies*. She is also interested in psychosocial research, and her writing on psychoanalysis, feminist pedagogy and racism is available in *Women's Studies International Forum*, and *Race, Ethnicity and Education*. Jessica is writing a book: *Postfeminist Education? Girls and the Sexual Politics of Schooling* (Routledge).

Farzana Shain is Senior Lecturer in Education in the School of Public Policy and Professional Practice at Keele University. She has written widely on issues of professionalism and managerialism in Further Education, but is known more recently for her work on youth and schooling. She is author of *The Schooling and Identity of Asian Girls* (Trentham, 2003) and *The New Folk Devils: Muslim Boys and Education in England* (Trentham, 2010).

Joan Stead is Senior Research Fellow at the University of Edinburgh. Her research interests include Restorative Approaches in schools; disciplinary exclusion from school; multi-agency working in schools; ADHD (Attention Deficit Hyperactivity Disorder). She has published widely on these topics.

Elisabet Weedon is Deputy Director in the Centre for Research in Education Inclusion and Diversity at Moray House School of Education, University of Edinburgh. Her main research interests are in the area of lifelong learning. She is currently working on a number of projects within the Centre including religious education in a multi-cultural society, dispute-resolution mechanisms in relation to additional support for learning, lifelong learning in Europe, and learning in the workplace, and has published research in this area.

Acknowledgements

This collection brings together research presented and discussed during a series of six seminars funded by the Economic and Social Research Council (ESRC; RES-452-25-4117). We are very grateful to the ESRC for their support. We also thank the Gender and Education Association (GEA) for providing co-funding, and Cardiff University, Goldsmiths, University of London, and Lancaster University for providing the venues.

The series was successful because of the enthusiasm, input and insights of all participants. The presentations and discussions were rich and engaging. The collaborations and friendships that were established and developed through the series are testimony to the stimulating and supportive nature of the events. We thank all participants.

Presenters, not all of whom have chapters in this collection, deserve particular thanks: Alexandra Allen, Louise Archer, Shereen Benjamin, Sheryl Clark, Michelle Cohen, Fin Cullen, Jannette Elwood, Debbie Epstein, Becky Francis, Rosalyn George, Valerie Hey, Laura Hills, Gabrielle Ivinson, Carolyn Jackson, Colette Jones, Jackie Marsh, Audrey Osler, Carrie Paechter, Emma Renold, Sheila Riddell, Jessica Ringrose, Farzana Shain, Valerie Walkerdine, Deborah Youdell.

Finally, we have decided to donate personal proceeds from this book to Camfed, 'an international organisation dedicated to eradicating poverty in Africa through the education of girls and the empowerment of young women' (see: http://uk.camfed.org/).

Introduction

Carolyn Jackson, Carrie Paechter and Emma Renold

This collection brings together UK-based research presented and debated at a seminar series also entitled Girls and Education 3–16: Continuing Concerns, New Agendas.[1] Our impetus for the series, which ran from 2005 to 2007, was a shared concern that issues relating to girls' schooling and femininities were sidelined and depoliticized in British education agendas. As we write this introduction – just over four years after preparing our seminar series proposal – we remain depressed by, indeed angry at, current policy agendas in which girls remain marginalized and boys continue to be a central focus. As Osler and Vincent (2003: 169) note, 'the efforts of policy-makers to address the needs of boys, examining apparent 'underachievement' and disaffection, have led to a neglect of girls' social and educational needs'.

The foregrounding of boys in educational policy has been driven and fuelled by various concerns about young males, but most notably by data suggesting that more girls than boys achieve A*–C benchmark grades in GCSE examinations taken in England, Wales and Northern Ireland (generally at age 16, the end of compulsory schooling), and by similar patterns in Scottish examination results. The narrowness of these drivers, which reflect the current emphasis on educational standards, means that policy concerns are centred almost exclusively on attainment and, more specifically, on raising boys' attainment (e.g. DfES 2003, 2007; DCSF 2007).

While it is clearly important to raise the educational outcomes of all students, the strategies implemented to raise boys' attainment can have negative consequences for girls. Charlton et al. document an example of this in their aptly titled article 'Sacrificial Girls' (2007), in which they discuss research undertaken in an Australian school that was renowned within the state for implementing boys' education programmes. Their study revealed that as part of one such programme some of the girls were placed in lower sets/streams than equally or lower-performing boys to ensure a gender balance across the groups. Charlton et al. highlight that 'the use of streaming and setting in the case study school demonstrates inequitable practices in that the process was not based upon concepts of merit . . . but upon a need to improve boys' academic outcomes through striking an artificial gender balance . . . We see this as part of a bigger picture occurring in education where boys' needs are prioritised over those of girls' (p. 460).

Although academic research is broader in focus than educational policy, studies of boys' schooling experiences have, nevertheless, dominated recent gender and education research: there has been what Weaver-Hightower (2003) referred to as a 'boy turn' in the field. Both the seminar series and this collection were prompted by our desires to add to the work that attempts to counter these two key trends, namely, the narrow focus on boys' attainment in educational policy and the more general turn to boys and masculinities in gender and education research. For too long the 'poor boys discourse' (Epstein et al. 1998) has overshadowed the problems faced by girls, and the assumption that 'girls are fine' (e.g. Williams et al. 2008) needs challenging. Our aim was and is to highlight some of the important issues faced by girls in Britain today, and to contribute to the important, and now growing, body of work that endeavours to put girls back on the educational agenda.

This refocus on girls and femininities is important as girls' experiences inside and outside school remain problematic in a number of ways. For example, it has been demonstrated that many girls face exclusion from schools (Osler and Vincent 2003); where choice is possible, subject choices tend to be gendered (Mendick 2006; DCSF 2007; EOC 2007); rates of smoking and drinking alcohol are high among some groups of girls (Fuller 2008; NHS Information Centre 2008); not all girls are academically successful (Francis and Skelton 2005; Connolly 2006); for some girls (perhaps especially middle-class girls) striving for excellence can be damaging for their bodies and subjectivities (Walkerdine et al. 2001; Evans et al. 2004; McSharry 2009; Rich and Evans 2009); the list could go on.

Countering claims that we are in 'post-feminist' times in which girls 'have it all' and can do, and be, whatever they like, the papers in this collection explore some of the current concerns of, and about, girls today. Many of the issues we raise have relatively long histories: they echo concerns about girls' experiences expressed by feminists in the 1970s, 1980s, and earlier (see Ivinson and Murphy 2007; Skelton and Francis 2009). Some continue to be relatively unchanged, for example, those about boys' domination of school space, and of teacher time and attention (Spender 1982/1989; Younger and Warrington 2005) and about the differential schooling experiences of working- and middle-class girls (Steedman 1982; Reay 2006a). In some cases the underlying problems continue, but they are manifest in different forms in 'new' times. For example, concerns about the ways in which girls (and boys) are portrayed in stereotyped ways in texts are certainly not new, but different contexts and spaces, for example virtual spaces and sites, provide new challenges and possibilities. Less commonly, new socio-political and educational landscapes produce novel concerns. For example, we are worried about the effects on girls of the requirements and pressures to succeed in all spheres of life, which emerge from what Harris (2004: 48) refers to as the 'fiction that all young women can be self-inventing, high-flying, and ideally placed to seize power in the new economy'. Throughout this collection, contributors attempt to grapple with the complexities of old, new and hybrid concerns and agendas for girls of different ages – from early years to the end of secondary schooling.

The concerns and agendas addressed by the various authors, while inevitably partial, reflect the particular socio-political, historical juncture at which we are located: a juncture at which neo-liberalism 'has achieved cultural hegemony' (Davies and Saltmarsh 2007: 3). Neo-liberalism is defined by Phoenix (2004: 228) as

> an economic system and philosophy based on laissez-faire free market values and freedom of globalized corporations. It enshrines values of competition, entrepreneurialism, market participation, privatization, lack of state intervention, individual responsibility (e.g., employability), surveillance, assessment, and managerialism.

Neo-liberal philosophy 'espouses survival of the fittest' (Davies and Saltmarsh 2007: 3), and the neo-liberal subject is expected to be flexible, autonomous, self-managing, and to invent and re-invent herself in order to be 'successful' (Walkerdine and Ringrose 2006). Furthermore, because neo-liberalism 'promotes a social world where the individual is fully self-responsible' (Aapola et al. 2005: 36), any problems are read as individual failings. It is within this context and climate that the contributors explore key issues facing contemporary girls: girls who are expected to negotiate enduring and new pressures in a 'post-feminist climate', and to navigate the problems and possibilities of femininity in the 21st century (Ringrose 2007; Renold and Ringrose, forthcoming). These explorations are organized in terms of three interrelated spheres of schoolgirls' lives, around which we have structured this collection: academic attainment; experiences inside school; and the relationship between girls' out-of-school experiences and school life. The next part of this chapter introduces these three spheres, and the chapters that relate to each of them. The final section of the Introduction offers some reflections on where this collection takes us, and why we should continue to be concerned about girls' in- and out-of-school lives.

Girls and Academic Achievement

The rise of the neo-liberal, market-driven, competitive state has led to a media-fuelled, government obsession with statistical measurements of academic 'achievement' (Francis and Skelton 2005). Over the last two decades we have witnessed an unrelenting education policy discourse of 'standards' and 'excellence', embedded in a performance and audit culture of testing, targets and tables. In this climate, success in examinations has been treated largely as an unqualified good. There has been little to no concern about what it means to struggle for, or accomplish, 'success', or about how the narrowly conceived 'standards' discourse, with its culture of excellence, relies upon and creates classed, gendered, racialized cultures of educational failure. In a chapter called 'Girls Will Be Girls and Boys Will Be First', Pat Mahony (1998) highlighted that the obsession with statistical comparisons was central to the production of the 'failing boys' discourse (Epstein et al. 1998). As predicted, this well-worn discourse of 'failing boys' continues both to contribute to a reactive, celebratory, post-feminist discourse of over-successful girls (Ringrose 2007) and to commonsense notions that girls have achieved equality with boys, or even surpassed them, in the educational race (Walkerdine and Ringrose 2006). In this gendered, zero-sum game, gender inequality is seen as no longer existing (Harris 2004), and boys and men are regarded as victims of the cultural shifts of the perceived new 'gender order' (Connell 1987).

For well over a decade the 'failing boys' discourse has been challenged by educational researchers in Britain and elsewhere, and it continues to be subject to critical scrutiny. However, despite these long-standing challenges, recent developments in policy and guidance suggest that the seductive discourse of successful girls and failing boys remains dominant. Although the UK Department for Children, Schools and Families (DCSF) acknowledges that 'many girls face significant challenges' (DCSF 2007: 6), and even that gender is not the main predictor of differential attainment, documents, guidelines and initiatives continue to foreground boys (DCSF 2007) and gender gaps (DCSF 'Gender Agenda' 2007–9). Policy discourse continues to treat social class as an outdated concept, despite enduring class inequalities (Reay 2006b).

In the context of the socio-political climate outlined earlier, this first section of the collection – 'Girls and Academic Achievement' – focuses on girls' relationships to, and with, achievement, 'success', and 'failure' (Archer 2005). The first two chapters (Francis and Elwood) outline the multiple effects of the persistent 'gender gap' discourse upon policy, assessment, and classroom practice. The remaining three chapters (Allan, Shain and Renold) offer intersectional analyses of the problematic relationship between 'femininity' and 'success' within contemporary neoliberal schooling, spanning 'failing girls' to 'supergirls'.

Drawing on Foucault's (1980) notion of the 'discursive unsaid', Becky Francis documents the marginalizing effects for girls of positioning them as the relational achievers to boys' 'under-achievement'. Francis illustrates how this process continues to 'count girls out' (Walkerdine et al. 1989) by ignoring those girls who do not achieve, and by failing to acknowledge the fraught relationship between social and academic 'success'. She draws upon recent research on the relationship between high achievement and 'femininity' to stress the challenges that secondary-school girls face, highlighting in particular the heterofeminine performances demanded of high-achieving girls if they are to avoid being constituted as unfeminine 'boffins'.

Taking issue with simplistic assumptions that fuel statistical representations of the gender gap, Janette Elwood illustrates how assessment instruments themselves create such performance differences by divorcing the 'socio-cultural' from the 'intellectual'. Foregrounding the inter-relationships of learning, mind and assessment as cultural practice, Elwood illustrates the danger of regarding any measuring instrument as gender neutral. She demonstrates how tests and tasks get disembedded from the social and cultural world of schooling, thus complicating any 'truths' about gender gaps as reflecting boys' and girls' real achievements. Elwood illustrates how teachers' gendered views of what girls can or cannot do mirror gendered legacies about girls' over-conscientiousness or boys' potential (see also Ivinson and Murphy 2007; Jackson and Dempster 2009).

Alexandra Allan draws upon a two-year ethnographic study of a single-sex selective school to explore middle-class girls' relationships to achievement and, in particular, the subjectification of 'success'. Allan analyses the experiences of girls in an elite, high-achieving school who were getting good results but were deemed by their teachers to be 'underachievers' because they were not performing as well as their very high-achieving peers. Hence, she suggests, even middle-class achievement is not a simple success story. She also explores the role of privilege in the subversion of normative femininity (e.g. 'rebel girls', 'bad girls' and 'misbehavers') and the classed and gendered antagonisms at play in the creation of insider and outsider cultures in an elite school.

Farzana Shain examines the relationship between achievement and the performance of Asian femininity. Drawing upon two research projects she focuses on low-achieving girls to explore: girls' collective response to institutionalized raced and sexual Othering; the significance of culture *and* class in girls' attitudes towards education; and the social and emotional impossibility of pursuing academic success and 'rebel' femininity. Shain suggests that we need to scrutinize the process by which the 'failure' of some Asian girls to conform to dominant representations of Asian femininity comes to be translated into academic failure. She urges us to consider critically the effects of assimilation and integration discourses that foreground the cultural practices of Muslim girls, and that shift attention away from economic problems and concerns affecting girls of South-East Asian heritage.

Emma Renold's chapter draws upon biographical case-study data from an ethnographic project of the everyday lives, identities and relationship cultures of children in public care. Through close analysis of one young woman's narrated journey through two years of school life (age 13–15), Renold explores what it means for marginalized girls to negotiate, and be positioned through, individualized and competitive cultures of schooling. Dovetailing policy analysis with empirical research, Renold examines the dynamic social, emotional and psychic costs and consequences, for girls in care, of surviving and succeeding at school. It is a story of the multiple ruptures and sutures (with friends, carers and teachers) required for the embodiment of success within the classed and gendered micro-socialities of schooling. The chapter highlights a theme that runs throughout this section and others, namely, the tensions that emerge for marginalized girls when they are compelled to perform passive, quietly clever (Jackson, this volume) 'girl-in-school'.

Collectively, the chapters in this section raise a number of ongoing and well rehearsed concerns regarding girls' complex relationships to achievement. The empirical analyses offered in each point to the persistent, uneasy fit between 'femininity' and 'success'. While the dynamics of this troubled relationship were documented by Valerie Walkerdine and others in the 1980s, the tensions seem to have intensified recently, as competing discourses simultaneously deny femininity, through notions of the individual learner, and demand particular versions of femininity.

However, while girls of all social groups are expected to embody nurturing good-girl femininity while acting as competitive neo-liberal learners, Renold and Shain's chapters point to the differential impact that such contradictory discourses have upon those positioned outside and inside normative, white, middle-class femininity. The social and emotional costs of girls' struggles to conform to, or resist, white middle-class norms can be high. The social aspects of success, and the relationships between girls and their families and communities more widely, are themes that punctuate the next two sections. These are themes that are largely ignored in the contemporary educational terrain, which is narrowly focused on disembodied asocial 'learners'.

Girls' Experiences in the Schooling System

The dominance of the 'standards' discourse and the concomitant focus on attainment has led to issues and concerns about pupils' *experiences* of schooling being sidelined or obscured. Given that school is one of the most significant social and cultural sites for the construction of identities and (peer) relations, the relative neglect of these areas is problematic. Furthermore, work that has been conducted on these aspects of schooling suggests there is cause for concern. For example, researchers have found problems for girls in terms of: teacher attention being dominated by boys and their concerns (Browne 2004; Francis 2005); alienation from 'masculine' subjects (Warrington and Younger 2000; Mendick 2006; Ivinson and Murphy 2007); homophobic and heterosexualized violence (Epstein et al. 2003); peer scrutiny and exclusionary hierarchies between girls (Hey 1997); and the everyday negotiation and performance of self under a growing number of public gazes (Eglinton 2008). These concerns have effects that last well beyond the period of compulsory schooling, from employment (Adkins 2002; Li et al. 2008) and motherhood (Thomson et al. 2008) to domestic and sexual violence (Walby and Allen 2004). In sum, the social learning that occurs in everyday school life – in classrooms, playgrounds, corridors and toilets (Gordon et al. 2006) – has significant effects on, and important implications for, girls' learning, school lives, and post-school experiences and prospects (Leathwood and Francis 2006; Paechter 2007). We do not have space in this section to cover all these key issues (see Arnot and Mac an Ghaill 2006; Francis et al. 2006; Skelton and Francis 2009 for more comprehensive overviews). We focus principally on power relations and the production of 'femininity' within the social world of the school. Each chapter picks up key themes from the previous section, developing, in particular, ideas about the significance for girls of their relationships with, and evaluations of, each other in complex circuits of power and knowledge. These social and cultural circuits both include and exclude, and produce yet another hierarchy of winners and losers, intensified by the competitive cultures embedded in schools' own official evaluation systems.

In the first chapter of the section, Rosalyn George develops the concerns raised by Shain around the politics of race and identity in relation to achievement. George does this through an analysis of the social dynamics of friendship during girls' transition from primary to secondary school. She investigates mothers' motivations for choosing particular schools for their daughters, and how these motivations influence the girls' relationships with their schools and peers. Like Shain, George contributes to the literature on what constitutes a 'successful' girl student by drawing on rich case study data from a longitudinal project. She explores how academically 'bright', Nigerian-born Leila and African-Caribbean Shumi use their friendship networks to renegotiate their relative marginality and reconstruct 'appropriate' femininities within white bourgeois school cultures. Both girls and their mothers articulate the need to tread a fine line between 'speaking up' and 'fitting in' to ensure academic success.

Contradictory demands from friends, family and community are constantly managed and negotiated. George joins Renold and Shain in calling for greater recognition of how discourses of resilience, strength and assertiveness challenge normative 'good-girl' femininity, yet continue to mediate 'black' dis/engagement with schooling and education. George argues that it is important not to treat 'race' as a unifying concept, but to consider it alongside other factors such as religion, family structures, and economic circumstances.

Laura Hills continues the exploration of how girls' friendships and social networks operate to construct and police 'appropriate' femininity, and how intellectual competence (academic achievement) is just one of many forms of capital influencing girls' school lives. Her longitudinal ethnographic research into early teenage girls' experiences of Physical Education (PE) brings issues of embodiment and physical capital to the fore. Drawing on Young's (1990) notion of a hierarchical 'scaling of bodies', Hills demonstrates the social importance of physical capital – from displaying the 'right' kind of body or sporting skills to the 'right' kind of clothes – by showing how it acts to consolidate social capital and recreate or confirm girls' existing social hierarchies. She notes how education discourses that privilege competition and elitism intensify public scrutiny, and exacerbate girls' 'defensive behaviours' as they strive to avoid failure.

Carrie Paechter and Sheryl Clark's chapter draws upon case study research into three all-girl friendship groups – the 'cool girls', the 'achievers', and the 'nice girls' – at a predominantly white, highly competitive, middle-class, outer London primary school. They explore the ways in which power/knowledge relations operate between and within groups of girls in ways that allow knowledge to be 'traded, accumulated, used and performed' and suggest that these are 'important for understanding the operation of competing friendship groups among girls at this age'. Paechter and Clark conclude that power/knowledge relations within and between girl groups have complex and multiple effects on girls' friendships, social status, and well-being in school. Their research suggests that what might appear as benign talk can be seriously destructive, as girls are caught in a power/knowledge nexus in which they might be objectified and humiliated, even as they attempt to consolidate their position in the hierarchy of girls by objectifying and humiliating others.

Barbara Martin's chapter takes us into the nursery to demonstrate how important it is for 3–4-year-olds to be 'correctly gendered'. Martin's observations illustrate how the colour 'pink' (on toys and clothes) continues to operate as one of the most powerful visual signifiers of 'girl'. Furthermore, it is drawn upon by both boys and girls to simultaneously uphold and subvert the symbolic gender binary system that keeps boys' and girls' social and cultural worlds apart. Martin discusses girls' heterofeminine desires and fantasies – reminiscent of Walkerdine's findings in the 1980s – where girls 'make themselves beautiful' for princes and imaginary 'boyfriends' (Blaise 2005). However, we also see examples of the girls' reappropriation of pink through discourses of girl power. For example, they claim territory and reinstate their domination by feminizing the climbing frame, and chanting, with fists in the air, 'this is girls' pink house, boys not allowed in'. Martin also draws our attention to the ways in which some teachers curb, through open disapproval, girls' reappropriation of power, while overlooking boys' everyday territorialization of space and materials. Martin calls for critical pedagogic discourses and practices that can intervene in the increasingly individualized discourses of developmentally appropriate practice, which ignore socio-cultural and structural power relations and continues to treat the symbolic gender order as a 'naturally' occurring state of affairs.

In the final chapter of this section, Sheila Riddell, Jean Kane, Gwynedd Lloyd, Gillean McCluskey, Joan Stead and Elisabet Weedon focus on school discipline and the construction of gender. In a context where boys continue to outnumber girls by 3 to 1 for both serious and daily acts of 'transgression', the team explore the gendered implications of 'gender-neutral' policies – in this case new disciplinary regimes – for addressing problematic behaviour. Riddell et al. critically evaluate a pilot project implemented in 18 Scottish schools. The project involved introducing restorative practice programmes to tackle problem behaviour (usually that of boys). Restorative practice approaches encourage students to resolve conflict through negotiation and mediation. The team argue that while restorative practices represent a new approach to behaviour management, they are steeped in traditional assumptions about girls and women, particularly regarding their responsibilities for curbing the destructive behaviour of boys and young men. The authors conclude that for restorative practices to disrupt rather than reinforce gendered power relations and normative performances in schools, boys and men must be involved more fully in the difficult processes of negotiation and mediation.

Relationships between Girls' Out-of-school Experiences and School life

This section explores the complex ways in which girls' experiences in school are mediated by local and global structures, networks and relations beyond school. Feminist scholars, particularly those working within the field of critical girlhood studies, are increasingly exploring these dynamic relationships (Aapola et al. 2005; Harris 2004; Mitchell et al. 2005, 2008; Nayak and Kehily 2008). As the work in this book shows, the gains made by some girls in education are represented and experienced in ways that can undo their 'successes', because of a reframing of what constitutes 'successful' femininity in the 'post-feminist' terrain. Representations of socially acceptable and marginalized femininities are increasingly central to this analysis. The chapters in this section point to how classed, racialized and sexualized discourses of 'new' femininities, such as 'girl power', co-exist alongside discourses of 'old' femininities in which girls are seen as being 'in crisis', or 'creating crisis' (Gonick 2004). This creates tensions and contradictions for, and between, girls, which we explore from various perspectives.

Each chapter highlights the balancing acts that mesh old and new regulatory discourses around the reputation, respectability and risk taking of 'good girls' and 'bad girls' (Griffin 2004). For example, they highlight the compulsory negotiations of 'sexy but not too sexy', and 'up for it' but 'not out of it' drinking femininities. New technologies and the temporal and spatial practices of consumption and commodification are central here. For example, we see that pre-school girls continue to navigate the heteronormative fantasy world of Barbie (Browne and Ross 1995), but now in the realm of the virtual. Gendered and sexualized objectification, subjectification and pathologization (Renold 2005; Youdell 2006) are key themes punctuating each chapter but with different and uneven effects, thus highlighting the continuing inequitable effects of social class. The final chapter (Hey) draws these themes together to explore contemporary gendered and classed deficit discourses representing girls, and how girls internalize and externalize the competing pressures of 'doing girl'.

Carolyn Jackson's chapter develops themes from the first section on girls' relationships to success by drawing on a study that explored 'laddishness' among 13–14-year-old girls and boys. Jackson considers the parallel and contradictory pressures on girls both to succeed academically and to appear not to work hard. She demonstrates how the masculinized notion of 'effortless achievement', previously considered to be a problem only for boys, is also an issue for girls. She documents how these pressures apply, and how girls deal with balancing academic and social demands, taking up many of the issues raised by Francis in the first section. The imperative to socialize with friends and perform hyper-femininities, in order to defend against the label 'boffin' or 'swot', is a constant feature of these girls' out-of-school experiences. Continuing a theme from previous chapters, Jackson highlights persistent issues of class inequalities, as the performance of the 'cool', 'have it all' girl demands access to particular sets of resources.

What constitutes 'cool', yet 'appropriate' femininity is taken up by Ringrose (in her discussion of 'pornification' and discourses of 'sexy') and Cullen (in her analysis of the drinking stories of girls). Jessica Ringrose discusses the ways in which girls and young women's online social networking sites reflect the increasing normalization of pornographic and sexual imagery. Old balancing acts between 'slag' and 'drag' reputations endure (Cowie and Lees 1981), while the 'pornification' of sexual culture is something that contemporary girls must navigate and appropriate. Exploring the blurring of on-line and off-line realities, Ringrose points to the complexity and contradictions involved in girls' collective social rejection and regulation of overt sexualization and sexual objectification in face-to-face contexts, while presenting highly sexualized images on their online sites. She argues that schools need urgently to find ways to address such contradictions and support girls in resisting this sexual commodification of their bodies.

Fin Cullen explores how teenage girls navigate appropriately 'risky' femininities through an analysis of their out-of-school drinking stories. She highlights how 'doing girl' successfully involves careful monitoring of drinking identities to ensure 'respectability' (Skeggs 1997) within increasingly competitive friendship cultures. Cullen reveals how drinking to excess incites contradictory discourses of individualization and conformity. Her chapter points to the importance of seeing girls' drinking as embedded within highly regulated social landscapes, and as contingent upon context, location and time.

Returning to the relationship between media and popular culture, and the gendered technologies of children's digital literacy, Jackie Marsh discusses the frequently overlooked relationship of young girls' home and school literacy practices. As in the nursery discussed by Martin, pink technologies abound in social networking sites for young girls, and the heterosexual matrix is writ large. The virtual world 'Barbie Girls' (which has 17 million registered users worldwide) operates as a young shopping heaven (see Russell and Tyler 2002) in ways that blur on-line and off-line practices and construct the young child firmly as a gendered consumer. Marsh argues that policymakers show little to no concern about the literacy practices and 'achievements' of girls, and so the gender equity issues associated with girls' digital literacy practices at home go unrecognized. She concludes that we need a critical literacy agenda that engages with girls' and boys' relationships to technology and popular culture in ways that challenge traditional constructions of classed and raced 'gender'.

The final chapter, by Valerie Hey, is a theoretical piece that takes up many of the key issues raised in this section and the collection as a whole. Hey considers academic and media representations of young women through a critique of Angela McRobbie's book, *The Aftermath of Feminism: Gender, Culture and Social Change* (2009). Many of the themes addressed in McRobbie's book have been taken up in direct and indirect ways in other chapters in this collection. Foregrounding girls and social class, Hey suggests that we need to continue to be mindful of the material and cultural aspects of difference, and how such differences are often articulated between girls, through what she calls 'the sociality of subjectification'. She argues that we need to interrogate the knowledge claims of contemporary girlhood studies, and to consider the legacy of feminism both for the girls under scrutiny and the scrutinizing researchers. Her psycho-social analysis of how research should provide a critical commentary of what it means for all girls to live in, and through, the individualizing logic of late neoliberal capitalist societies is an important one both for researching the 'can do girls' (including feminist academics), and those girls who are unmoved by appeals to 'get on' and 'get out'.

Where Does This Collection Take Us?

Where does this collection take and leave us? What should we conclude from the papers presented here? What remains to be done? Of course, collections such as this can only give a snapshot of what is happening, both in terms of time and in terms of focus. This is particularly true of this one, because of our desire to bring together research from across the age span of 3–16 years. On the other hand, including such a wide range of papers allows us to see broad commonalities and to illuminate some specific areas that should continue to concern researchers and practitioners working with school age girls.

It is clear from the papers in this collection that we are right to have continuing concerns about girls' experiences at school. The story told in both media and policy arenas of girls' unrelenting educational success, often at the expense of boys, is belied by the research presented here. First, success is clearly problematic for girls and brings with it a number of serious difficulties, including the need to preserve other aspects of self, and to project a public persona that is acceptable within the local girls' community. Second, there seems to be an unrelenting pressure on 'successful' girls to maintain high achievement in all aspects of their lives, not just in education: there is no let-up in the hothouse of some girls' worlds. Third, not all girls are able to attain educational success, and the continued exclusion of some not only remains strongly raced and classed, but has increasingly serious implications for future exclusion from social, working and public life. As we write, we are moving into an economic recession in which educational, social, and physical capital will matter more than ever before. The exclusion of some girls from the attainment of all three of these is therefore an increasingly pressing concern.

This collection also brings to the fore the extent to which some aspects of girlhood are important right through the 3–16 age range. The presentation of self as a 'proper' girl is particularly significant here. Although how this is demonstrated varies in age-relevant ways, the presentation of forms of peer-acceptable girlhood is shown by these papers to be a strong and perpetual element of what it is to be a girl in Britain today. From the ubiquitous wearing of pink at age 3 to the sexualized display of young women's bodies on Facebook at age 16, girls expect each other to conform to and display particular forms of femininity. Similarly, though girls' expected behaviour changes as they get older, the assumption that one will conform to gendered norms does not: girls expect each other, and are expected by boys and adults, to conform to particular stereotypes, and failure to do so is met by exclusion from the group and, in some cases, public moralizing.

That girls remain subordinate to boys in many aspects of their social lives is also apparent from the research shown here. While girls are described in the press as dominating educational arenas, and while some girls are extremely successful in school examinations, they have not been able to change gender hierarchies in classrooms or playgrounds. They are expected by teachers to service or support boys' achievement, subordinating their own learning needs to those of their male peers. They are excluded from areas within schools which have been taken over by boys, giving them, despite efforts on the part of many schools, less play and social space than is available to boys. Furthermore, despite girls' seemingly greater ability than boys to manipulate social worlds, they are unable to attain the summit of the classroom pecking-order, which remains reserved for dominant boys. All of this means that, as researchers and teachers, we need to continually remind ourselves that all girls, and their concerns, matter, despite the relative academic success of some of their number. This will require us to sustain our focus on the social and cultural aspects of girls' lives, both in and out of school, while maintaining a watchful eye on their academic performance and curriculum choices.

Finally, it is evident from the research reported here that, despite enthusiastic media discussion of the 'post-feminist world', in which the new young woman has an infinite variety of possibilities at her feet, this world is constructed in such a way as to exclude many girls. Of course such a world is in any case highly problematic: Angela McRobbie (2009: 130) describes it as 'a kind of anti-feminism, which is reliant, paradoxically, on an assumption that feminism has been taken into account', and, of course, it requires that the gendered oppressions detailed in this book no longer exist. However, even post-feminism as imagined by the media is strongly exclusionary. Where are the girls discussed by Renold or George? How can they possibly fit into such a supposedly liberated existence? The media hype about how girls and young women now 'have it all' simply indicates an increasing blindness to the realities of the lives of many of their number, who are not educationally, socially, or materially successful, whose bodies do not reflect popular stereotypes, and who, in the current hegemonic emphasis on boys, continue to be excluded from consideration. If, through this collection, we are able to show how important it is to continue to research and support all girls, within and beyond schooling, then we will have succeeded.

Note

1. Funded by the Economic and Social Research Council (RES-452-25-4117) and the Gender and Education Association.

References

Aapola, S., Gonick, M. and Harris, A. (2005). *Young Femininity: Girlhood, Power and Social Change*. Basingstoke: Palgrave MacMillan.

Adkins, L. (2002) *Revisions: Gender and Sexuality in Late Modernity*. Buckingham: Open University Press.

Archer, L. (2005) The impossibility of girls' educational 'success': entanglements of gender, 'race', class and sexuality in the production and problematisation of educational femininities. Paper presented at the ESRC-funded seminar series, *Girls in Education 3–16: Continuing Concerns, New Agendas*, Cardiff University, 24 November.

Arnot, M. and Mac an Ghaill, M. (2006) (eds) *The RoutledgeFalmer Reader in Gender and Education*. London: RoutledgeFalmer.

Blaise, M. (2005) *Playing It Straight*. London: Routledge.

Browne, N. and Ross, C. (1995) 'Girls' stuff and boys' stuff': young children talking and playing, in J. Holland, M. Blair and S. Sheldon (eds), *Debates and Issues in Feminist Research and Pedagogy*. Milton Keynes: Open University Press.

Charlton, E., Mills, M., Martino, W. and Beckett, L. (2007) Sacrificial girls: a case study of the impact of streaming and setting on gender reform, *British Educational Research Journal*, 33(4): 459–78.

Connell, R.W. (1987) *Gender and Power*. Stanford, CA: Stanford University Press.

Connolly, P. (2006) The effects of social class and ethnicity on gender differences in GCSE attainment: a secondary analysis of the Youth Cohort Study of England and Wales 1997–2001, *British Educational Research Journal*, 32(1): 3–21.

Cowie, C. and Lees, S. (1981) Slags or drags, *Feminist Review*, 9: 17–31.

Davies, B. and Saltmarsh, S. (2007) Gender ecomomies: literacy and the gendered production of neo-liberal subjectivities, *Gender and Education*, 19(1): 1–20.

Department for Children, Schools and Families (DCSF) (2007) *Confident, Capable and Creative: Supporting Boys' Achievements. Guidance for Practitioners in the Early Years Foundation Stage*. Norwich: DCSF Publications.

Department for Education and Schools (DfES) (2003) *Key Stage 3 National Strategy Gender: Raising Boys' Achievement – Key Messages*. Available at: http://publications.teachernet.gov.uk/default.aspx?PageFunction= productdetails&PageMode=publications&ProductId=DfES+0487+ 2003& (accessed 17/04/09).

Department for Education and Schools (DfES) (2007) *Gender and Education: The Evidence on Pupils in England*. Nottingham: DFES Publications.

Eglinton, K.A. (2008) Making selves, making worlds: an ethnographic account of young people's use of visual material culture. Unpublished PhD thesis, University of Cambridge.

Epstein, D., Elwood, J., Hey, V. and Maw, J. (eds) (1998) *Failing Boys? Issues in Gender and Achievement*. Buckingham: Open University Press.

Epstein, D., O'Flynn, S. and Telford, D. (2003) *Silenced Sexualities in Schools and Universities*. Stoke on Trent: Trentham Books.

Equal Opportunities Commission (EOC) (2006) *Facts About Men and Women in Great Britain*. Manchester: EOC.

Equal Opportunities Commission (EOC) (2007) *The Gender Equality Duty and Schools: Guidance for Public Authorities in England*. Available at: http://www.equalityhumanrights.com/en/forbusinessesandorganisa tion/publicauthorities/Gender_equality_duty/Pages/Genderequality dutydocuments.aspx (accessed 18/10/07).

Evans, J., Rich, E. and Holroyd, R. (2004) Disordered eating and disordered schooling: what schools do to middle class girls, *British Journal of Sociology of Education*, 25(2): 123–42.

Foucault, M. (1980) *Power/Knowledge: Selected Interviews and Other Writings*, 1972–1977. New York: Pantheon.

Francis, B. (2005) Not/knowing their place: gendered classroom behaviour, in G. Lloyd (ed.), *Problem Girls: Understanding and Supporting Troubled and Troublesome Girls*. London: Routledge.

Francis, B. and Skelton, C. (2005) *Reassessing Gender and Achievement: Questioning Contemporary Key Debates*. London: Routledge.

Fuller, E. (ed.) (2008) *Drug Use, Smoking and Drinking among Young People in England in 2007*. Available at: http://www.ic.nhs.uk/statistics-and-data-collections/health-and-lifestyles-related-surveys/smoking-drink ing-and-drug-use-among-young-people-in-england/drug-use-smok ing-and-drinking-among-young-people-in-england-2007 (accessed 14/4/09).

Gonick, M. (2004) Old plots and new identities: ambivalent femininities in late modernity, *Discourse: Studies in the Cultural Politics of Education*, 25(2): 189–209.

Gordon, T., Holland, J. and Lahelma, E. (2006) *Making Spaces: Citizenship and Difference in Schools*. Basingstoke: Palgrave Macmillan.

Griffin, C. (2004) Good girls, bad girls: Anglocentricism and diversity in the constitution of contemporary girlhood, in A. Harris (ed.) *All About the Girl: Culture, Power and Identity*. London: Routledge Falmer.

Harris, A. (2004) *Future Girl: Young Women in the Twenty-First Century*. London: Routledge.

Hey, V. (1997) *The Company She Keeps: An Ethnography of Girls' Friendship*. Maidenhead: Open University Press.

Ivinson, G. and Murphy, P. (2007) *Rethinking Single-Sex Teaching: Gender, Subject Knowledge and Learning*. Maidenhead: Open University Press.

Jackson, C. and Dempster, S. (2009) 'I sat back on my computer ... with a bottle of whisky next to me': Constructing 'cool' masculinity through 'effortless' achievement in secondary and higher education. Paper presented at the *Gender and Education Association 7th International Conference*, Institute of Education, London, 25–27 March.

Leathwood, C. and Francis, B. (eds) (2006) *Gender and Lifelong Learning*. London: Routledge.

Li, Y., Devine, F. and Heath, A. (2008) *Equality Group Inequalities in Education, Employment and Earnings: A Research Review and Analysis of Trends over Time*. Manchester: Equality and Human Rights Commission.

Lloyd, G. (ed.) *'Problem' Girls: Understanding and Supporting Troubled and Troublesome Girls*. London: Routledge.

McRobbie, A. (2009) *The Aftermath of Feminism: Gender, Culture and Social Change*. London: Sage.

McSharry, M. (2009) *Schooled Bodies? Negotiating Adolescent Validation through Press, Peers and Parents*. Stoke on Trent: Trentham.

Mahony, P. (1998) Girls will be girls and boys will be first, in D. Epstein, J. Elwood, V. Hey and J. Maw (eds), *Failing Boys? Issues in Gender and Achievement*. London: Routledge.

Mendick, H. (2006) *Masculinities in Mathematics*. Maidenhead: Open University Press.

Mitchell, C. and Reid-Walsh, J. (eds) (2005) *Seven Going on Seventeen: Tween Studies in the Culture of Girlhood*. New York: Peter Lang.

Mitchell, C., Reid-Walsh, J. and Kirk, J. (2008) Editorial, *Girlhood Studies*, 1(1): vii–xv.

Nayak, A. and Kehily, M.J. (2008) *Gender, Youth and Culture: Young Masculinities and Femininities*. Basingstoke: Palgrave Macmillan.

NHS Information Centre (2008) *Statistics on Alcohol: England, 2008*. Available at: http://www.ic.nhs.uk/statistics-and-data-collections/health-and-lifestyles/alcohol/statistics-on-alcohol:-england-2008-%5Bns%5D (accessed 14/4/09).

Osgood, J., Francis, B. and Archer, L. (2006) Gendered identities and work placement: why don't boys care? *Journal of Education Policy*, 21(3): 305–21.

Osler, A. and Vincent, K. (2003) *Girls and Exclusion: Rethinking the Agenda*. London: RoutlegeFalmer.

Paechter, C. (2007) *Being Boys, Being Girls: Learning Masculinities and Femininities*. Maidenhead: Open University Press.

Phoenix, A. (2004) Neoliberalism and masculinity: racialization and the contradictions of schooling for 11- to 14-year-olds, *Youth and Society*, 36(2): 227–46.

Reay, D. (2006a) Compounding inequalities of gender and class, in B. Francis, C. Skelton and L. Smulyan (eds), *Handbook on Gender and Education*. London: Sage.

Reay, D. (2006b) The zombie stalking English schools: social class and educational inequality, *British Journal of Educational Studies*, 54(3): 288–307.

Renold, E. (2005) *Girls, Boys and Junior Sexualities*. London: Routledge.

Renold, E. and Ringrose, J. (forthcoming) Phallic girls? Girls' negotiations of phallogocentric power, in N. Rodriguez and J. Landreau (eds), *Queer Masculinities: A Critical Reader in Education*. Dordrecht: Springer.

Rich, E. and Evans, J. (2009) Now I am NObody, see me for who I am: the paradox of performativity, *Gender and Education*, 21(1): 1–16.

Ringrose, J. (2007) Successful girls? Complicating post-feminist, neo-liberal discourses of educational achievement and gender equality, *Gender and Education*, 19(4): 471–89.

Russell, R. and Tyler, M. (2002) 'Thank heaven for little girls': 'girl heaven' and the commercial context of feminine childhood, *Sociology*, 36(3): 619–37.

Skeggs, B. (1997) *Formations of Class and Gender: Becoming Respectable*. London: Sage.

Skelton, C. and Francis, B. (2009) *Feminism and the Schooling Scandal*. London: Routledge.

Spender, D. (1982/1989) *Invisible Women: The Schooling Scandal*. London: The Women's Press.

Steedman, C. (1982) *The Tidy House*. London: Virago.

Thomson, R., Kehily, M.J., Hadfield, L. and Sharp, S. (2008) *The Making of Modern Motherhood: Memories, Representations and Practices* (Research Report). Available at: http://www.open.ac.uk/hsc/_assets/yqwnotatstun71rdbl.pdf (accessed 17/4/09).

Walby, S. and Allen, J. (2004) *Domestic Violence, Sexual Assault and Stalking: Findings from the British Crime Survey*. Home Office Research Study 276. London: Home Office.

Walkerdine, V. and the Girls and Mathematics Unit (1989) *Counting Girls Out*. London: Virago.

Walkerdine, V. and Ringrose, J. (2006) Femininity: reclassifying upward mobility and the neo-liberal subject, in C. Skelton, B. Francis and L. Smulyan (eds), *Sage Handbook of Gender and Education*. Thousand Oaks, CA: Sage.

Walkerdine, V., Lucey, H. and Melody, J. (2001) *Growing Up Girl: Psychosocial Explorations of Gender and Class*. Basingstoke: Palgrave.

Warrington, M. and Younger, M. (2000) The other side of the gender gap, *Gender and Education*, 12(4): 493–508.

Weaver-Hightower, M. (2003) The 'boy turn' in research on gender and education, *Review of Educational Research*, 73(4): 471–98.

Williams, K., Jamieson, F. and Hollingworth, S. (2008) 'He was a bit of a delicate thing': white middle-class boys, gender, school choice and parental anxiety, *Gender and Education*, 20(4): 399–408.

Youdell, D. (2006) *Impossible Bodies, Impossible Selves: Exclusions and Student Subjectivities*. Dordrecht: Springer.

Young, I.M. (1990) *Justice and the Politics of Difference*. Princeton: Princeton University Press.

Younger, M. and Warrington, M. (2005) *Raising Boys' Achievement in Secondary Schools*. Maidenhead: Open University Press.

Part 1

Girls and academic achievement

1 Girls' achievement: contesting the positioning of girls as the relational 'achievers' to 'boys' underachievement'

Becky Francis

Introduction

In the ongoing hyperbolic debate over 'boys' underachievement', it has become commonplace to assume that 'girls' do not warrant educational concern: as the discursive 'unsaid' (Foucault 1980) of boys' underachievement, they are the Achieving, or even Over-achieving, Girls. As such, while 'boys' continue to provoke anxiety and resources, 'girls' are seen as managing very well on their own.

Indeed, it is the unfortunate case that this ignorance of diversity among girls and their educational achievements, experiences and needs has extended beyond unawareness into actual projection of blame to girls for boys' apparent underperformance (Francis and Skelton 2005). For it seems that girls are absent from media and policy debates, *except* where they are invoked as the beneficiaries of apparent 'feminization' of schooling, and of equal opportunities policies that favoured girls at boys' expense. Of course there is a raft of feminist scholarship that both questions the extent of these imagined interventions on behalf of girls (Arnot et al. 1999) and explodes notions of 'feminization' of schooling (Epstein et al. 1998; Elwood 2005; Francis and Skelton 2005; Ivinson and Murphy 2007). Such discourses of disparagement and blame are clearly steeped in misogyny, and social priorities elevating the masculine can be identified from the very way in which the debate is coined as '*boys*' underachievement' (rather than 'gender and achievement'). As Skelton and I observe, there has been scant interest in, or attention to, the improved attainment of girls in some traditionally masculine curriculum areas, and possible explanations. Research funding has tended to be directed at research investigating the needs of boys, rather than girls, and the former research has received more attention from media and policymakers. We argue that this absence of discussion of girls constitutes a silent 'unsaid' in the discourse, revealing 'the marginalisation of girls, how their school performance is seen as peripheral to that of boys, how they *do not count*' (Francis and Skelton 2005: 104).

Therefore I want to use this chapter to counter some of the myths manifest in the panic about boys' educational achievement. Some might query the validity of another chapter focusing on gender and achievement. After all, the contemporary obsession with educational achievement, and the understanding of the expression of achievement as constituted exclusively by exam credentials, are products of twin neo-liberal trends. Namely, the human capitalist belief in skilled labour to ensure national competitiveness in a global marketplace (and exam credentials as indicators of 'skill'); and the belief that a marketized and differentiated education system can best ensure 'excellence' (or possibly will win best favour with key middle-class voters). These neo-liberal drives have certainly excluded alternative understandings of the value of, or what counts as, education. However, given their power, and their consequent effect 'on the ground' in terms of what and how teachers teach young people, and young people's consequent experiences of schooling, I feel it is vital that we continue to engage and challenge these discourses around achievement. Such 'speaking-back' may appear to fall on stony ground regarding policy influence, and perhaps may be seen to become repetitive, but I believe that by drawing on our research resources to insist on the inaccuracies of the dominant discourse, we at least maintain the existence of alternative discourses. Hence keeping open the possibility that these frail counter discourses may be mobilized and developed by researchers and practitioners working against the status quo.

Therefore, I shall attend to deconstructing two myths: that girls are unproblematically achieving in schools; and that high achievement is not problematic in relation to girls' social identities at schools. I begin by analysing the extent to which girls are 'achieving' in the education system, with attention to variables such as social class and ethnicity, in order to emphasize that not all girls *are* achieving. Having analysed the achievement figures, I then move to discuss research evidence that the policy focus on boys' achievement is further marginalizing these underachieving girls, with discussion of the consequences of strategies designed to 'raise boys' achievement'. There is increasing evidence that strategies introduced in schools to improve boys' attainment are negatively impacting on girls in terms of both achievement and experiences. Finally, I attend to tensions between high educational attainment and social identity for girls, drawing on recent research that illustrates how gender–sexuality discourses work to regulate girls and their productions of gender and achievement in the classroom.

Achievement Patterns in England

Even a cursory look at national achievement data, and the UK data presented in the OECD's (2007) PISA study, shows that in the UK, social class, rather than gender, is the primary predictor of achievement. This has been pointed out by very many educational researchers, and there have been a host of recent detailed statistical studies which illuminate these patterns (e.g. Blanden and Machin 2007; Cassen and Kingdon 2007). Table 1.1 illustrates this point in the case of England, using the indicator of Free School Meals (FSM) as a proxy for relative poverty.[1] Table 1.1 reports achievement at GCSE, the exams taken by all pupils age 16 at the end of Key Stage 4, the final stage in compulsory schooling.

Table 1.1 reveals a gender gap for both FSM and non-FSM groups (9 per cent for FSM pupils; 10 per cent for non-FSM pupils). But it simultaneously highlights a wider gap according to FSM: nearly double the proportion of girls and boys not taking FSM achieve 5 or more GCSE A*–C grades, compared with counterparts taking FSM. And this includes a gap of 19 percentage points between boys not taking FSM (56 per cent) and girls taking FSM (37 per cent); highlighting how (indicatively) middle-class boys tend to out-perform (indicatively) working-class girls. These GCSE results for 2006 provide a striking illustration of the way that in England, the social class gap dwarfs the gender gap for achievement.

Gender and race inflect with social class in sometimes unpredictable ways – social class and gender have a less significant impact on the achievement of some ethnic groups than others – but as the key predictor for the majority, we must not lose sight of social class in discussion of social justice

Table 1.1 Achievements at Key Stage 4 GCSE qualifications in 2006, by FSM and gender

| | 5 or more A*–C | | | | | |
| | Eligible pupils | | | %Achieving | | |
GCSE	Boys	Girls	Total	Boys	Girls	Total
FSM	39,498	38,589	78,087	28.7	37.4	33.0
Non FSM	261,971	252,545	514,516	56.2	66.0	61.0
Unclassified	814	717	1,531	42.3	47.7	44.8
All pupils	302,283	291,851	594,134	52.6	62.2	57.3

Source: standards.dfes.gov.uk/genderandachievement/understanding/analysis/.

and education; or of the point that this inequality remains a particularly British phenomenon (see OECD 2007).

Tables 1.2a and 1.2b are included to demonstrate the complexity in terms of patterns of achievement once ethnicity and social class (as indicated by FSM) are taken into account with gender.

Even if we concentrate exclusively on the most substantial pupil groups (as the numbers for some ethnic groups are very small), Tables 1.2a and 1.2b show the diversity of achievement patterning by ethnicity, social class and gender. The tables illustrate the trend to smaller social class gaps in minority ethnic groups irrespective of gender. So, for example, while there is a staggering gap of 35 percentage points between White British girls gaining 5 A*–C (non-FSM 66 per cent, FSM 31 per cent), and of 32 percentage points for White British boys (non-FSM 56 per cent; FSM 24 per cent), the social class gap is smaller for nearly all other groups. These figures reflect other data showing how some groups, such as young people of Black African, and Pakistani heritage – particularly girls – have increased achievement in recent years (Bhavnani 2006). And Indian heritage (and the smaller group of Chinese heritage) pupils continue to out-perform other groups. Conversely, the tables illuminate how, among groups of girls taking FSM, the largest group – White British girls – have virtually the lowest achievement figure at 31 per cent (excluding the 102 girls of Traveller/gypsy/Roma background). It seems important to point out that this puts this group of girls below the achievement of virtually all groups of boys not taking FSM, illustrating again the significance of social class for the White majority of pupils in the English education system. And the tables highlight the marginalization of working-class White British boys and those of Caribbean heritage, at 14 and 15 per cent gaining 5 A*–C grades (including Maths and English) at GCSE respectively.

In terms of gender, it is clearly the case that there is a profound gap for language and literacy. Even in this area some middle-class boys still out-perform working-class girls, but the gap is much smaller than for other areas, and the gender gap for literacy (especially wide for writing) extends across all ethnic and social class groups. This gender gap for literacy also extends across the OECD and partner nations, where in all cases the gap favouring girls is broad – indeed the UK has one of the smallest gender gaps for literacy, at (still substantial) 29 points (OECD 2007). The OECD PISA study tests 15-year-old students across 57 different countries (2006 assessments), and its results are useful for putting the panic over 'boys' achievement' into perspective. Of the subject areas measured, the UK has somewhat above-average achievement at science, and average achievement at maths and literacy. Average science performance for 15-year-olds showed no gender difference in the majority of countries, and where there were differences in either direction these were small. But there remain

Table 1.2a Achievements at Key Stage 4 GCSE and Equivalent in 2006 by ethnicity, FSM and gender (females)

	Non FSM				FSM			
		% achieving				% achieving		
	Eligible pupils	5 A* to C	5 A* to C including E and M	Any Passes	Eligible pupils	5 A* to C	5 A* to C including E and M	Any Passes
Ethnicity								
Girls								
White	217,990	65.7	52.0	98.3	26,901	31.6	18.4	93.8
White British	212,013	65.6	51.9	98.3	25,655	31.3	18.1	93.8
Irish	939	70.8	59.7	98.1	192	32.8	22.4	93.2
Traveller of Irish Heritage	36	41.7	27.8	88.9	33	3.0	0.0	69.7
Gypsy / Roma	70	15.7	7.1	72.9	69	5.8	4.3	82.6
Any other White background	4,932	68.9	55.8	98.1	952	43.5	26.6	96.6
Mixed	5,346	66.4	52.7	97.9	1,474	40.4	25.1	95.3
White and Black Caribbean	1,978	58.9	42.7	97.8	647	38.2	20.6	94.4
White and Black African	475	67.2	53.5	97.5	165	44.2	29.1	95.2
White and Asian	1,036	77.4	67.9	98.1	196	42.9	34.2	95.4
Any other mixed background	1,857	68.1	54.7	98.1	466	41.2	26.2	96.4

(continues)

Table 1.2a (continued)

| | Non FSM | | | | FSM | | | |
| | Eligible pupils | % achieving | | Any Passes | Eligible pupils | 5 A* to C | % achieving | Any Passes |
		5 A* to C	5 A* to C including E and M				5 A* to C including E and M	
Asian	12,881	70.6	56.5	99.0	5,111	56.7	36.5	98.3
Indian	5,732	78.3	66.6	99.5	749	62.6	45.5	98.0
Pakistani	4,249	60.5	43.0	98.4	2,359	52.4	31.2	98.0
Bangladeshi	1,322	64.4	46.5	99.4	1,628	59.7	38.5	99.3
Any other Asian background	1,578	75.0	64.5	98.7	375	59.5	43.5	96.8
Black	7,601	59.3	44.5	98.5	3,344	43.9	28.2	97.3
Black Caribbean	3,333	55.9	39.4	98.9	1,054	41.6	23.9	97.3
Black African	3,348	62.9	50.4	98.4	1,956	44.5	30.4	97.4
Any other Black background	920	58.8	41.5	97.4	334	47.3	28.7	96.4
Chinese	954	84.9	73.6	98.7	130	80.0	60.0	99.2
Any other other ethnic group	1,521	66.3	52.9	97.4	796	53.1	33.4	96.4
All Pupils3	252,625	65.7	52.0	98.3	38,625	37.0	22.3	94.9

Source: standards.dfes.gov.uk/genderandachievement/understanding/analysis/.

Table 1.2b Achievements at Key Stage 4 GCSE and Equivalent in 2006 by ethnicity, FSM and gender (males)

	Non FSM				FSM			
		% achieving				% achieving		
	Eligible pupils	5 A* to C	5 A* to C including E and M	Any Passes	Eligible pupils	5 A* to C	5 A* to C including E and M	Any Passes
Ethnicity								
Boys								
White	226,037	56.0	43.5	97.4	27,356	24.4	13.9	91.1
White British	220,081	56.0	43.4	97.5	26,011	24.0	13.6	90.9
Irish	848	63.4	52.6	96.5	182	26.4	16.5	92.3
Traveller of Irish Heritage	36	22.2	11.1	77.8	21	0.0	0.0	61.9
Gypsy / Roma	101	10.9	3.0	72.3	72	6.9	1.4	84.7
Any other White background	4,971	58.4	46.8	96.9	1,070	36.1	20.6	96.3
Mixed	5,123	55.8	43.8	97.1	1,377	29.2	18.2	93.5
White and Black Caribbean	1,803	43.6	31.6	96.2	613	26.8	15.0	93.6
White and Black African	475	56.2	43.2	97.9	126	34.1	20.6	92.9
White and Asian	1,050	70.2	60.3	98.3	163	34.4	27.0	94.5
Any other mixed background	1,795	59.6	46.7	97.0	475	29.3	18.7	93.3

(continues)

Table 1.2b (continued)

| | Non FSM | | | | FSM | | | |
| | | % achieving | | | | | % achieving | | |
	Eligible pupils	5 A* to C	5 A* to C including E and M	Any Passes	Eligible pupils	5 A* to C	5 A* to C including E and M	Any Passes
Asian	13,863	59.8	46.6	98.0	5,502	43.0	27.2	97.3
Indian	6,202	69.2	56.7	98.9	824	48.3	33.4	98.2
Pakistani	4,627	48.9	34.5	97.7	2,624	37.8	23.0	96.9
Bangladeshi	1,304	52.8	39.6	97.2	1,553	48.2	31.3	97.7
Any other Asian background	1,730	60.6	47.8	96.1	501	45.3	26.7	96.2
Black	7,456	44.5	31.2	97.0	3,350	31.1	17.7	95.8
Black Caribbean	3,177	38.8	25.0	96.6	1,024	27.1	14.7	94.9
Black African	3,272	50.6	38.0	97.4	1,939	33.7	20.1	96.9
Any other Black background	1,007	42.9	29.0	96.9	387	28.4	13.4	92.5
Chinese	1,019	75.8	60.7	99.0	123	65.0	46.3	98.4
Any other other ethnic group	1,700	55.5	43.2	96.2	934	41.0	26.0	95.5
All Pupils[3]	262,154	55.8	43.2	97.4	39,554	28.3	16.6	92.5

Source: standards.dfes.gov.uk/genderandachievement/understanding/analysis/.

gendered trends in perceptions of science and science ability which may explain later trends in subject take-up: males performed substantially better than females when answering 'physical systems questions'; and in the UK boys had significantly more positive attitudes to science than girls. The largest gender difference was in self-concept regarding science – males tended to think significantly more highly of their own science abilities than did females (echoing a raft of feminist work showing how boys tend to articulate greater confidence in their academic abilities than do girls). And males tend to out-perform females at maths: in 35 of 57 countries, males performed significantly better at the PISA assessments, including in the UK whereas females performed better in only one country, Qatar.

I have elaborated the complicated picture regarding gender and achievement, and the integral influence of factors such as social class and ethnicity on these patterns, to highlight the error of perceptions of boys as uniformly 'underachieving', and girls as achieving. I now turn to highlight the impact of such simplistic readings of 'boys' underachievement' on practice in schools.

Consequences for Girls of the Moral Panic Around 'Boys' Achievement'

Skelton and I have recently undertaken reviews of the literature concerning gender and achievement (Francis and Skelton 2005; Skelton et al. 2007). We identify a long list of explanations for the gender gap emerging from this literature, but the only one based on substantive research evidence is the social constructionist thesis that young people's gender constructions encourage them to adopt particular behaviours, some of which are less condusive to learning, or to identification with particular subject areas, than others. Classroom strategies that are based on notions of gendered learning styles and innate sex difference are not only lacking a basis in research but are shown to be ineffectual over a decade of application, wherein achievement results have altered very little.

However, the policy preoccupation with this issue has driven application of these strategies (often conceived as 'boy-friendly' teaching strategies and curriculum materials) so that they have been widely adopted in primary and secondary classrooms, often resulting in a range of inequalities. I include two notable examples of research evidence here to illustrate this trend.

First, research in an Australian case study school by Charlton and colleagues (2007) revealed ability sets being engineered so that the 'problem of boys' underachievement' was magically addressed – by allocating some girls to a set below their level so that they could be replaced in higher sets by lower-achieving boys. This school was offered to the research team as a case of potential good practice because it had as many boys as girls allocated as high-achieving. It was only on investigation that the researchers uncovered the practices used to achieve 'gender-equitable' streams. Simultaneous to this practice of moving boys into the high sets, a similar move was being made with the low sets, where lower-achieving boys were replacing higher-achieving girls in the middle set, with the unfortunate girls moved to the problematic bottom set, overtly as a classroom-management strategy to 'calm' this group of boys. It was these practices that led the researchers to title their paper on the subject 'Sacrifical Girls'.

Second, investigating English primary schools, Skelton and colleagues found a widespread reversion to teaching and management strategies based on gender, prioritizing the perceived needs of boys (Skelton and Read 2006; Skelton et al. 2009). They found that the discourse of 'boys' underachievement' established by policymakers in the 1990s had resulted in the rejection of many 'gender-equitable' practices established in the 1980s, in favour of teaching and classroom organizational approaches based on assumptions of essential gender difference. These included teaching to imagined 'gender learning styles' (though in fact these were usually geared to *boys*' perceived learning styles), and use of 'boy-friendly' teaching materials and curriculum content (usually premised on the basest stereotypes of what 'boys' like). Such normalization of assumptions about gender difference were shown to be infecting broader aspects of school life and organization, with practices such as lining boys and girls up separately after break and so on re-emerging (Francis et al. 2008).

Many of these strategies to 'raise boys' achievement' assume that educational attainment is unproblematic for girls. However, recent research contests such presumptions, as I illustrate next.

Problematic Relationships between Femininity and Educational Achievement

The reviews alluded to earlier have included the substantial feminist research evidence on the relative educational achievement of girls from different social class and ethnic groups; the different experiences and positionings of such girls within school settings, and the psychic and emotional impacts of such differing levels of achievement for those concerned (see chapters on girls and schooling in Francis and Skelton 2005, and Skelton and Francis 2009). It is not my intention to repeat that elaboration here (indeed, many of the authors in this collection have contributed to the body of work to which I refer, and their chapters are likely to develop these themes). However, I attend briefly to the continuing discursive tension between high achievement and femininity, in order to demonstrate how assumptions reflected in media and policy literature, that girls have an unproblematic relationship with achievement, are misguided.

Findings from a current research project on high-achieving pupils' gendered subjectivities[2] stress the challenges for these pupils in achieving the 'balance' between sociability and high achievement required to avoid being Othered as a 'Boffin' or swot (Jackson 2006; Renold and Allan 2006). The study is focused on Year 8 (12–13-year-olds) high-achieving pupils across nine secondary schools in urban, suburban and rural areas in Southern England. Research methods include classroom observation and individual interviews. We found that the largest group of the 71 high-achieving pupils sampled considered the 'balance' between high achievement and sociability particularly difficult for boys to achieve (see also Jackson 2006). It was often maintained by pupils that girls were under less pressure than boys to 'dumb down', as girls were less judgemental and more academically oriented than boys (Francis 2009). However, a considerable group of pupils (12) argued it is harder for *girls* to be popular and high achieving, and a further 18 maintained this 'balance' is equally difficult for girls and boys, lending support for that research illustrating the risks for girls in performing high achievement. As Renold and Allan (2006: 469) observe, "being the best" is rarely a desirable option for "nice girls" and "good pupils" (good citizens?), where sharing, caring, and essentially "fitting in" and conforming to normative and conventional feminine traits take precedence'.

Various feminist researchers have highlighted a specific tension for girls between academic and social success, given the powerful association of female academic attainment with a-sexuality. Walkerdine (1990) discusses how this discursive production draws on gendered binaries that locate rationality, reason and mind as masculine; irrationality, emotion and body as feminine. She maintains that for girls to produce themselves as academically successful involves an identification with the (masculine) Other. Perhaps no surprise, then, that various Second Wave feminist studies of schoolgirls in the 1980s found that in order to maintain heterosexual attractiveness girls played down their academic abilities (Gaskell 1992). Such tendencies are shown to remain evident today (Renold and Allan 2006). There is evidence from contemporary work that constructions of girlhood have broadened somewhat and, at least for some girls,[3] incorporate more positive views of academic achievement than in the past (Francis 2000; Renold and Allan 2006; Renold and Ringrose 2009). However, this is not to lend credence to the populist view of girls as 'having it all' (Harris 2004): the continuing social restraints that impact on girls in different ways depending on their social locations and identities have been well established. A number of researchers have emphasized the continuing tension between academic success and heterosexual attractiveness for girls (Hey 1997; Renold and Allan 2006). Mendick et al. (2008) assert that this tension is less acute for men: they point out that in the scripts of successful Hollywood movies such as *Good Will Hunting*, *A Beautiful Mind* and *Enigma*, some conventionally beautiful women are attracted by the male central characters' mathematical brilliance whereas no comparative scripts exist for mathematically brilliant women. Such themes were corroborated in our research on high-achieving pupils, with contributions such as that from Fred (Ironoaks School), who maintains that many boys would say 'eeugh' at the prospect of a clever girl, adding, 'as if to say like [in disgusted voice] "I don't want my girlfriend being smart and bodrick like"'. Similarly, the emphasis on 'looks' for girls as important for maintaining popularity simultaneous with educational achievement, emerged strongly in our data. Renold and Ringrose (forthcoming) argue that investment in aesthetic performances of hyper-femininity is one strategy via which some high-achieving girls maintain their construction of femininity.

As an aspect of this study, I have analysed the construction and Othering of 'Boffins'[4] in secondary school. Drawing on Butler's (2004) work on sexuality and abjection, it becomes possible to argue that boffins are abjected by other pupils for their lack of conformity to dominant accepted orders among the peer group. Discussing queer sexualities, Butler speaks of how the abjected Other (the queer) is symbolically cast out in a ritual performance necessary to draw and maintain the boundaries of 'normal' (heterosexual) sexualities. In this sense, the demonization of the identified abject, and the process of abjection, polices those incorporated within behaviours ascribed 'normal', by accentuating binaries of self and Other, and serving as a reminder as to the social consequences of 'abnormality' (or failure to conform). This analogy can also be applied to boffins, in their abjection for failure to conform to the dominant, gendered, social expectations of the classroom, and their subsequent marginalization as ridiculed and despised. In this sense it can be argued that boffins constitute Queers in the classroom. This argument is lent further support by the tendency we found for pupils to construct Boffins in terms of sexuality – male boffins as effete and/or gay, and female boffins as a-sexual (Epstein and Johnson 1998). The link between failure to 'do' hyper-femininity (with its inherent link to heterosexuality) and popularity is recognized by one of our Year 8 respondents, Stella (White, middle-class): she comments of her and her friends, 'If we didn't do well in school and we wore more make-up or we wore mini skirts we might be able to join the gang'. She discusses at length what she perceives as her lack of 'fit' because she is not prepared to compromise her high achievement, and does not wear make up or hyper-feminine fashionable clothing. Her words evoke the powerful heterosexualization of schools, and the observations by the researchers noted earlier concerning the firm associations of female academic achievement with a-sexuality. Further, Stella's interview indicates the painful consequences of such positioning as a-sexual for girls – in her case, the consequent interpolation to boffin status, which I characterize as that of Pariah (Arendt 1978; see Francis 2009). The normalizing heterosexual matrix produces girls/women as sexually available for men (Holland et al. 1998; Youdell 2005), and perhaps the female Boffin's lack of 'balance', prioritizing the academic over aesthetics, renders her Other in this regard. She is thus abjected in classroom relations and 'queer' in her lack of conformity to the demands of the heterosexual matrix (see also Epstein and Johnson 1998).

That one would need to engage 'girling' in terms of production of self, via both attire and demonstrated romantic interest in boys, in order to be more popular, is evident to Stella. Commenting that 'there's quite a lot of pressures to be in the popular group', she describes the efforts of one of her less popular friends to gain inclusion to the popular groups thus:

> R: . . . My best friend Launa she, she acts a lot more grown up than her own age and she's a proper emo[5] and then she decided she was going to get a pink Just Do It[6] bag and I was like 'no you're an emo, *pink?* you know, emos don't get pink Just Do It bags' and she got one, and then she decided she wanted to go out with four different people who are in the chavvy[7] group so, these two boys um, one of them is in my tutor group and one of them's in a different tutor group, they're like some of the heads of the chavvy boys – they took her out to Lewisham to try turn her into a normal person which is, like, a chav. Unfortunately all the money had been stolen off their card.
>
> I: oh no
>
> R: yeh but she didn't get turned into one, but she did *want* to be one, so that she could kind of be in the popular group and then go out with these people. I don't know, she's kind of gradually turning chav, but I don't want to say it to her cos she'd get really annoyed.

Clearly myriad themes emerge in this extract, including in/authenticity, remaking, gender production, betrayal, 'balance', heterosexuality and social class. Stella's account illustrates how the overt identity work undertaken by her friend to reposition herself as more popular sits in opposition to powerful discourses of authenticity that were hegemonic among our teenage respondents (who frequently articulated the importance of 'just being yourself'). And the way in which Launa's 'remaking' has involved her 'girling' and heterosexualization – which Stella, positioned as 'queer' Boffin, experiences as something of a betrayal.

Classed aesthetics of femininity and feminine popularity also emerge as a strong theme. In the context of her largely working-class school, the established (popular) feminine subject – the 'normal person', as Stella puts it – is what she constructs as 'chavvy'. White middle-class Stella positions herself as outside such normality, as the boffin-pariah. Yet her use of the word 'chav' serves to undermine this locally dominant working-class subjecthood, and reposition it as Other, via the middle-class discourses of excess and pathologization of working-class embodiment that the term 'chav' bears (see Skeggs 2004).[8] Hence wider social discourses circulating beyond the school are brought to bear in order to disrupt local constructions and reassert middle-class power. In this sense, middle-class boffins may draw on particular social discourses to rebuff or invest in their interpolation as boffins, and hence to reap educational capitals ensuing from this positioning. This is not, however, to downplay the painful psychic effects that Stella and other boffins have to endure in their interpolation to the category 'Boffin', which for Stella had involved processes of bullying and exclusion, and her contemporary ironic but somewhat resentful acceptance of her place in the social pecking-order.

The a-sexualization of the female 'boffins' explored in this study recalls similar a-sexualization applied to high-achieving British-Chinese girls in a previous study (Archer and Francis 2007), as well as one of the cases discussed in Renold and Allan's (2006) study of high-achieving girls. Elsewhere I discuss how for boys, Boffinhood is associated with (Other) sexuality but for girls with a-sexuality, and consider historic precedents for this dualism (Francis 2009). In terms of the female construction, for example, we may recall 18th- and 19th-century caricatures of the spinster governess or school mistress, and concerns that 'rigorous' education might render female scholars infertile. And in the early 20th century, the stereotype of the blue stocking; women more interested in academic pursuits than in heterosexual marriage. Significantly, lesbianism is the discursive 'unsaid' of such stereotypes: occasionally hinted at, but rarely openly articulated, in these demonizations (as too shocking a possibility to openly contend). Hence affirming the argument that in their refusal of/outsiderness to the heterosexual matrix, female 'boffins' signify as queer in the classroom. Such findings highlight the ongoing tensions between productions of femininity, educational attainment, and heterosexuality, illustrating the point that relationships between academic achievement and social identity are far from straightforward.

Conclusion

What is clear is that girls' academic attainment remains an important and complex issue. At a macro level, the extent of girls 'achievement' is patterned by variables such as ethnicity and social class and is as well concentrated around particular areas of the curriculum which reflect social constructions of gender. The silencing of such inequalities by the exclusive focus on boys reflected in recent policy making and media commentary constitutes an important issue for (lack of) gender justice. And I hope to have illustrated how, at the micro level, girls' relationship with academic achievement remains socially and psychically fraught, given the still prevalent binary productions that position heterosexual femininity as in tension with cleverness. Feminist research in this field is playing a vital role in contesting discourses that dismiss girls' academic attainment as beyond concern.

Notes

1. It is acknowledged that Free School Meals is an unsatisfactory indicator of social class, yet it is the only indicative record maintained by schools (Archer and Francis 2007).
2. ESRC-funded project 'The Gendered Subjectivities of High Achieving Pupils' (RES062230462), by Francis, Skelton and Read.
3. Often middle-class and/or minority ethnic girls, but sometimes working-class White girls too.
4. Variously termed 'keenos', 'keeners', 'nerds', 'boffs', 'bods', 'bodricks', 'geeks'. All these terms to some extent evoke academic achievement and poor social skills (Francis 2009).
5. 'Emo' represents an 'alternative look', tending towards the 'goth' fashions of black, scruffy clothes and a rejection of hyper-masculine or feminine aesthetics.
6. Nike sportswear slogan.
7. 'Chav' denotes a person from working-class/deprived social background who wears ostentatious designer clothes and sportswear. The term evokes the notion of 'common' attitudes and aesthetic expression, fundamentally producing an essentialization of poverty.
8. Although the term 'chav' was used by both middle- and working-class pupils, it was effectively applied to working-class pupils, and not 'owned' by any pupils we interviewed.

References

Archer, L. and Francis, B. (2007) *Understanding Minority Ethnic Achievement.* London: Routledge.

Arendt, H. (1978) *The Jew as Pariah: Jewish Identity and Politics in the Modern Age.* New York: Grove Press.

Arnot, M., David, M. and Weiner, G. (1999) *Closing the Gender Gap*. Cambridge: Polity Press.

Bhavnani, R. (2006) *Ahead of the Game: The Changing Aspirations of Young Ethnic Minority Women*. Manchester: Equal Opportunities Commission.

Blanden, J. and Machin, S. (2007) *Recent Changes in Intergenerational Mobility in Britain*. London: The Sutton Trust.

Butler, J. (2004) *Undoing Gender*. London: Routledge.

Cassen, R. and Kingdon, G. (2007) *Tackling Low Educational Achievement*. York: Joseph Rowntree Foundation.

Charlton, E., Mills, M., Martino, W. and Beckett, L. (2007) Sacrificial girls: a case study of the impact of streaming and setting on gender reform, *British Educational Research Journal*, 33(4): 459–78.

Elwood, J. (2005) Gender and achievement: what have exams got to do with it?, *Oxford Review of Education*, 31(3): 373–93.

Epstein, D. and Johnson, R. (1998) *Schooling Sexualities*. Buckingham: Open University Press.

Epstein, D., Elwood, J., Hey, V. and Maw, J. (eds) (1998) *Failing Boys?* Buckingham: Open University Press.

Foucault, M. (1980) *Power/Knowledge: Selected Interviews and Other Writings, 1972–1977*. New York: Pantheon.

Francis, B. (2000) *Boys, Girls and Achievement*. London: Routledge/Falmer.

Francis, B. (2009) The role of The Boffin as abject Other in gendered performances of school achievement, *The Sociological Review* 57(4).

Francis, B. and Skelton, C. (2005) *Reassessing Gender and Achievement*. London: Routledge.

Francis, B., Skelton, C., Carrington, B., Hutchings, M., Read, B. and Hall, I. (2008) A perfect match? Pupils' and teachers' views of the impact of matching educators and learners by gender, *Research Papers in Education*, 23(1): 21–36.

Gaskell, E. (1992) *Gender Matters from School to Work*. Buckingham: Open University Press.

Harris, A. (2004) *Future Girl: Young Women in the Twenty-first Century*. London: Routledge.

Hey, V. (1997) *The Company She Keeps: An Ethnography of Girls' Friendships*. Buckingham: Open University Press.

Holland, J., Ramazanoglu, C., Sharpe, S. and Thomson, R. (1998) *The Male in the Head: Young People, Heterosexuality and Power*. London: Tufnell Press.

Ivinson, G. and Murphy, P. (2007) *Rethinking Single Sex Teaching*. Maidenhead: Open University Press.

Jackson, C. (2006) *Lads and Ladettes in School: Gender and a Fear of Failure*. Maidenhead: Open University Press.

Mendick, H., Moreau, M. and Hollingworth, S. (2008) *Mathematical Images and Gender Identities*. London: IPSE.

Organization for Economic Co-operation and Development (OECD) (2007) *PISA 2006: Science Competencies for Tomorrow's World Executive Summary*. Available at: www.pisa.oecd.org.

Renold, E. and Allan, A. (2006) Bright and beautiful: high achieving girls, ambivalent femininities, and the feminisation of success in the primary school, *Discourse*, 27(4): 457–73.

Renold, E. and Ringrose, J. (forthcoming) Phallic girls? Girls' negotiations of phallogocentric power, in N. Rodriguez (ed.), *Queer Masculinities: A Critical Reader in Education*. Dordrecht: Springer.

Skeggs, B. (2004) *Class, Self, Culture*. London: Routledge.

Skelton, C. and Francis, B. (2009) *Feminism and the Schooling Scandal*. London: Routledge.

Skelton, C. and Read, B. (2006) Male and female teachers' evaluative responses to gender and the learning environments of primary age pupils, *International Studies in Sociology of Education*, 16(2): 105–20.

Skelton, C., Carrington, B., Francis, B., Hutchings, M., Read, B. and Hall, I. (2009) Gender 'matters' in the primary classroom: pupils' and teachers' perspectives, *British Educational Research Journal,* 35(2): 187–204.

Skelton, C., Francis, B. and Valkanova, Y. (2007) *Breaking Down the Stereotypes: Gender and Achievement in Schools*. Manchester: Equal Opportunities Commission.

Walkerdine, V. (1990) *Schoolgirl Fictions*. London: Verso.

Youdell, D. (2005) *Impossible Bodies, Impossible Selves*. Dordrecht: Springer.

2   Exploring girls' relationship to and with achievement: linking assessment, learning, mind and gender

Jannette Elwood

Introduction

Gender differences in assessment outcomes continue to be a very popular area of debate and research. Every summer, the release of A level and GCSE results[1] prompts comparisons between the overall performances of boys and girls, which become the focus of various commentaries about why such differences (which are quite large in some subjects) occur. Since the mid 1990s the concern expressed in many of the commentaries has been the underachievement of boys relative to girls, in other words, that girls' levels of achievement at important stages of schooling have far surpassed those of boys, and that girls leave schooling better qualified than their male counterparts (Elwood 2005).

Responses to these perceived gender disparities in examination performances have been policy and research agendas that have focused on raising the achievements of boys. While the rhetoric associated with both large- and small-scale educational innovations has promoted the raising of achievement standards of all pupils (i.e. boys and girls), research has shown that many such innovations have primarily geared themselves towards solutions to boys' underachievement (Younger et al. 2005). Initiatives have included shifting classroom practices, reforming pedagogy and changing curriculum contexts so that they are more interesting and beneficial to boys, with often little or no consideration afforded to the possible effects such strategies may have on girls' achievements. Thus improvements in girls' performances overall have occurred despite experiences in schools of strategies that may not have their own educational opportunities at heart, for example being seated next to boys to act as 'civilizing' influences to help the boys learn; engaging with texts and reading materials that are focused on boys' learning needs, and being organized into single-sex classes in mixed schools across various subjects to help raise the achievements of their male peers (Jackson 2002; Ivinson and Murphy 2007). However, a limited amount of research exists which focuses on the longer-term impact of such strategies on boys' and girls' achievements and on their experiences of schooling under such conditions. It is not fully understood how the effects of such strategies are manifest in gendered differences in outcomes, and/or in boys' and girls' successes in school more generally. Furthermore, treating boys and girls as homogenous groups of students often accentuates differences that are small or of little statistical significance (Hyde 2005). There are far more similarities between boys' and girls' performances than differences; bigger differences occur within girl and within boy groupings. So while overall figures may present all girls as being successful, this is far from the case; the roles of ethnicity and social class interacting with gender contribute a very different pattern of outcomes in terms of variations in girls' successes.

This chapter argues that general assumptions about boys' and girls' performances in examinations, and popular explanations about them, are simplistic and belie the complex web of factors that interact with gender to create the performances observed. Moreover, the chapter is not only concerned with gender and how that concept is defined and used in relation to how we understand students' achievements, but also with the contribution that examinations and assessment instruments themselves make to how achievement is defined and constructed, as well as the role that such techniques and systems play in creating the differences obtained. Researchers who are concerned with the social consequences of assessment practices recognize that any form of assessment system will have repercussions for boys' and girls' achievements, as will the multiple contexts in which assessment, learning and achieving take place (Elwood 2006a). Thus, from a perspective that sees assessment and examining as a social activity, there emerges a complex relationship between assessment processes, outcomes and gender that has to also understand their relationship to, and with, learning and mind. How we consider these four interconnected concepts shapes our understanding of achievement and how it is manifested differently between boys and girls. Thus, this chapter will explore girls' relationships to, and with, achievement by considering the links between the concepts of assessment, learning, mind and gender. It will also consider how and why assessment and testing influence the achievement of both boys and girls, and how and why different perspectives on the learner, how they learn, and how that learning is assessed differentially, affect the achievements of boys and girls.

Linking Gender, Assessment, Learning and Mind

A key area of focus of research in assessment is concerned with the links that exist between learning and assessment, especially how different models of assessment align to particular models of the learner (Murphy 1998; Elwood 2006b; James 2006). This research suggests that we cannot consider systems of assessment and testing without acknowledging their relationship to the model of the learner they wish to promote. There is a connection between learning and assessment, which is fundamental, yet changes depending on the view of the learner adopted. For example, within a sociocultural view of learning and assessment, the cultural life and experience of the learner is fundamental to understanding how they come to know. Furthermore, within this view, gender is seen as a cultural manifestation that needs to be considered in all its complexity. This is because how gender mediates learning has a profound impact on how boys and girls achieve and on how students and teachers experience assessment practice and its influence on educational success.

A vast range of learning theories exist that consider how we learn and what learning is (Murphy 1998). Such theories are often collated into larger groupings or families to help define and categorize key ideas and concepts. Common categorizations tend to link (i) theories of behaviourism in which learning is conceptualized as fixed and innate, and is seen to occur through transmission; (ii) theories of constructivism or social constructivism where learning is seen to happen through social relations, and the role of language in learning and development is prioritized; and (iii) theories of socioculturalism where learning is seen as a cultural activity and our social, cultural, linguistic and historical contexts are regarded as fundamental to the process of learning (Murphy 1998; Elwood 2006b). Aligned to these theories of learning there are associated theories of mind which, like theories of learning, can be categorized into families of thought. Common categorizations consider (i) a symbolic view of mind which is concerned with an individual's mental processing as a way to understanding learning – the learner is separate from their environment and learning is 'stored' in the head of the learner; and (ii) a situated view of mind which is concerned with how the social world is integral to learning – the learner is inseparable from their environment, and mind is between learners, not in the head of the learner (Murphy 1998; Elwood 2006b).

Associated with these different categories of learning and of mind are different views on how students should be assessed and how gender is considered. For example, views of assessment that align to the behaviourist models of learning and a symbolic view of mind see assessment as a neutral, independent instrument that measures an individual's learning. There are underlying assumptions about fixed psychological attributes that can be observed and evaluated through responses to test items. The view of gender within this model is traditional, where it is seen as the same as the sex of the test taker (i.e. male or female). It is treated as a dichotomous variable against which differences in performance can be analysed and reported. A further assumption here in relation to the gender gap in performance is that if no difference between boys and girls is observed, then gender equality is suggested and no issues in relation to differential treatment or opportunity need be explored.

However, more recent considerations of assessment are aligned to sociocultural theories of learning and situated views of mind. Views of assessment within this position consider the practice a cultural activity and acknowledge the influence of the social and cultural mediation of teachers and students in the assessment process. Gender is regarded as a social representation, a set of social norms, conventions and associations within society that has definition within our community (Ivinson and Murphy 2007). Thus, boys and girls create and are created by their entangled, social interactions with teachers and others, and it is their gendered appropriated subject knowledge, thought processes and lived experiences that are assessed. Viewing gender, assessment, learning and mind in this way has profound implications for how we understand gender and achievement through assessment outcomes.

Patterns of Achievement and Gender

Definitions of achievement and considerations about whether one gender is performing better or worse than another are generally based on the outcome measures of performance in assessments and examinations. Within the assessment and testing systems across the countries of England, Wales and Northern Ireland benchmark figures have been set over time which have come to denote and define national standards of success and achievement, both for individual pupils and for schools overall. The benchmarks for schools range from the proportion of 7-year-olds achieving level 2 or above in national curriculum assessments in English and maths, to the proportion of 18-year-olds achieving A–C grades (or their equivalent) in GCE A levels or vocational qualifications. For individual pupils there are average levels specified as targets for age-related national curriculum tests and assessments. For example, level 4 is the average target level for 11-year-olds in national tests and teacher assessments in English, maths and science. There are also targets for the number of GCSEs and A levels to be obtained (5+ and 3+ respectively) at the top grades (C or above). Commonly a benchmark of 5+ GCSEs at grade C or above is needed for students to gain entry into advanced level study.

These benchmarks have become increasingly important but they also continue to be contentious as they are used both to rank schools in league tables – with severe consequences for some schools if they do not meet the set standards (i.e. they are put into special measures) – and also to position and label boys and girls as failures or successes among their peers. Thus, the social consequences of these benchmarks are significant and extend way beyond the valid uses to which such assessment results should be applied.

If we take gender as a variable against which data can be reported, then reviewing examination data from all major examination boards across England, Wales and Northern Ireland for males and females who take key qualifications at ages 16 (GCSEs) and 18 (A levels) some important patterns emerge. The following data represent percentage point differences in the proportion of girls and boys entering and passing GCSEs and A levels:

- slightly more females than males are entered for examinations at 16 years old – in 2008 51 per cent of the entry for GCSE were female
- at 16 years old females leave school with more GCSEs than males of that age – in 2008 there was a difference of 7.2 per cent in the numbers of females obtaining GCSEs at grades A*–C compared to the number of males (this is a drop in the percentage difference from 9 per cent in 2003)
- there were more males classified as absent (i.e. those who were entered but did not complete the examinations and those who did not enter at all); in 2008 53 per cent of absentees were males
- more females enter for examinations at 18 years old (A levels) – in 2008 54 per cent of A level entrants were female (compared to 38 per cent 30 years ago)
- at 18 years old females perform better than males in the proportion of top grades achieved – in 2008 overall statistics showed that females did better, with 5.3 per cent difference in A–C grades (again this is a drop in the percentage difference from 7 per cent in 2003).

(JCGQ 2008a, 2008b)

On the face of it, the above statistics denote some large differences in entry and performance patterns between males and females. Since the mid 1990s, similar patterns, year-on-year, have focused concern on the underachievement of boys relative to girls.[2] Yet much is hidden behind these overall statistics. A more in-depth look at entry and result patterns reveals distinct variations at the individual-grade level that suggest a more complex overall picture. For example, these figures ignore the relative proportions of males and females not entered for examinations (more males are not entered at age 16 than females), and they also hide a cross-over in performance patterns between males and females at ages 16 and 18 in particular subjects that show the differences in top grades awarded reversed. For example, in French in 2008, females were 57 per cent of the entry at GCSE in this subject and obtained 10 per cent more A*–C grades than males, whereas at A level, while a greater proportion of entrants for French were girls (at 69 per cent), boys obtained 0.5 per cent more A–C grades than girls. There is much that is not explicit in overall result patterns, and much that impacts significantly on the achievements of boys and girls in the various subjects they choose to study. The choices made by boys and girls affect their experiences of schooling and their opportunities for success.

Subjects have their own historical legacies that Murphy (2008: 163) suggests are associated with 'cultural scripts about how people are or how they figure in the world [which] are . . . played out in oppositional terms . . . of masculinity and femininity [which] are culturally specific'. Moreover, subjects also have historical preferences for ways of assessing knowledge within that subject, and the assessment techniques chosen to evaluate student learning reflect these subject culture influences, which in turn in-fluence gender differences in results. Taking results at face-value, although helpful in terms of overall patterns of performance, represents the tra-ditional, deterministic view of performance differences, which sees the measuring instrument as neutral, gender as a static variable, and any gen-der gap in assessment results denoting some 'truth' about boys' and girls' real achievements. However, such a view is not helpful in understand-ing the complex relationships to, and with, achievement that are created through the interaction of gender and assessment practices. To better un-derstand such complexities we are forced to consider other positions that see: learning as integral to the contexts in which we learn; assessments as problematic and not socially neutral; and any gender gap in performance as coming about through the interaction of the assessment instruments used (either tasks or tests) and boys' and girls' learning experiences in the cultural worlds within which they live.

The Role of Assessment Techniques

Research in the 1990s from the UK (Stobart et al. 1992; Elwood and Comber 1996) had as its critical focus how the social nature of assessment influences the experiences of teachers and students and the subjects they teach and study. The social consequences of assessment activity mould boys' and girls' perceptions of subject knowledge and understanding and their own identities as successes or failures at particular stages of schooling and in particular subject areas. The research identified key factors that contributed significantly to differences in performance between boys and girls which were associated with the design, structure and use of tests and examinations. Factors identified included: the type and mode of item response; teacher-assessed coursework; different levels of examinations with restricted grade ranges within the same qualification (known as tiering); the use of real-life contexts in assessment items and tasks; and the sampling of subject content on test papers (Elwood 2005).

For example, since the introduction of teacher-assessed coursework into examinations in the 1990s there has tended to be a widespread perception that such non-standard forms of assessment (which require continuous assessment through extended writing and redrafting of work) tend to favour girls, and so any increase in girls' performances in examinations was due to the inclusion of such assessment techniques (Stobart et al. 1992). Research into the contribution of coursework to the overall grades of boys and girls found that across a range of subjects girls' mean coursework marks were higher than those of boys and that these differences were statistically significant. Coursework marks were slightly more 'bunched' for girls than for boys; there was also less variation in the marks awarded to girls than those awarded to boys. This 'bunching' of marks (i.e. awarding similar marks, usually towards the top end of the mark range) creates an interesting technical contradiction between coursework and examination components in relation to gender. If coursework marks are 'bunched' and examination marks spread more widely across the mark range then it is the examination marks that will determine the final rank order of students and hence their overall grade. The outcome of this was that coursework marks actually contributed more to the final outcomes of boys than for girls. Moreover, girls were also found to be doing as well as, or better than, boys on the examination components with girls' achieving higher mean marks on these components across a range of subjects (Elwood 2001). So girls' higher grades (relative to those of boys) in the examinations overall were a result of them doing well on both types of components.

What this research showed was that different assessment components can operate differently in practice for boys and for girls. This is an important point given the different attention paid by girls and boys to different assessment tasks, and teachers' perceptions of how different types of assessment contribute to girls' and boys' final grades. For example, Elwood (1998) considered teachers' views regarding differences in the ways in which boys and girls approached and dealt with examinations and coursework. Teachers did not go as far as to suggest that coursework might be a critical factor in girls' better performance, but they were inclined to suggest that girls had a certain advantage in this type of assessment:

> We were unhappy about the shift away from coursework ... although that's one of the factors that mitigated against boys in the past. The exam suits boys better than it does girls ...
> (Female English teacher quoted in Elwood 1998: 178)

However, perceptions that females panic more in examination situations and are better at coursework are not reflected to any degree in their examination performance. Thus, the *actual* influence of coursework in contributing to girls' and boys' success is quite different to its *perceived* influence as understood by teachers and students. The way in which different assessment modes interact and operate differently for boys and girls affects the validity of any inferences made from the results awarded. The social consequences of assessment modes differentially affecting boys' and girls' performances can create backwash effects into the curriculum and the learning experiences of students; the negative consequence of which may provide misrepresentations of boys' and girls' success.

Thus, to understand the interaction between gender and assessment more fully we are forced to look into those spaces where formal learning takes place (i.e. classrooms) and where decisions about girls' and boys' abilities and achievements are made. Such a position demands that we see classrooms as cultural settings which 'foreground subjective experiences within local contexts' (Murphy and Ivinson 2008: 148) and acknowledge that teacher–student and student–student relationships within these settings are gendered, complex and problematic. Furthermore, such relationships and interactions are created, enacted, developed and experienced by girls and boys in very different ways, which has major implications for how we assess boys and girls and how we define achievement.

Assessment and Gender as Cultural Activities

New interests in the field of gender and assessment are adopting positions that consider sociocultural perspectives on learning and situated views of mind. I have argued elsewhere (Elwood 2006b) that such a view positions learning, mind, gender and assessment as culturally generated and mediated, and that we must consider the complex interactions and relationships of these concepts if we are to understand the impact of assessment practices in schools and classrooms. Assessment within this view becomes a cultural artifact that only has meaning in relationship with, and between, the teacher and the students and/or peer and the context in which it occurs; the outcomes are relational and cannot be abstracted away from the situation in which they were created. The social, cultural and historical experiences that students and teachers bring to learning and assessment situations are integral to how we understand students' performance on examinations and assessments; it is only by looking into students' and teachers' histories, their 'forms of life' (McGinn 1997),[3] that can we fully understand their achievements.

Thus, to understand the achievements of boys and girls we need to consider them as relational to, and with, the interaction of learning with assessment practice. The relationships between teachers, students, their learning and how this learning is assessed are entangled, as are the gendered lives of students and teachers and their understandings of subject knowledge(s). All these factors come into play in comprehending how boys and girls learn and how this is represented in outcomes on assessment tasks and tests. From this perspective, to understand boys' and girls' learning through assessment we need to see gender as located 'within' the outcomes observed.

Murphy and Ivinson (2008) argue that teachers, through their practice and interactions with students, can directly and indirectly mediate the historical, gendered positioning of their subjects and their own views about boys' and girls' participation and belonging within these. Furthermore, teachers present to students what they consider valued subject knowledge, and their notions of what constitutes a successful examination candidate and how this equates with achievement. For example, Elwood and Comber (1996) found that through the structure and type of assessment technique selected by examiners within GCSEs and A levels, a shift could be seen in the definition of achievement between the two stages of examining. This was illustrated through the variation in mode of response presented to candidates as well as in the quality and type of response required. This shift in how achievement and success were defined between the two stages of examining seemed to impact differentially on boys and girls and tended to affect how teachers viewed success for girls and for boys at the different stages of assessment and in the different subjects assessed:

> I think the boy's approach [in A level English] is much more effective . . . he will write you a side-and-a-half where others are writing four or five pages . . . it's like a knife through butter, almost notes but not quite, a very sparse style of writing . . . I've never seen a girl do that . . .
> (Female English teacher quoted in Elwood 1998: 177)

Teachers who hold such views may be judging girls to have less command of the subjects they teach and fewer capabilities for advanced-level study when the opposite is true, and such messages may, in the long term, restrict girls' achievements. Furthermore, gendered views of what boys and girls can or cannot do closely mirror historical, essentialist perspectives of males and females with regard to over-strain, over-conscientiousness and potential. Even though girls are performing at very high levels at ages 16 and 18, their success is still being attributed not to their brilliance, but to their hard work which is also seen as finite and limited, as is their potential to excel. In the cultural settings of the classroom, the interactions and relationships between teachers and students, which are the essence of teaching and learning, create descriptions and definitions of successful and non-successful students which provide messages about what type of achievement aligns with success. Often the non-explicit nature of these messages means that some students (either boys or girls) can or cannot meet the teachers' criteria for success. Thus, how teachers view success in the community of the subject, its conventions, forms, practices and cultural settings can significantly influence their judgements of boys' and girls' abilities.

Conclusion

This chapter explored the links between the concepts of gender, assessment, learning and mind as a way of understanding more fully girls' relationship with, and to, achievement. Discourses around gender and achievement that present gender as something that is fixed (a static variable against which results can be reported), and assessment as neutral, give us a distorted view of boys' and girls' achievements. The positioning of girls' results relative to those of boys' and vice-versa limits our comprehension of the multiple and complex ways in which girls and boys succeed in examinations and assessment situations, and the influences that create differences in performance. Indeed, considering girls and boys as homogenous groups prevents more in-depth consideration of variations within these groups by ethnicity and/or social class which would tell a more profound story. Thus, adopting a position that is less about looking at boys and girls as two opposing groups and more about looking at girls' educational successes (and boys' educational successes) in the context of their own goals and expectations would allow for a better consideration of the influences and experiences that interact with assessment situations. To reflect critically on achievement as it relates to, and with, gender we need to see that girls' and boys' forms of life – in relationship with those of their teachers and peers – are crucial to any valid interpretations and judgements that are made about what constitutes successful achievement for girls and boys at these significant stages of schooling.

Notes

1. The General Certificate of Secondary Education (GCSE) is the main examination taken by 16-year-olds in England, Wales and Northern Ireland at the end of compulsory schooling. Passing grades are A*–G; the benchmark for higher performances is A*–C, and the proportion

of students obtaining five or more GCSEs at grades A*–C is used as an indicator of accountability for schools. The General Certificate of Education (GCE) Advanced (A) Level is the main examination taken by 18-year-olds in England, Wales and Northern Ireland. Passing grades are A–E, and results in these examinations are used (primarily) for entrance to university. Results in these examinations are also used to evaluate schools.

2. The extensive debates and research emerging out of these considerations of boys' underachievement and girls' overachievement are well documented by many of the contributors to this volume as well as others (e.g. Arnot et al. 1998; Epstein et al. 1998; Francis 2000; Skelton et al. 2006).

3. 'Form of Life' is a Wittgensteinian concept defined as the underlying consensus of linguistic and non-linguistic behaviour, assumptions, practices, traditions and natural propensities which humans as social beings share with one another and which is therefore presupposed in the language they use (Grayling 2001: 97).

References

Arnot, M., Gray, J., James, M. and Ruddock J. (1998) *Recent Research on Gender and Educational Performance*. London: OFSTED.

Elwood, J. (1998) *Gender and Performance at A Level: Gender-equity and the 'Gold Standard'*. Unpublished PhD thesis, University of London Institute of Education.

Elwood, J. (2001) Examination techniques: issues of validity and effects on pupils' performance, in D. Scott (ed.), *Curriculum and Assessment*. Westport, CA: Ablex.

Elwood, J. (2005) Gender and achievement: what have exams got to do with it?, *Oxford Review of Education*, 31(3): 373–93.

Elwood, J. (2006a) Formative assessment: possibilities, boundaries and limitations, *Assessment in Education*, 13 (2): 215–32.

Elwood, J. (2006b) Gender issues in testing and assessment, in C. Skelton, B. Francis and L. Smulyan (eds), *The Handbook of Gender and Education*. London: Sage.

Elwood, J. and Comber, C. (1996) *Gender Differences in Examinations at 18+: Final Report*. London: Institute of Education for the Nuffield Foundation.

Epstein, D., Elwood, J., Hey, V. and Maw, J. (eds) (1998) *Failing Boys? Issues in Gender and Achievement*. Buckingham: Open University Press.

Francis, B. (2000) *Boys, Girls and Achievement: Addressing Classroom Issues*. London: RoutledgeFalmer.

Grayling, A.C. (2001) *Wittgenstein: A Very Short Introduction*. Oxford: Oxford Paperbacks.

Hyde, J.S. (2005) The gender similarities hypothesis, *American Psychologist*, 60: 581–92.

Ivinson, G. and Murphy, P. (2007) *Re-thinking Single-sex Teaching: Gender, School Subjects and Learning*. Buckingham: Open University Press.

Jackson, C. (2002) Can single-sex classes in co-educational schools enhance the learning experiences of girls and/or boys? An exploration of pupils' perceptions, *British Educational Research Journal*, 28(1): 37–48.

James, M. (2006) Assessment, teaching and theories of learning, in J. Gardner (ed.), *Assessment and Learning*. London: Sage.

Joint Council for General Qualifications (JCGQ) (2008a) *National Provisional GCSE Full Course Results (All UK candidates)*. Available at: www.jcgq.org.uk/exam-result-data/gcse-statistics-summer.2008.pdf (accessed 21 August 2008).

Joint Council for General Qualifications (JCGQ) (2008b) *National Provisional GCE A level Results (All UK candidates)*. Available at: www.jcgq.org.uk/exam-result-data/gce-statistics-summer.2008.pdf (accessed 18 August 2008).

McGinn, M. (1997) *Wittgenstein and the Philosophical Investigations*. London: Routledge.

Murphy, P. (ed.) (1998) *Learners, Learning and Assessment*. London: Paul Chapman.

Murphy, P. (2008) Gender and subject cultures in practice, in P. Murphy and K. Hall (eds), *Learning and Practice: Agency and Identities*. London: Sage/Open University Press.

Murphy, P. and Ivinson, G. (2008) Gender, assessment and students' literacy learning, in K. Hall, P. Murphy and J. Soler (eds), *Pedagogy and Practice: Culture and Identities*. London: Sage/Open University Press.

Skelton, C., Francis, B. and Smulyan, L. (eds) (2006) *The Handbook of Gender and Education*. London: Sage.

Stobart, G., Elwood, J. and Quinlan, M. (1992) Gender bias in examinations: how equal are the opportunities? *British Educational Research Journal*, 18(3): 261–76.

Younger, M., Warrington, M. and McLellan, R. (2005) *Raising Boys' Achievements in Secondary Schools: Issues, Dilemmas and Opportunities*. Maidenhead: Open University Press.

3 'Rebels', 'bad girls' and 'misbehavers': exploring 'underachievement' in single-sex, selective schooling

Alexandra Allan

Introduction

Over the last 20 years, middle-class, female educational achievement has been portrayed as a celebration story with no cause for concern. As Francis (2000: 11) suggests, girls have been performing increasingly well in education since the early 1990s and the current image of girls' success seems far removed from the 'grim picture of rampant inequality' that was reported by feminists in the 1970s and 1980s. A recent Department for Children Schools and Families (DCSF 2007) publication reported that girls are outperforming boys at almost every level of the education system, particularly in subjects like English and in GCSE examinations taken at the end of secondary schooling.

In recent years a number of researchers have endeavoured to explore the story of female academic achievement in more depth; to examine the complex interweaving of gendered, raced and classed discourses with educational achievement (Archer and Francis 2006; Renold and Allan 2006; Reay 2008). Authors such as Ringrose (2007) and McRobbie (2007) have also begun to question what success actually means for those 'top' and 'super' girls who are able to achieve the most spectacular results in the education system. Yet even within this literature very little empirical evidence is drawn upon to outline these girls' experiences and to investigate their perceptions of schooling and success.

Drawing upon data generated during a two-year ethnographic study (involving individual interviews, focused group interviews, observation and photography) in one single-sex, selective school in south Britain (Allan 2007), this chapter explores young middle-class girls' educational achievements. Concentrating on the educational achievements of one group of 25 girls (11–12 years old) I explore the different ways in which they negotiated their identities as middle-class girls, pupils and academic achievers. In particular, the chapter focuses on those girls who were described by their teachers as 'underachievers' (as girls who were 'failing to reach their potential') and by their peers as 'rebels', 'bad girls' and 'misbehavers'. I examine the classed and gendered discourses available to the girls, and explore what it means to be an 'underachiever' in a 'high-achieving' school.

Background to the Study: Success and the Single-sex, Selective School

Taylor's Girls' School,[1] the institution where my research was based, was often described to me by members of the local community as a white, upper middle-class[2] suburban haven. Indeed, almost all of the girls in the study described themselves as 'white' (with only one describing herself as 'mixed-race') and all claimed that they were middle class (with a few suggesting that they were 'rather more upper than middle'). These were girls whose parents could largely be described as professionals, with only a few parents whose work could more accurately be described as managerial. All of the girls in the study could also, in a formal sense (based on examination marks), be described as high academic achievers. At the end of Year 6, when the girls collected their results for their Standard Assessment Tests (SATs), 19 of them had achieved the highest levels possible. The remaining six pupils had achieved only slightly lower levels, with results that were still significantly above the national average. This was a school that felt able to celebrate its pupils' achievements as 'exceptional and extra-ordinary' and to describe pupils as 'motivated', 'confident', 'independent' and 'intuitive'.

The 'Rebels', 'Bad Girls' and 'Misbehavers'

Given the school's examination results and the selective nature of its intake, I was extremely surprised to find a number of girls who were identified by their teachers as 'low achievers'. Less surprising, however, was the fact that these girls were still achieving quite highly on tests (significantly above national averages for their age group) and that they were not being described as 'failures' but as 'underachievers', that is, girls who were not fulfilling their (high) potentials (Jones and Myhill 2004a, 2004b). As Lucey (2001) explains, academic achievement is always relative, and as such there will be winners and losers in every school. Even in this selective school there had to be pupils who were deemed to be 'underachieving' in order for others to be identified as high achievers.

Many of the girls who were identified as underachieving were pupils who were new to the school, often having been educated in state schools before they joined the school's senior department at 11–12 years old. Although as 'new girls' they were part of a large and heterogeneous group, many of whom were not described as underachieving, they were often talked about by some of their teachers as pupils who struggled due to 'a lack of knowledge' and previous 'inferior' educational training. The girls themselves also described their struggle to 'keep up at school', as this interview extract demonstrates:

> *AA:* So are you happy with the work you have done so far?
> *Elissa:* I don't know . . . I am not sure.
> *Millie:* I think I did better in my old school . . . it was just easier.
> *Elissa:* I think it is harder here because like in my old school I was popular and really smart but here I don't seem very smart.
> *Millie:* I think I am able to mess around less here . . . I have to be serious now.

These were girls who were also identified by their peers as 'rebels', 'bad girls' and 'misbehavers' – girls who, many of the other pupils felt, did not want to achieve at school, who 'didn't put any effort in' and 'preferred to mess around' instead of getting on with work.

However, it was not just the 'new' girls who were identified in these ways. A number of the girls who had been in the school for a long time (often from reception class) were also pointed out to me as underachievers and misbehavers. Gayle, for example, was a girl to whom my attention was drawn on my first day in the school. One of her teachers told me that although they believed that she was quite academically able, she was 'always in trouble', 'never on track with her work', 'always distracting others in the group' and 'the cause of 99 per cent of trouble in the class'. In interviews, Gayle's peers talked about her as both a 'troublemaker' and a 'joker'. Gayle's best friend Eva was described in a similar manner. Even though Eva's teachers felt that she was 'actually very capable' they said that she was easily distracted from her work and often misbehaving. Eva's classmates told me that she was the leader of the rebel gang (an interesting idea, given that they did not seem to know who else was a part of this gang!) and that she was 'just known for being bad'.

The girls' (so called) misbehaviour at school and in lessons appeared to revolve around humour and, in particular, playing practical jokes. During my time observing lessons I often saw Gayle trying to catch people's eyes as the teacher was explaining a concept from the front of the class; Gayle was trying to make other pupils laugh by making faces at them, writing notes to them or drawing funny pictures in their books. One of Eva and Gayle's favourite pastimes was drawing caricatures of teachers in a sketch book that they took to each lesson. After drawing a cartoon image they would make up a fictitious personality, list of hobbies and pastimes for the teacher and would accompany all of this with a title (taken from one of the teacher's 'famous sayings'). During lessons these were often passed round to other pupils in the class to distract them and make them laugh.

Often these smaller jokes would delight and amuse the class, it was only when the girls went further and jeopardized the other girls' reputations as good students that they were criticized severely and brought back into line by their classmates, as the following field notes demonstrate:

> Today was the third English lesson that the girls were to have in the library – a lesson where they are allowed to work by themselves to devise their own drama. During the lesson many of the girls sat and worked quietly at the library desks, writing their scripts before they moved on to act them out. It was only one group who appeared to be making an enormous amount of noise. When I peered behind the book shelves to see where the noise was coming from, I was greeted by Elsie, Gayle, Eva and Genella. Sure enough the girls were acting out a storyline from a book that they had chosen, but they appeared to have exaggerated the characters and to have added in a new storyline where all of the characters had been at the pub and were subsequently extremely drunk. As the lesson progressed the story became more and more exaggerated and the girls staggered between the library aisles, laughing hysterically and pulling out books from between the shelves. Up until this point the girls' classmates had been looking on, seemingly amused by the action. But as the girls became more rowdy – climbing over the library shelves and fighting with their props – a few of their classmates tried to intervene to tell them to calm down. It is at this point that the class teacher walks back into the room, horrified by what she sees. She quickly sends the entire class back to their form room for a break-time detention.
>
> During break time she expresses her disappointment and tells the class that as she can no longer trust them they will not be allowed to do any more drama work for the rest of term. Many of the girls are extremely disappointed by the ban and are furious that they have become involved in a situation that was effectively not of their own making. By the end of the day a few of the girls decide that they will have to go to the teacher to tell her who was really involved in the incident – after all it is all of their reputations at stake, and what if the teacher was to tell the school's senior department that they had behaved in this way?

In this instance Gayle appeared to be quite ashamed by the way she had behaved, or at least by being caught and punished for her actions. However, in many of the interviews I held with her she was quite keen to boast about her misbehaviour in class. In fact in one interview she told me that she felt that it was her mission to make people laugh, to misbehave and have fun, rather than to get bothered by school work. She said that she despised the 'wussy' way that others in her class did what they were told and just got on with their work. In a similar manner, Eva would often talk about how much she hated school, how she felt that her classmates were all geeks, and that making her stay and learn at school when she wanted to be doing other things was 'child abuse'.

'Too Cool for School': Humour and Underachievement

'Rebellious' behaviours like those performed by the rebel girls are not uncommon in schools. Humour has often been used by pupils to avoid school work. As Woods (1990: 185) explains, humorous practices have often been regarded as 'natural products and responses to the exigencies of the institution, such as boredom, ritual, routine, regulation and oppressive authority'. Indeed, in recent years there have been many reports of increases in this sort of rebellious misbehaviour in schools. Although commonly characterized as 'laddish' behaviour more typical of boys than girls, the 'uncool to work' discourse has been recognized as one of the major problems affecting pupils' educational achievements in schools today (DfEE 2000).

One explanation for this type of behaviour is based upon arguments developed by Jackson (2006). Drawing upon Covington's (1992) work, Jackson argues that certain behaviours – like humour, shouting out in class, and distracting others – can be attractive to pupils for a number of reasons. One reason is that any educational 'failures' can be attributed to these behaviours (messing around in class) rather than to a lack of ability. This is particularly important in the current climate, one in which ability is valued very highly and is 'measured' by academic results, and many pupils face considerable pressure to 'succeed'. In such climates self-worth is inextricably tied to ability – to lack ability is to lack worth. It is, therefore, much more desirable for pupils to be able to explain 'failure' in terms of a lack of effort rather than a lack of ability. In the words of one of Jackson's (2006: 24) 13–14-year-old interviewees: 'If you've tried your best and you've got a low mark then it's sort of like "oh you can't do it and you're stupid". But if you didn't try and you got a low mark it's like "oh I couldn't be bothered doing it so I only tried a little bit" '. This may well have been one of the reasons why the rebel girls in my study engaged in humour as a way of avoiding their school work. In fact, Gayle told me in one interview that she often did not try hard at school so it did not really matter if she achieved highly or not.

Another reason given for pupils investing in this rebellious behaviour at school relates to their positioning through gendered discourses. Many educational researchers have drawn upon Connell's (1995) notion of hegemonic masculinity to suggest that boys find it particularly hard to show interest in academic work at school because it is equated with femininity. As Francis and Skelton (2005: 129) propose, 'learning and academic achievement is not so socially stigmatised for girls as it is for many boys . . . and hence they are less deterred from application by social considerations'. However, this theory has been critiqued by researchers who argue that it fails to account for the experiences of girls who have been identified (or as a result of this view, fail to be identified) as 'underachievers' in school (Jones and Myhill 2004a).

Jackson (2005, 2006) is one author who has argued strongly that it is not only boys who invest in these 'laddish behaviours' or who claim that it is 'uncool' to work in school. Many girls also experience pressures to downplay their effort and to misbehave. This is not to suggest that Jackson does not see gender as an important factor, but rather that she believes that we need to understand how 'uncool to work' discourses affect both boys and girls, and to realize that some girls may also underachieve because school work is also not equated with some popular forms of femininity.

Like the girls in Jackson's (2006) study it could be argued that the rebel girls in my research were also investing in a type of 'laddish' behaviour in order to avoid being seen as a 'geek' or a 'swot' and in order to be seen as a particular type of girl. Both Eva and Gayle told me that they felt they were 'different to the other girls in their class' and that they wanted to distinguish themselves from the 'passive' and 'girly' behaviour of most of their classmates. The rebel girl identity appeared to provide a space that allowed them to perform this difference. Through their investment in humour and misbehaviour, Gayle and Eva were able to take up these laddish (and many would argue, powerful) subject positions.

Posh and Pretentious: Social Class and Academic Achievement

However, it was not just as girls or as rebels that these girls claimed that they were different, and so gender and self-worth protection cannot be regarded as the only reasons why they misbehaved in class. One of the main things that the rebel girls stressed to me in interviews was that they were different to their classmates because they were 'common girls'. Many of the rebel girls felt that they did not fit in with the other girls in their class and said that they did not want to become posh or pretentious like their peers.

The 'new' girls talked about this in terms of feeling lost in such a privileged and high-achieving environment. These girls could be compared to a group of students in Reay's (2001) study, a group who found it impossible to fit into the educational institutions they attended and who described themselves as losing a sense of who they 'really were' as they were forced to perform new acceptable middle-class personas. Although almost all of the 'new' girls could be described as middle class, they too felt lost in school due to a lack of relevant cultural and economic capital. As one girl told me,

> The junior girls have just been brought up well while they were young and they have been to private schools which means you are taught better because you pay for the privilege. You can tell they are different because they are just so confident ... Not like me, I am not confident. I have not been trained in the same way to do well at school.

Although Gayle and Eva were not new to the school and were regarded as being from a slightly higher-class background than the new girls, they talked about class and achievement in a similar manner to the 'new' girls. Gayle, for example, spoke about lacking the 'right know how' (cultural capital) to compete with peers at school. Although she did not talk about class directly, she talked about having enough money (economic capital) to succeed in social terms at school (indeed she was often the centre of attention in the summer term when her 'famous' pool party invites were being handed out) but felt that she still stood out because 'well, I just didn't know the things the other girls did when I came to this school, I was different and some would call me dumb'.

Eva, on the other hand, told me that she felt she had the 'correct knowledge' to succeed at school but that she lacked the money to succeed socially. She explained this in terms of her Dad being a Professor and having impressed the value of education on her from a young age (cultural capital), but lacking the money needed to pay school fees (economic capital).

Social class seemed to be a major reason why they did not feel 'at home' or successful at school. One of the ways in which the rebel girls appeared to deal with these feelings of 'class failure' was to critique their classmates for being posh and pretentious:

> *Iyana:* Some people are so posh in this school and they judge you
> on your work saying you are not good enough. Like they ask
> you how you pronounce scone and stuff! I just say 'shut your
> face!'.
> *Isla:* Yeah we say scones [s-gone-s] anyway we are not posh!
> *AA:* What does being posh mean then?
> *Iyana:* Well it can be if you are a hard worker but it could also
> mean that you have lots of money. Not all people with money
> are posh but if they brag about it then they definitely are!

The term posh was used by the girls to mean a number of different things: to describe girls who were wealthy, 'stuck up', overly confident and who spoke with a 'haughty' accent. As the above extract demonstrates, however, it was also used to refer to girls who they felt worked too hard at school. Posh was a term that they used to criticize girls who achieved highly in school, especially if they did it publicly and seemingly unashamedly. In interviews and informal conversations the girls would often publicly devalue academic achievement, claiming that academic work was something that only posh people cared about. The rebel girls also downgraded their peers' achievements by suggesting that the pupils who achieved in this school 'were not really clever' but that their parents had used their money to make them clever. Eva was a particular proponent of this view, which turned out to be one of the dominant reasons why she downplayed her own achievement, because she felt that it had been achieved in the wrong way and that her grades would not have been the same if she had attended a state school.

By critiquing the other girls in this way, the rebel girls were able to devalue those who devalued them. By critiquing their classmates' success and downplaying the importance of academic achievement they were able to lever themselves into a more powerful position as 'normal girls'. Once again, the rebel girl identity appeared to offer them a space where they were able to be different and to legitimately distinguish themselves from others in the school.

'It's Not That I Don't Care About School Work . . .': The Struggle to Succeed

However, the girls' attempts to devalue academic achievement and to invest in a form of anti-pretentiousness also appeared to operate as a mechanism to keep them in place. For while they successfully challenged their classmates, they also made barriers to their own success, making it virtually impossible for them to be recognized as high achievers in the school

(Skeggs 2004). By devaluing academic achievement, the rebel girls found it extremely hard to invest in any behaviour that would seem 'pro-school', even when they felt that they needed to.

Gayle, in particular, often pushed her 'laddish' behaviour to the limit and risked school exclusion as well as being ostracized by her classmates. There were times when Gayle clearly wanted to achieve at school, if not for herself then for her parents (who she told me expected great things from her). However, when Gayle tried to behave she struggled with the comments of her classmates and the criticism that she received from teachers who refused to believe that she was really behaving well. Eva also struggled to be consistently recognized as a high achiever, although in contrast to Gayle she appeared to maintain this balance far more successfully. By avoiding engaging in the openly challenging behaviour that Gayle invested in, and by resisting quietly (completing her work but only by doing the bare minimum, challenging her teachers but not so that they could hear, and complaining about school but only to her friends), she was able to carefully manage a high-achieving identity for herself as well as retain her identity as a rebel.

The girls' struggle to be different middle-class girls and to simultaneously achieve at school is best summed up in a photograph that they took as part of the research. The picture portrayed Gayle in a Superman pose being wheeled across the classroom on the teacher's chair. The photograph was aptly labelled 'rebel Supergirl' and seemed to combine all of the different elements of the identities that they struggled to balance. The girls explained to me that they felt the photograph symbolized the ways in which they were expected to behave at school, as 'Supergirls' who could achieve anything and behave perfectly all of the time. Yet they also felt that the picture was a humorous 'take' on this identity as it showed the girls rebelling from these norms and hinted at other possible ways of being. The fact that both of these identities were combined in the photograph demonstrates the struggles that the girls faced in being 'different' – the powerful discourses to which they were subjected and the dominant ways in which they had to behave if they wanted to succeed.

Conclusion

All of these perceived hardships must be kept in context, for ultimately these were privileged girls who were achieving very well at school and had the desire to succeed (even if they did not always demonstrate this publicly). Because of their privileged positions it appeared as though many of them were actually able to 'play' with their inscriptions as 'laddish underachievers', to manoeuvre themselves into more powerful positions, and to ultimately be recognized as good (if not high) achievers (Skeggs 2004).

What this chapter has demonstrated, however, is that even middle-class female educational achievement cannot be celebrated as a simple success story. The position of girls in relation to educational achievement has changed in recent years, with girls increasingly being seen as 'active and aspirational' educational subjects (McRobbie 2007: 727). But as McRobbie (2007) reminds us, not all girls will reach the high standards expected of them, meaning that some will be singled out as failures more forcefully than ever before, while others will attain glittering academic prizes as part of an elite and competitive group. Yet, if even these upper-middle-class girls (who were privileged enough to attend a private, single-sex, selective institution) struggle to be recognized as high achievers and to publicly own academic success for themselves, we may ask what this means for those girls who have no choice but to be fixed in position as low achievers and who lack the capital to be recognized in these expected and dominant ways.

The 'gender agenda' may have shifted in schools in recent years (though like McRobbie I would question the extent of this shift) but social class does not seem to have changed in the same ways (Lucey 2001). Class is a factor that is often overlooked in these debates, yet as the experiences of the rebel girls demonstrate, it is an important factor and one that needs to be examined in more depth – not just in terms of the economic resources that pupils have available to them, but also in terms of the other forms of capital that they are able to deploy, the intra-class differences that emerge, and the ways in which class positionings allow access to different academic discourses and identities. By looking at the experiences of the 'underachieving girls' in this school, I hope that the chapter has demonstrated the need to look at the multiplicity of discourses that fuse together to determine the range of possible identities open to students as pupils and achievers (Youdell 2006).

Notes

1. The school and individual participants are referred to by pseudonyms.
2. The term upper middle class is used in this chapter to refer to the girls' similar social positions (as daughters of wealthy top-end professional workers). However, in line with Bourdieu's (1987) theoretical propositions, class is understood to be about more than economic capital or employment relations. Rather, social class is viewed as a structure of relationships where class positioning depends upon the different forms of capital (social, economic and cultural) that people possess. Class is

also seen as a set of fictional discourses marked on people's bodies and minds; producing identities that are deeply lived (Walkerdine et al. 2001).

References

Allan, A. (2007) *Struggling for Success: An Ethnographic Exploration of the Construction of Young Femininities in a Selective, Single-sex School.* Unpublished doctoral thesis, Cardiff University.

Archer, L. and Francis, B. (2006) *Understanding Minority Ethnic Achievement.* London: Routledge.

Bourdieu, P. (1987) What makes a social class? On the theoretical and practical existence of groups, *Berkeley Journal of Sociology*, 22: 1–17.

Connell, R. (1995) *Masculinities.* Cambridge: Polity Press.

Covington, M.V. (1992) *Making the Grade: A Self-worth Perspective on Motivation and School Reform.* Cambridge: Cambridge University Press.

Department for Children, Schools and Families (DCSF) (2007) *Gender and Education: The Evidence on Pupils in England.* Available at: www.dcsf. gov.uk/research/data/uploadfiles/RTP01-07.pdf (accessed 18/2/09).

Department for Education and Employment (DfEE) (2000) *Boys Must Improve at Same Rates as Girls* – Blunkett. Available at: www.dfee.gov.uk/ pns/DisplayPN.cgi?pn_id=2000_0368 (accessed 18/08/08).

Francis, B. (2000) *Boys, Girls and Achievement: Addressing the Classroom Issues.* London: RoutledgeFalmer.

Francis, B. and Skelton, C. (2005) *Reassessing Gender and Achievement: Questioning Contemporary Key Debates.* London: Routledge.

Jackson, C. (2005) The bad girls don't really work hard and then they get really popular: an exploration of girls' attitudes and approaches to schoolwork. Paper presented at The British Educational Research Association Conference, 14–17 September, University of Glamorgan.

Jackson, C. (2006) *Lads and Ladettes in School: Gender and a Fear of Failure.* Maidenhead: Open University Press.

Jones, S. and Myhill, D. (2004a) Seeing things differently: teachers' constructions of underachievement, *Gender and Education*, 16(4): 531–46.

Jones, S. and Myhill, D. (2004b) 'Troublesome boys' and 'compliant girls': gender identity and perceptions of achievement and underachievement', *British Journal of Sociology of Education*, 25(5): 547–61.

Lucey, H. (2001) Social class, gender and schooling, in B. Francis and C. Skelton (eds), *Investigating Gender: Contemporary Perspectives in Education.* Buckingham: Open University Press.

McRobbie, A. (2007) Top girls?, *Cultural Studies*, 21(4): 718–37.

Reay, D. (2001) Finding or losing yourself?: working-class relationships to education, *Journal of Education Policy*, 16(4): 333–46.

Reay, D. (2008) Class out of place: the white middle classes and intersectionalities of class and 'race' in urban state schooling in England, in L. Weis (ed.), *The Way Class Works*. New York: Routledge.

Renold, E. and Allan, A. (2006) Bright and beautiful: high-achieving girls, ambivalent femininities, and the feminisation of success in the primary school, *Discourse*, 27(4): 457–73.

Ringrose, J. (2007) Successful girls? Complicating post-feminist, neo-liberal discourses of educational achievement and gender equality, *Gender and Education*, 19(4): 471–89.

Skeggs, B. (2004) *Class, Self, Culture*. London: Routledge.

Walkerdine, V., Lucey, H. and Melody, J. (2001) *Growing Up Girl: Psychosocial Explorations of Gender and Class*. Buckingham: Palgrave.

Woods, P. (1990) Having a laugh: an antidote to schooling, in M. Hammersley and P. Woods (eds), *The Process of Schooling: A Sociological Reader*. London: Routledge and Kegan Paul.

Youdell, D. (2006) *Impossible Bodies, Impossible Selves: Exclusions and Student Subjectivities*. London: Springer.

4 Refusing to integrate? Asian girls, achievement and the experience of schooling

Farzana Shain

Introduction

This chapter focuses on achievement with specific reference to Asian girls' experiences of schooling. Since the early 1990s education policy in England has been preoccupied with academic 'success' as measured by public examination results. New Labour's record on education in particular has been marked by an unrelenting focus on 'success', 'standards' and 'achievement' (Bradford and Hey 2007) set in the broader context of policies of marketization, privatization and managerialism. This not only marks continuity with the neo-liberal policies of earlier conservative governments but has also had the effect of exacerbating division and disadvantage rather than equalizing educational opportunities (Gerwirtz 2002). Despite the rhetoric of inclusion, the overt focus on achievement which also features heavily in recent government documents on gender and ethnicity (see DCSF 2007) has enabled so called model minorities (Mirza 2005) such as middle-class south Asians (mainly Indians) and some Chinese students to be held out as evidence of 'meritocracy at work'. For the vast majority of minoritized and working-class students, however, the dominant version of 'success' remains illusive.

The picture on Asian girls' achievement is quite varied, although statistics generally show Indian girls who tend to be from more middle-class backgrounds outperforming working-class Pakistani and Bangladeshi girls (see DfES 2006). While recent research has focused on high achievement among working-class Asian girls (Ahmad 2001; Abbas 2002; Dwyer et al. 2006; Renold and Allan 2006), less attention has been paid to the educational experiences of Asian girls who are defined as 'low achievers'. This chapter draws on empirical data from two studies to explore the ways in which Asian girls are both positioned and positioned themselves in relation to dominant notions of success as well as ideal versions of Asian femininity and the particular consequences of these negotiations for their experiences of achievement and schooling.

Asian Girls in Public and Policy Discourses

Media and public interest in Asian girls, especially those from Muslim backgrounds, has spiralled in recent years. Culture clash, forced marriages, honour killings and Islamic modes of dress have been among the controversial topics that have served to reinforce and rework historic (colonial) representations of Asian women as the passive victims of oppressive cultures. Intense public and policy debate in the aftermath of the urban unrest in English towns in 2001 and the 2005 London bombings has focused on the 'limits' of multi-culturalism and the extent to which Muslims can integrate into a 'British way of life'. Against this background, the repositioning of Muslim males (who were once regarded as passive and law abiding) as dangerous fanatics has impacted on representations of Muslim women. Since femininity is defined in relation to masculinity, the more dangerous, volatile, and aggressive Asian and Muslim men and boys appear to be, the more passive, controlled and vulnerable Asian and Muslim girls and women are assumed to be (Shain 2003).

Controversies over Islamic dress such as the veil affair in 2006, have further cast Muslim women as the bearers or symbols of backward and barbaric cultures (Brah 1996). Set in the context of broader debate about the management of ethnic diversity and policy initiatives promoting social and community cohesion as the solution to economic problems (Cheong et al. 2007), the controversy sparked by Cabinet minister Jack Straw's comments that the veil is a 'visible marker of separation' enabled Muslim girls to be drawn as outward symbols of a 'refusal to integrate'. This was further echoed in Tony Blair's (2006) assimilationist call to Muslims and new migrants to adopt British values in order to be accepted into British society. While policies for the management of ethnic diversity since the 1960s have been based on a complex range of ideologies including 'assimilation', 'integration' and 'multi-culturalism' (Cheong et al. 2007), Grosvenor (1997: 49–50) has argued that 'these identified shifts in policy are more apparent than real . . . they exist in the sphere of articulation rather than in practice' and that 'a clear, coherent consistent and uniform' policy goal can in fact be readily identified as running through government circulars, advisory notes, select committee documents and political speeches during the same period, which reflects 'an enduring commitment to assimilation'. As I argue, the pressure to assimilate has and continues to be a daily reality for Asian girls.

Theorizing Asian Girls' Experiences of Schooling and Achievement

Since the 1980s feminist research focusing on intersections of 'race', class and gender (Basit 1997; Dwyer 2000; Archer 2003; Shain 2003) has challenged popular representations and earlier culture-clash frameworks that positioned Asian girls as 'helpless victims' (Watson 1976) focusing instead on the more active role played by British-born Asian youth in negotiating identities drawn from both residual 'home' cultures and the local cultures they currently inhabit (Dwyer 2000; Archer 2003; Shain 2003).

In relation to achievement, recent feminist research exploring girls' relationships to success has shown that even girls who achieve the highest grades may experience success as fragile or problematic (Walkerdine et al. 2001; Archer 2005) and are often viewed as possessing the 'wrong sort of femininity' for success – they are either 'too loud', 'too working class', or 'too hardworking'. Dominant characterizations of Asian girls as 'quiet', 'passive' and 'demure' resonate to some extent with the idealized and de-sexualized middle-class femininity of the sort performed by Reay's (2001) 'nice girls' and Renold's (2001) 'square girls', but Asian girls are still often read as the Other of academic success because of the assumption that cultural constraints prevent them from realizing their full academic potential. The tight discipline that is believed to characterize Asian family life is also often associated with strong educational values encouraging 'hard work' and 'studiousness'. Yet when Asian girls do not succeed, it is this same tight discipline that is cited in pathology frameworks as placing a burden on girls to conform to family pressures surrounding for example, arranged marriages (Archer 2003; Shain 2003).

Research on primary-school-aged Asian girls has also focused on the 'impossibility' of combining academic success with peer popularity. In Renold and Allan's (2006) research, Shamilla, a high-achieving Asian girl, was extremely popular with peers in part because she downplayed her academic success. Nyla, another high achiever, was described by her peers as a 'loner' and 'miserable' because she refused to diminish her achievements for the sake of popularity. The importance of the peer group and its relationship to academic 'success' and 'failure' is a central theme in the schooling of Asian girls that I take up in the next section.

The Asian Girls (AG) Project

In this section I draw on research conducted as part of a wider study on Asian girls' experiences of schooling (Shain 2003). This research, completed in the mid 1990s, did not set out to explore achievement but a reanalysis of the data suggests that setting by ability across the schools was a critical factor in friendship formations which were central to the girls' active negotiations of their academic and social experiences through schooling. The research focused on the strategies that girls used to deal with schooling and drew on interviews (as part of a broader ethnographic approach) with 44 Asian girls across eight schools in Greater Manchester and Staffordshire. The girls were aged 13–16 years and were from Pakistani, Indian and Bangladeshi backgrounds with Pakistani Muslims in the majority (over 80 per cent). Despite sharing common class and regional locations in economically deprived areas that had suffered from the decline of manufacturing, and while also being subject to common cultural definitions of them as passive, timid and over-controlled, the girls were able to take up a range of identity positions which I refer to as strategies. Through an analysis of the girls' accounts of schooling, friendships, family and peer relations, four main strategies emerged which are not intended to be static or fixed but illustrate the range of Asian femininities being 'struggled over' within the context of schooling:

1. *Resistance through culture* – the 'Gang Girls' were both positioned and positioned themselves in opposition to the dominant culture of the school, which they defined as white and racist.
2. *Survival* – the 'Survivors', whose strategy of apparent conformity was part of an overall conscious drive to achieve academic success, prioritized neither racism, nor sexism though they experienced both.
3. *Rebellion* – the 'Rebels' as teachers referred to them, prioritized uneven gender relations within their communities. Without actively resisting these, they were critical of parental and community values and they actively dissociated themselves from the Gang girls.
4. *Religious prioritization* – the 'Faith Girls' prioritized religion but were well integrated in terms of mixed friendships and pursued a 'survival' strategy to achieve academic success.

In this section I focus on the first category, which featured an overwhelmingly large number of 'low achievers'. Underachievement is defined here as a combination of the girls' own expectations, their location in the lower sets and teacher predictions of further exam success. The 'Gang girls'–adopted an 'us and them' approach to schooling as in Willis's (1977) study, but unlike the lads, their experiences were defined primarily with reference to racism and their positive assertion of 'Asian' identities. The 14 girls in this category were both positioned and positioned themselves in opposition to the dominant culture of the school, which they defined as white and racist. It was the experience of racism in the school that led to the formation of an all-Asian female sub-culture from which white students and teachers and Asian students who appeared to ally with whites in the school were excluded.

Racist Name Calling

The majority of the girls in the AG study (not just the Gang girls) were subjected to some form of verbal abuse with terms such as 'Paki' and 'black bitch' being routinely employed. In the Muslim girls study these racist terms of abuse had not lost currency but insults such as 'terrorist' and 'suicide bomber' had been added to this usual repertoire of racist insults. But the girls who occupied the lower sets and who chose all Asian friendship groups were the particular targets of racist name calling. These girls were also the most likely to actively resist name calling both individually and collectively within the context of the female friendship group and included both verbal and physical resistance:

> I just swear back . . . [laughs]. Well you know they call me 'black bitch' and I just call them 'white bastard'. (YA)

> Yeah I've been called things like because of my colour. 'Paki', 'black bitch' I don't care. I just turn around and call them back. I was born in this country and I'll stay in it. (TH)

> This boy called me a 'Paki' but I got him back. I called him white 'B'. If someone calls me, I call them back. If they want to have a fight, I'll have a fight. (PA)

These comments reveal practices of 'sexual Othering' (Connolly 1998) in Asian girls' experiences of schooling. Because the girls did not passively accept racism and were prepared to defend themselves, they fell outside the dominant stereotypes associated with both conventional 'nice girl' (Reay 2001) white femininity and 'passive' Asian femininity. Boys were prepared to physically attack them, including punching and kicking them. The girls' willingness to fight back could be read as a form of reactive violence (Osler and Starkey 2005) which further reinforced their status as deserving of abuse and characterizations of them as 'volatile', 'angry' and 'aggressive' – more resonant with current discourses surrounding Asian masculinity (Archer 2003; Shain 2010).

Dress and Language

The Gang girls were also highly visible because of their preference for traditional dress and their 'home languages', which became important visible markers of their 'Asian' identities. They fiercely defended

traditional Asian dress, which was allowed by most schools in school uniform colours. While this enabled them to identify positively with other
similarly dressed Asian girls, it also marked them out for further racist
name calling because it was read against the schools' dominant white
culture as a 'refusal to integrate'. Like dress, language was an important
vehicle for expressing identities and eight of the Gang girls admitted deliberately using their home language at school to exclude other groups
from their conversation:

> I speak [my language] at school sometimes with friends . . . like
> when you want to say something and you don't want others to
> know like when there's Christian people present . . . They say speak
> in our language . . . We [say], 'No, we're not saying anything about
> you, it's just our culture'. [Laughs]. English people speak English,
> Asian people speak their own language. (TH)

This use of 'home' language further marked the girls out as separate and
'isolationist' but for the girls it was one way to 'win space' and defeat the
boredom they experienced in the lower sets.

Friendships and the Policing of Sexuality and
Sexual Reputation

The importance of the peer group and the role friendship groups play in
defining and performing femininity has been well documented in feminist
studies of schooling (see Hey 1997; Walkerdine et al. 2001; Renold 2001;
George 2007; Ringrose 2008) but for the 'low achievers' in the AG study,
this was a defining feature of their experience of schooling. The Gang
girls were characterized by their all-Asian female friendship groups, to
the exclusion of boys (White and Asian) and White students generally.
They claimed to mix with their 'own kind' also for security, friendship
and empathy: 'I mix with Pakistanis – they understand my ways' (PD).
An important reason, however, was the shield from verbal and physical
abuse that Asian girl groups were seen to provide: 'Pakistanis don't bully
you' (KB) and 'the English don't treat us very well. They just ignore us and
batter us. I used to hang around with English people but Asians understand
better' (NN).

Girls' friendships and hostilities show an ongoing fascination with 'de-
ciphering the relationship between gender and sexuality' (Ali 2003: 275).
Like Ali's girls, the Gang girls vocalized strongly their ideas about what
constituted appropriate kinds of femininity. They employed sexist and
abusive language (Hey 1997; Youdell 2005) to refer to Asian girls who befriended White girls and boys. They were most scathing in their comments

about girls who engaged in interracial relationships who they labelled as 'sluts' or 'slags' (Hey 1997; Ali 2003):

> There's a girl [****], in the third year. She acts like she's English. She goes out with boys like she hangs round with boys in school like she's got no Asian friends and just every time hanging round with boys white boys. [People] swear, to her face and behind her back, 'slag', 'bitch', anything that comes into our minds, because she's stupid going out with an English boy and she's Asian. (PA)

As Ringrose (2008) argues, sexual regulation is integral to the micro-dynamics of girls' friendship groups. These scathing remarks were one way in which the girls were able to seize power in their relations with other Asian girls. The comments were directed mainly at Rebel girls who, by dissociating themselves from the Gang girls and mixing mainly with white students (boys and girls), were often read by peers and teachers to be performing a more acceptable version of Asian femininity. The Rebels were more likely to dress in western clothes, which in relational terms further marked the Gang girls out as 'refusing to integrate'. In relation to current policy, the Rebels' appropriation of often hyper-feminine western-ized forms of dress (short skirts) could be read as illustrative of the ways in which social integration may be achieved [ironically] at the expense of the social alienation of Others who have not adopted the language and culture of the dominant mainstream (Cheong et al. 2007).

Negative Relations with Staff and the Withdrawal from Learning

A major consequence of 'being' a Gang girl was negative relations with staff. This was largely because they appeared to challenge dominant passive Asian femininity. Teachers often spoke unfavourably of them, in terms such as 'troublemakers' with some openly confessing dislike because of the girls' involvement in 'gangs'. The gang label has masculine connotations, associated with boys, violence and 'laddishness' and connects with wider current discourses on Asian masculinity. Immediate gratification was another major Gang characteristic and like Keely in Renold's chapter (this volume) the characterization of them as 'bad girls' led to a cycle of negative relations with staff and their location in the lower sets further reinforced teachers' perceptions of them as academically incapable. The girls claimed to receive little or no encouragement from the school and staff and thus resorted to strategies to defeat boredom, such as breaking school rules, truancy and being late for lessons. With few positive reports from the school and rare contact between the school and their families, it was a foregone conclusion that the Gang girls would not pursue further studies.

The gradual withdrawal or self-exclusion from learning is illustrated in the following example:

> *AP:* I can't read or write. I just don't be bothered. It's boring English. I just don't like the teacher he's always picking on us, all the Asian girls.
>
> *FS:* Can you comment on your progress?
>
> *AP:* I don't know, I hardly come into school. I'm in the lower sets.
>
> *FS:* Do you have any career plans?
>
> *AP:* I'm not interested. I don't want to do anything. I just like coming to meet my friends.

By challenging the dominant stereotypes, the girls played an active role in creating an Asian femininity from which Others were excluded. Identifying the main cause of their oppression as racism, they appeared to accept and provide justification for their likely exclusion from further education and careers. It was their definition and acceptance of the inevitability of this situation that influenced their approach to schooling. Consequently, school became a place to have fun and defeat boredom. Inherent in their attempts to convince other girls of the inevitability of their future roles as wives and mothers was a fatalism owing as much to their class locations in England than to their cultural backgrounds (see also Plummer 2000; Walkerdine et al. 2001) and as such the girls played an active part in the reproduction of the conditions of their oppression.

The Muslim Girls (MG) Study

In a pilot study carried out in 2006, I interviewed six girls who in various ways described themselves as Muslims, not all of whom were practising. Four were of Pakistani descent, one was Bangladeshi and one from Afghanistan whose family had migrated to England post-2001. The girls were aged 14–16 years and were all from the same Staffordshire school. Two were 'high achievers', two were in middle sets and two were 'low achievers'. I refer briefly to the 'low achievers' before focusing on one high-achieving girl whose account both supports and complicates the wider findings of the AG study.

The two 'low-achieving' girls' accounts resonated with the experiences of Gang girls except that they primarily identified as Muslim rather than Asian even though, like the Gang girls, they were not practising Muslims and religion played little part in their lives. This identification as Muslim reflects the wider impact of the politicization of Muslim identities in the last two decades when groups who were previously identified and identifying as Asian, Pakistani or Bengali have come to be defined or define themselves as Muslim. This process has been driven further by policy frameworks that have given prominence to 'faith' over ethnicity (Worley 2005).

Like the Gang girls, the two low achievers also expected arranged marriages and saw schooling as primarily a place to have fun and defeat boredom. They defined school space as racist and differentiated themselves from other Asian girls who they described as 'sell-outs' for mixing across gender and ethnic groups. They spoke their home language in school and defended Asian cultural practices such as arranged marriages.

Humaira, a 'high-achieving' Bangladeshi girl was labelled by girls in the lower sets as a 'sell-out' because she was seen to mix mainly with White students in school. Like a number in the AG study, she spoke at length about a racist incident that she had encountered, including being asked whether she was a suicide bomber. Within the school though, and like a number of the Rebels in the AG study, Humaira largely dissociated herself from what she described as 'stereotypical Pakistani girls':

> *Humaira:* I don't want to be seen as one of those stereotypical Pakistani girls.
> *FS:* And what are they?
> *Humaira:* Well you know, they like hang together in a big crowd and don't mix with anyone else. Some of them you see, they do mix in their classes, but as soon as they get out they go back to their [Asian] mates as if . . . y'know no one else is good enough. And I think that's just rude and I don't want to be like that.

As this comment suggests, the 'stereotypical Pakistani girls' like the Gang girls, were highly visible because of their preference for other Asian female friends. Humaira justifies her dissociation from these girls by drawing on the dominant discourse of segregation – 'they hang together in a big crowd', 'no one else is good enough', 'it's rude' – implying that the girls engage in a process of self-segregation (Cantle 2001). She positions herself outside of this discourse – 'I don't want to be like that' – and expresses a strong dislike for what she regards as an instrumental attitude on the part of Asian girls who happily mix in their classes with White students but outside of class show a strong own-ethnic group preference. Her account thus resonated with several of the Survivors in the AG study who also felt excluded by the girl groups but, more significantly, Humaira like some of the Survivors and Rebels, seemed to pay a considerable cost for pursuing academic success. This included being disliked or viewed as 'stuck up' by other Asian students for being a high achiever (she was predicted A* grades in her GCSE exams) but in also being routinely compared favourably with the Asian girls groups she had to be accepting of some racist comments from her own friends:

I hang out mainly with these girls who y'know who smoke and drink and are labelled as 'bad girls' [i.e. popular White working-class girls]. My friends are always saying to me, 'you're alright you are; you're dead safe; you don't get offended if we call you Paki like these other Asian girls'. I mean I really don't mind being called a Paki because it depends on who is saying it, how they're saying it.

In choosing not to define these comments as racist, Humaira performed a Rebel femininity but what complicates a straight reading-off of her account as a Rebel however, is her wearing of the hijab. But unlike hijab-wearing Faith girls, this was not initially for religious reasons. Rather, a hair-cut 'gone wrong' had led to the take-up of the headscarf at 11 and she now felt 'naked without it'. It was interesting that in Humaira's case the hijab was far less provocative than being part of an Asian girl-group. Across the two studies, which were conducted 10 years apart, it seems that the Asian girl-group had not lost its symbolic power. It was just as threatening in the Muslim girls study as in the Asian girls study.

Conclusion

While there is now a considerable body of literature challenging dominant representations of Asian femininity, Asian girls, especially those from Muslim backgrounds, continue to be represented in media and public discourses in contradictory ways that reinforce historic assumptions about their femininities. Themes of culture clash, subordination and increasingly a 'refusal to integrate' suggest a reworking of old colonial stereotypes in new times.

A number of research studies now focus on Asian girls' high academic achievements but there is still a paucity of research on the experiences of low-achieving Asian girls. Although I did not set out to address the issue of achievement, I did find some correspondence between academic achievement and a range of ways of performing Asian femininity.

A number of issues emerge from a reading of the Gang girls' experiences of schooling. These include the complexity of the process by which the girls gradually withdraw from learning. While family (low) expectations played a part it also emerged from the study that parents were often prepared to allow their daughters to proceed to further and higher education as long as they received positive reports about their daughters' progress from the school. In some cases parental permission was actually withdrawn when school reports failed to support the standard expected by parents. This suggests we need to look more closely at the process by which the failure on the part of some Asian girls to conform to the dominant representations of Asian femininity comes to be translated also as academic failure.

Perhaps the most urgent issue relates to the immense pressure on Asian girls to be 'seen to integrate' in the context of schooling or, more specifically, to avoid all-Asian girl friendships. I would argue that the same pressures do not exist for White girls to integrate with other ethnic groups. Much of the pressure for Asian girls to conform to a westernized version of Asian femininity predates, but has been reinforced by, recent policy discourses on integration and community cohesion which shift attention from economic problems to the cultural practices of Muslims. This places a large burden particularly on Muslim girls who adopt Islamic dress and who are seen as the most visible and outward symbols of a 'refusal to integrate'. In the MG study there was evidence that despite the introduction of various schemes aimed at promoting 'racial tolerance', friendship patterns remained much the same as in the AG study with high achievers paying considerable costs in return for social acceptance. Humaira, a high-achieving Bangladeshi girl commented on the racist abuse that she chooses to ignore on a daily basis as part of her dissociation from Ganggirl femininity which was positioned by the school's dominant culture as the least desirable version of Asian femininity available. That there was an immense pressure on Asian girls to be 'seen to integrate' also suggests, as Grosvenor (1997) has argued, that an enduring commitment to assimilation has been central to shaping education over the last four decades.

References

Abbas, T. (2003) The impact of religo-cultural norms and values on the education of young south Asian women, *British Journal of Sociology of Education*, 24(4): 411–28.

Ahmad, F. (2001) Modern traditions? British muslim women and academic achievement, *Gender and Education*. 13(2): 137–52.

Ali, S. (2003) To be a girl: culture and class in schools, *Gender and Education*, 15(3): 269–83.

Archer, L. (2003) *Race, Masculinity and Schooling*. Maidenhead: Open University Press.

Archer, L. (2005) The impossibility of girls' educational 'success': entanglements of gender, 'race', class and sexuality in the production and problematisation of educational femininities. Paper presented at the ESRC Seminar Series *Girls in Education 3–16*, Cardiff, 24 November.

Basit, T. (1997) *Eastern Values, Western Milieu: Identities and Aspirations of Adolescent British Muslim Girls*. Aldershot: Ashgate.

Blair, T. (2006) The duty to integrate, speech at Downing Street, 8 December.

Bradford, S. and Hey, V. (2007) Successful subjectivities? The successification of class, ethnic and gender positions, *Journal of Education Policy*, 22(6): 595–614.

Brah, A. (1996) *Cartographies of Diaspora, Contesting Identities*. London: Routledge.

Brah, A. and Phoenix, A. (2004) Ain't I a woman? Revisiting intersectionality, *Journal of International Women's Studies*, 5(3): 75–87.

Cantle, T. (2001) *Community Cohesion*. London: Home Office.

Cheong, P., Edwards, R., Goldbourne, H. and Solomos, J. (2007) Immigration, social cohesion and social capital: a critical review, *Critical Social Policy*, 27(1): 24–49.

Connolly, P. (1998) *Racism, Gender and Primary School Identities*. London: Routledge.

DCSF (2007) *Gender and Education: The Evidence on Pupils in England*. Nottingham: DCSF.

DfES (2006) *Ethnicity and Education: The Evidence on Minority Ethnic pupils, Research topic paper: RTP01-0*. London: DfES.

Dwyer, C. (2000) Negotiating diasporic identities: young British south Asian Muslim women, *Women's Studies International Forum*, 23(4): 475–86.

Dwyer, C., Modood, T., Sanghera-Shah, B. and Thapar-Bjorkert, S. (2006) *Ethnicity as Social Capital? Explaining the Differential Educational Achievements of Young British Pakistani Men and Women*. Available at: http://www.bristol.ac.uk/sociology/leverhulme/conference/conferencepapers/dwyer.pdf (accessed 3/11/08).

George, R. (2007) Urban girls' 'race' friendship and school choice, changing schools, changing friendships, *Race, Ethnicity and Education*, 10(2): 115–29.

Gewirtz, S. (2002) *The Managerial School: Post-welfarism and Social Justice in Education*. London: Routledge.

Grosvenor, I. (1997) *Assimilating Identities*. London: Lawrence and Wishart.

Hey, V. (1997) *The Company She Keeps: An Ethnography of Girls' Friendship*. London: Routledge.

Mirza, H. (2005) *The More Things Change, the More They Stay the Same: Assessing Black Underachievement 35 Years On*. Available at: http://www.multiverse.ac.uk/attachments/06536150-1447-4bb9-8df6-c705a0793065.pdf (accessed 3/11/08).

Osler, A. and Starkey, H. (2005) Violence in schools and representations of young people: a critique of government policies in France and England, *Oxford Review of Education*, 31(2): 195–215.

Plummer, G. (2000) *Failing Working Class Girls*. Stoke-on-Trent: Trentham.

Reay, D. (2001) 'Spice girls', 'nice girls', 'girlies', and 'tomboys': gender discourses, girls' cultures and femininities in the primary classroom, Gender and Education, 13(2): 153–66.

Renold, E. (2001) 'Square-girls', femininity and the negotiation of academic success in the primary school, *British Education Research Journal*, 27(5): 577–88.

Renold, E. and Allan, A. (2006) Bright and beautiful: high-achieving girls, ambivalent femininities and the feminisation of success in the primary school, *Discourse: Studies in the Cultural Politics of Education*, 27(4): 547–73.

Ringrose, J. (2008) 'Just be friends': exposing the limits of educational bully discourses for understanding teen girls' heterosexualized friendships and conflicts, *British Journal of Sociology of Education*, 29(5): 509–22.

Shain, F. (2003) *The Schooling and Identity of Asian Girls*. Stoke-on-Trent: Trentham.

Shain, F. (2010) *The New Folk Devils: Muslim Boys and Education in Britain*: Stoke-on-Trent: Trentham.

Walkerdine, V., Lucey, H. and Melody, J. (2001) *Growing Up Girl: Psychosocial Explorations of Gender and Class*. Basingstoke: Palgrave.

Watson, J. (ed.) (1976) *Between Two Cultures: Migrants and Minorities in Britain*. Oxford: Blackwell.

Willis, P. (1977) *Learning to Labour*. Farnborough: Saxon House.

Worley, C. (2005) 'It's not about race. It's about the community': New Labour and community cohesion, *Critical Social Policy*, 25(4): 483–96.

Youdell, D. (2005) Sex-gender-sexuality: how sex, gender and sexuality constellations are constituted in secondary schools, *Gender and Education*, 17(3): 249–70.

5 Fighting for an education: succeeding *and* surviving for girls in care at school

Emma Renold

Introduction

This chapter draws upon biographical case-study data generated in an ESRC-funded research project that ethnographically explored the everyday lives, identities and relationship cultures of children in public care. These are young people who are subject to care orders and looked after by a local authority. They can be in foster or residential care, living with relatives, or placed at home. Sometimes, they are voluntarily accommodated away from home with the 'agreement' of their parents. A significant portion of the chapter involves close analysis of one young woman's narrated journey through school life over two years (aged 13–15), where multiple struggles to perform 'good-girl pupil' meet and mesh with the incitement to perform 'bad-girl pupil'. In so doing, it engages with contemporary post-feminist discourses in which girls and young women are imagined as the new model neo-liberal[1] citizens, free to adapt and reinvent themselves as successful rational educational subjects (see Walkerdine et al. 2001; Benjamin 2003; Gordon 2006; McRobbie 2007; Ringrose 2007; Baker 2008). This analysis draws on and contributes to two substantive literatures: the psycho-social affects of individualized and competitive cultures of schooling, and the pathologization of aggressive school-based femininities. The chapter foregrounds the dynamic social, emotional and psychical costs and consequences of surviving and succeeding for girls in care at school.

Contemporary Figurations of the Child-in-care as Potential Educational 'Waste'

Discourses of school success are totalizing in their reach. The expectation and fantasy of 'excellence for all' now include the most vulnerable and marginalized in society. Driven by a desire for sameness and equality, the latest working group report for transforming the schooling experiences of children in care 'combines high expectations and standards with inclusion' so that children in care 'achieve highly and gain results and qualifications which are every bit as good as their peers' (DCSF 2006: 9). Success, however, as Bradford and Hey (2007: 598) remind us, 'is a relational and dynamic concept and can only be understood as coming from the shadow of its Other: failure'. This figuration of the child as 'failed' educational Other, is embedded in a bigger suite of Otherness, all of which pivot around discourses of the child-at-risk. Cultural geographer Katz (2008: 9) conceptualizes this figuration as the 'spectre of a wasted childhood'. Despite the welcome shift to 'strengths-based' approaches in social work (which promote discourses of capacity and competencies), deficit discourses of the child as future waste continue to haunt recent policy documents. Such documents constitute the educational experiences of 'looked-after children', through discourses of lack, as potentially 'failed' educational subjects with 'failed' educational and occupational futures (DCSF 2006: 3). Ironically, the acronym used in everyday social work practice to refer to 'Looked After Children' is 'LAC', thus brutally reinforcing wider deficit discourses positioning and repositioning the child 'in care'.

Although the most recent document outlining Best Practice for children in care (DCFS 2007) reiterates their failed futures, it emphasizes the need to challenge stereotypes and expectations of the looked-after experience as an inevitable trajectory of unfulfilled potential. Here, the educational system, and schooling in particular, is constituted through a familiar affective register of its child-saving capacity (from a wasted future), with looked-after children discursively positioned as potential carriers of academic excellence. Difficult and troubled pasts, as catalysts for 'bad affects', are acknowledged and thus tolerated but are no reason not to pursue Benjamin's (2003) 'techno-rationalist ladder to success'. Throughout the DCSF (2007) document, the 'past/present experience' of looked-after children and its potential for unleashing unruly or bad affect (anger, pain, bullying) and wasted futures, mesh with the 'future experience' of the looked-after child and the potential for unleashing good affect (friendship, social cohesion) and successful futures. It is precisely this schizoid dynamic and the constellation of representations of the looked-after educational subject (as achiever/non-achiever, bully/friend), the role of the school (as a place of stability/instability) and the gendered and classed dynamic of the sacrificial logic of the neo-liberal drive for excellence (e.g. in the relinquishing of 'bad affect'), that focuses the rest of the chapter.

Method/ology: Researching and Theorizing Marginalized Subjectivities

The central methodological aim of the 'ExtraOrdinary Lives' (2006–8) project was to generate research encounters and opportunities using particular reflexive methodological practices through which young people (8 in total) could choose their own level of engagement to represent their everyday lives (pasts, presents and futures). They could also choose their own methods to record and represent aspects of their lives and identities: visually, textually, orally and aurally (see Holland et al. forthcoming for full discussion of the participatory methodology). It is the research relationship with one young person, Keely, and the analysis of data generated between us, predominantly in the car (recorded with a digital recorder) over an 18-month period, that this chapter focuses upon. We met Keely as a potential high achiever whose academic and vocational ambitions were supported by the school (a successful, yet often demonized, city comprehensive serving an area of multiple deprivation). The analysis in this chapter focuses specifically around multiple episodes of conflictual relational encounters in school, and Keely's struggle to realize her potential as aspirant achiever.

While the case study offers up analyses of only one young person to explore processes of subjectification and affectivity, theoretically, I am conceptualizing the making of subjectivity as thoroughly social, relational and contextually contingent. This has been central to our project's exploration of the everyday lives of children 'in care' because of the dominance of individualizing psychological and neo-liberal discourses which divide the normative rational subject from its pathological irrational Others (Baker 2008). Conceiving of the subject as always bound up with Others foregrounds how the subject cannot live without its Others (Butler 2005). This relational process of becoming a subject is thus always intersubjective and always social (see Walkerdine 2007). The significance of the relationality of affect and the classed and gendered dynamics of the way the Other works in, and through, the 'looked-after' girl subject is explored in the empirical sections that follow.

Bad Girls and the Schooling of Un/intelligible Femininities

'Doing girl' for some of the girls in our project involved negotiating some complex and contradictory positionings. Many had to routinely negotiate their discursive positioning as Other in relation to local social and cultural gender norms, what Butler (1990) terms culturally un/intelligible femininities. Such positionings and performances seemed to bring about feelings of shame, or what Ahmed (2004: 107) describes as 'the affective costs of not following the scripts of normative existence'. A significant strand in the analysis has thus been an exploration of the ways in which discourses of (in) crisis and (at) risk are mediated by contemporary conceptualizations of femininity. Indeed, the ways in which discourses of crisis and risk have infiltrated all social groups is particularly acute in recent theorizing within critical girlhood studies (Harris 2004; Aapola et al. 2005; Jiwani et al. 2006). Aapola et al.'s (2005) deconstruction of the US 'Reviving Ophelia' discourse, for example, is interpreted as a contemporary moral panic over the sustainability of previously privileged femininities of white, middle-class girls and young women. As Hey argues in Chapter 15, many of these representations, from girl power to girl in/creating crisis, continue to pivot around the luminous presence of the abject subject, for example, the 'bully' (Ringrose and Renold 2009), the 'chav' (Hayward and Yar 2006) and the 'ladette' (Jackson 2006) in a familiar and historically embedded class-based dichotomy of good girl/bad girl (Griffin 2004). Compare, for example, the classed pathologization of aggression in the psychological 'mean girl' discourse (White, middle class, see Ringrose 2006) with the physically violent bad-girl discourse (White, working-class and racialized other, see Chesney-Lind and Eliason 2006). While a number of studies demonstrate empirically how 'femininity' is increasingly becoming an impossible practice (Walkerdine et al. 2001; Griffin 2005; O'Flynn and Epstein 2005; Renold and Allan 2006; Youdell 2006; Archer et al. 2007; Renold and Ringrose 2009), this 'impossibility' is intensified when negotiated from the position of an already marginalized subject. This was certainly an emerging theme in Keely's negotiations of being in school and living in foster care. However, while the anger and accompanying violence following everyday negotiations of the abject positioning of being 'in care' are well documented in policy guidance, the gendering of these dynamics continues to rely on well-worn stereotypes. This chapter thus takes up and addresses some of the concerns raised by Hey (Chapter 15) around the norms of individualization and how the bodily practices of marginalized groups, even within 'demonized' (Reay 2004) schools, are constituted as outside the norms of acceptable femininities.

'I'm Not a Girlie Fighter': Angry Femininities

> *Keely:* She pulled my hair, so I hit her ... I'm not a girlie fighter.
> I don't do pulling hair and scrabbling (inaudible), just punch
> and kick.

. . .

> *Keely:* Because I don't give up, yeah. Never back down yeah ... I
> never back down in an argument ... if someone wants to fight
> me, I'll fight them back and I'll win.

Over the course of the fieldwork, we learned from Keely about the way she invested in a range of symbolically 'masculine' activities: from jumping off high walls, swimming in rivers, climbing trees/lampposts and doing dares (such as the 'punching competition', see below). With many of these episodes occurring in school, she was frequently constituted as aggressive 'bully', leading to a series of temporary school exclusions. Her refusal to covet nice-girl hyper-femininity is summed up in her phrase 'I'm no girly girl' which reaches into the domain of physical violence ('I'm no girlie fighter'); she preferred punching and kicking to hair pulling. As these quotes illustrate, meshing with the symbolic violence of being positioned through non-normative discourses of the nomadic girl-in-care were multiple episodes of verbal and physical violence – conflictual episodes that we learned over time had long affective histories.

While 'mean-girl' or 'bad-girl-bully' (Ringrose 2006) discourses might constitute these verbal and physical violences as deviant or pathological, a wider analytic lens might constitute such conflict as practices of survivability, pleasure or resistance as Keely negotiated the social battlefield of the school playground and the demands of performative neoliberal schooling (Ringrose and Renold 2009). The point I emphasize here is how such warrior femininities are disavowed and out of place, both within the context of schooling and the embodiment of the normative girl-pupil/child. There is an acknowledgement in policy discourse of the unruly affects (e.g. as 'bullies' and 'bullied', DCSF 2007) that might accompany the child-in-care into the social world of the school. These affects, however, are not explored in terms of their gendered dynamics, or more widely as the psycho-social affects of competitive individualism (e.g. 'I'll fight them back and I'll win).

As an example of this classed and gendered dynamic, the following extract illustrates how the compulsion for Keely to always speak her mind (see Archer et al. 2007) literally constitutes what Skeggs (2004) theorizes as noisy femininities – combative performances which severely disrupt the institutionalized docile body of the idealized good-girl pupil (Walkerdine 1990). Keely is relating what happened when her teacher brought her background to the foreground by disclosing to the class that her brothers had just 'gone into care'. Keely thought this 'outing' of her family life resulted from her 'kicking off' in a previous lesson:

> *Keely:* And now all he's [class teacher] done, is bring that up about
> my brothers, in front of the class!

Emma: Why would he bring that up though?

Keely: I dunno … 'cause I think that cause I kicked off in last lesson.

Emma: Oh, OK.

Keely: What he did, he goes, 'I know your family life and I know your brothers have just gone into care and all that'. I went, 'three people in this class knew that, I didn't want everyone knowing, they all gonna come up to me now right, and do my head in'. And then he went, 'Keely calm down', I went, 'screw you, you just like, blatantly just told everyone'. And he went, 'Keely there's no reason to get upset about it'. I went 'I'm not upset, I'm just mad at you for doing it like' … He was like, 'Keely calm down' and I was like 'get out of my face please' and then he just, then he sent me out … I was like that 'aaaaaaaaaaaaagh' (screams), so then he's like 'right, I'm gonna phone your carers now' and I just walked out. … I was in the time-out room and I just completely went mad … and then he said it again in the time-out room and there're people in different years know me and they don't know I'm in care or anything like that … oh I just went mad.

As Osler (2006: 578) notes in her article on excluded girls, the 'mundane tyrannies of everyday exclusion' are highly gendered. She outlines how a range of violences, particularly verbal abuse, are framed by many school staff as a domestic problem, normalized within pathological girlhood discourses and thus not the responsibility of school authorities. This extract provides a clear example of the ways in which girls' anger can be reconstituted as unjustifiable emotional outburst ('there's no reason to get upset'). It illustrates how such out-rage, in this case, against the institutionalized symbolic violence of being 'known' as troubled and troubling 'child-in-care', is intensified in the Otherization of the physically violent over-emotional girl (Chesney-Lind and Eliason 2006). However, Keely's refusal to have her rage feminized through a discourse of emotion ('I'm not upset, I am just mad' and 'screw you') disrupts another set of normative power relations (authoritative teacher and obedient pupil) and she is ejected from the classroom. Indeed, Keely's sustained 'outbursts' and 'talking back' to school authority figures often led to a series of journeys to the 'time-out room' – a room which repeatedly failed to keep the bad affect 'in' ('I went completely mad', 'I just walked out'). Nevertheless, Keely recognized early on that she must protect against self-sabotaging her road to success through the fights and dares that had long peppered the everyday socialities of school life. The following section explores further the processes of this realization when Keely literally fights for her education in an affective and physical battle with sparring partner Carly.

(Not) Fighting for an Education: The Making and Marking of the Achieving Educational Girl-subject

Gonick (2004) suggests that becoming the right sort of successful girl involves complex familial and peer-group dramas which are acknowledged but elided in policy discourse on raising the attainment of children in care. In the following extract, I first learn of the interpersonal conflict with Carly and the battle for academic capital ('I'm more intelligent than you'). Here, discourses of individualized competitiveness seemed to rupture existing social networks and affinities:

> *Nevaeh:* I had friends like that who wouldn't speak to me because I was higher than them in school.
> *Emma:* Really?
> *Nevaeh:* So I used to lie a lot and tell them that I was thick and . . .
> *Keely:* I did that.
> *Nevaeh:* Yeah.
> *Keely:* And then I moved up (sets) and then/she (Carly) kicks off, she's goes 'Keely you're not that intelligent', well I'm more intelligent than you now go away.

Over three months Keely related a series of conflictual negotiations at the level of local peer group sub-cultures and friendship dyads about being positioned as 'high achiever'. The following section explores these conflicts further as she negotiates the ambivalence of 'good-girl pupil'.

Negotiating the 'uneasy hybrid' (Lucey et al. 2003) of being bi-located, that is, living for the most part 'in care' (e.g. foster family) but negotiating the complexities of being 'on and off contact' with her birth family, Keely had already instigated a significant rupture to secure a 'better life'. This move, however, positioned her as 'the black sheep of the family' (Foster carer's words). Indeed, the chaos of belonging/not belonging to either birth family or foster family and being 'in' but not 'of' local communities, was paralleled in the social relationships forged at school and the multiple affective ties to rival peer group sub/cultures: the 'moshers/punks/emos'[2] (alternative sub-culture) and the 'chavs'[3] (normative dominant culture). When we first met Keely she invested in multiplicity and contradiction ('I'm a bit chav, bit mosher, bit emo, bit tomboy'). However, after moving up ability sets she reconfigured her dual affinities with the alternative emos/mosher/punk cliques predominantly occupying the higher-ability streams. A couple of weeks later, Keely announced that 'she don't do chavs no more'. However, part of not 'doing chav' involved a sustained break from 'frienemy'[4] Carly, who, unsurprisingly within such a competitive affective economy, resisted and resented Keely's attempts not to 'hang out' together:

> *Keely:* [describing the end of a fist fight with Carly] We must have been like that close to killing each other.
> *Emma:* Is this because you didn't want to hang around with her?
> *Keely:* Yeah . . . because of that. It's like I still see you outside school and stuff but not.
> *Emma:* But not inside.
> *Keely:* Well yeah, I say 'hello' to her and everything you know I'm gonna talk to you.
> *Emma:* Why not inside then?
> *Keely:* No, it's because inside the school, um my education and stuff innit? And I'm mixing with the wrong person at school like.
> *Emma:* But do you think that, or are people telling you that?
> *Keely:* Everyone is telling me and I – I'm thinking it so . . . on my own you know like I've said don't want to hang around with her. Not in school anyway. I can't.
> *Emma:* Does she know the reason why? Did you tell her why then?
> *Keely:* Yeah . . . that's why – why this argument started . . . because I've moved up, Carly's a bit dodgy with it.

In many ways Keely internalized the latest governmental message to take it upon herself ('on my own') to 'break contact with other children who are a bad influence' (DCSF 2008 press release). She reiterated in a later conversation how her foster carer wanted her 'to like be with nice people and everything. She wants me to do well (at school)'. Discourses of proximity ('to be with' to 'not hang around with') mesh with the contagion and inter-subjectivity of 'bad affect' ('mixing with the wrong person' – the polar opposite of 'nice', see Hey 1997; Ringrose 2006). However, as the line, 'we were nearly that close to killing each other' dramatically illustrates, she struggles to maintain her distance and keep her own 'bad affect' in. The following extract sees Carly draw Keely into a wall-punching competition which Keely ensures she wins even if it means hospitalization. It is one of many episodes through which Carly incites Keely to protect and project her 'hard-girl' identity, safe in the knowledge that Keely, in her words, 'will never back down':

> *Keely:* [We were] having this little competition like and um you just started off slow like that right . . . and you had to go hard in and the one with the worst bruise or something is the winner . . .

and then there was the final punch . . . so she goes first, banged it like and I was like, 'I am not going to beat that' and because she done it really hard she bruised her hand and I thought 'oh no I have got to beat that and it is really going to hurt', so then in the end I just went 'oh I can't be bothered like you know'. Bam! Hit the wall then and hurt my knuckles and had to go to hospital.

Keely articulates a hardened femininity that refuses to be beaten. Indeed, Keely's oft-repeated mantra 'I never back down' featured in almost every violent episode recounted during the fieldwork and seemed to Keely (in earlier conversations) to be an important psycho-social defence against earlier vulnerabilities (particularly her physical powerlessness as a young girl). The ways in which Keely rages and fights with and against Carly might also be interpreted through a psycho-social lens as an inner drama (with Carly representing the 'bad affect' which Keely is trying to keep inside) being played out in the social world (a kind of beating-up of her projected bad affect). Moving on and away from Carly, however, led to a series of fights and dares as Keely was not only frequently called upon to protect her 'hard' reputation but also incited to retaliate against the rumours and gossip through which Keely was accused as 'bad mouthing' her closest friends:

> *Keely:* . . . apparently, um 'cause I didn't wanna hang around them, like I said earlier like, and um we all go off our heads when we're together and everything . . . apparently it's [the ensuing fight] because I don't like Rosy [close friend], 'she's too small and she's ugly and she's a bitch' by the way. I was like that – what? . . . And then she went back and told her older cousins, they ran back and told them and . . . because so the rumour gets out and then there was meant to be a fight between us.

Throughout the fieldwork, Keely articulated the importance of friendships, and school seemed to be the only social arena through which she could forge close friendships (living away from the local catchment area). Indeed school friends were often identified as why she 'loves school' and thus the prospect of losing friends was one sacrifice too many. While the school worked hard, within a discourse of 'tolerance' to provide Keely with the educational support she needed by only temporarily excluding her and suggesting she make more use of the 'time-out' room, future fights in school led to threats of permanent exclusion, which operated to position her as 'intolerant' subject. As Keely was all too aware, that put her foster placement at risk.

However, over the months, while Keely began to talk about finding ways to 'do dares' *and* 'get on' at school, she related an increase in episodes of interpersonal conflict and violence, and her increased temporary exclusions impacted severely upon her school work. Within just under two years of meeting Keely, she moved from the top-ability stream to an alternative curriculum at an alternative venue, attending regular school only one day per week. Ironically, her 'fight' for success involved a series of impossible practices in a complex conflictual web of losses and belongings to peers, friends and families. Within rationalist policy discourse, she becomes a neo-liberal killjoy by failing to change and is reconfigured within well-worn discourses of lac/k. She shifts from exceptional educational subject, to tolerant educational subject, to intolerant educational Other.

Conclusion

Schools can be the most important institutions in the lives of children in care. They can provide a point of stability when other aspects of children's lives are in chaos. … Everyone who works in schools must be clear that children in care can succeed and should do all they can to support and enable them to do so.

(DCSF 2006: 6)

Keely's case study illustrates some of the psycho-social complexities of living relational subjectivities. It is a story of the multiple ruptures and sutures (with friends, carers and teachers) of embodying success within the classed and gendered micro-socialities of schooling. Her story highlights the continuing inequitous effects of how marginalized girls are compelled to negotiate the rough terrain of embodying normative (intelligible) 'girl-in-school'. Walkerdine et al. (2001) caution how 'getting on' and achieving in school for working-class girls is neither 'easy rebellion' nor 'simple resistance'. Rather, it involves some complex negotiations between home and school. This inter-relationship between 'home' and 'school' is perhaps intensified when 'home' for those 'in care' is fractured and in flux, and thus any transformation involves a substantial remaking of the subject in an affective economy of loss, difference and fragmentation. Indeed, we learn through Keely's narratives that the individualized and sacrificial logic demanded by the neo-liberal drive for academic excellence is too risky to be viable in terms of the social functioning of the subject and her relationality with others (Butler 2005). And it is these affective (and context specific) relationalities, and the real and symbolic violences of the social and cultural world of schooling, that education policy makers and future research agendas need to acknowledge and address so as to make bearable and survivable the journeys of young women, like Keely, through the 'chaos' and 'stability' of contemporary neo-liberal education systems.

Notes

1. Neo-liberalism is a form of government in which life trajectories are perceived to be the outcome of individual choice and constant self-invention and reinvention, making people responsible for their own successes and failings (see Walkerdine et al. 2001).
2. 'Emo', 'punk' and 'mosher' are music- and fashion-based sub-cultural identities. They are often portrayed as 'alternative' yet 'mainstream' in a post-punk era of multi-national record labels and the growth of global creative industries (see Huk 2006). Keely defined herself as 'emo' (short for 'emotional') because of her dark make-up, feelings of isolation, angst and music tastes (e.g. My Chemical Romance) and also as 'punk' and 'mosher' (as a transition from young 'tomboy-self') to refer to her rebellious anti-establishment 'F*** You' attitude.
3. The sub-cultural identity of 'the chav' has been popularized in media discourse to represent 'stereotypical notions of lower-class, disaffected urban youth' (Hayward and Yar 2006: 9). Interpretations of the acronym vary slightly, for example, 'council housed and violent' or 'council house vermin'. Seemingly unaware of the pathological gendered and classed dispositions and consumption practices of 'chav culture' (see Tyler 2008), Keely proudly declares her affinity with 'being chav' ('I'm the queen of chav'), aligning herself with the fashion and music of her favourite R&B singers and with the dominant youth sub-culture in school.
4. 'Frienemy' is a cultural term popularized by the US high school film *Meangirls* that denotes the blurred boundaries between friend and enemy.

References

Aapola, S., Gonick, M. and Harris, A. (2005) *Young Femininity: Girlhood, Power and Social Change*. Basingstoke: Palgrave.

Ahmed, S. (2004) *The Cultural Politics of Emotion*. Edinburgh: Edinburgh University Press.

Archer, L., Halsall, A. and Hollingworth, S. (2007) Inner-city femininities and education: 'race', class, gender and schooling in young women's lives, *Gender and Education*, 19(5): 549–69.

Baker, J. (2008) The ideology of choice: overstating progress and hiding injustice in the lives of young women, *Women's Studies International Forum*, 31: 53–64.

Benjamin, S. (2003) What counts as 'success'? Hierarchical discourses in a girls' comprehensive school, *Discourse: Studies in the Cultural Politics of Education*, 24(1): 105–18.

Bradford, S. and Hey, V. (2007) Successful subjectivities? The successification of class, ethnic and gender positions, *Journal of Education Policy*, 22(6): 595–614.

Butler, J. (2005) *Giving an Account of Oneself.* New York: Fordham University Press.

Chesney-Lind, M. and Eliason, M. (2006) From invisible to incorrigible: the demonization of marginalized women and girls, *Crime Media Culture*, 2(1): 29–47.

DCSF (2006) *Care Matters: Transforming the Lives of Children and Young People in Care.* London: HMSO.

DCSF (2007) *Care Matters: Best Practice in Schools Working Group Report.* London: HMSO.

DCSF (2008 press release) *Multidimensional Treatment Foster Care Pilot*, 23 May. Available at: http://www.dcsf.gov.uk/pns/DisplayPN.cgi?pn_id= 2008_0100 (accessed 1/10/2008).

Gonick, M. (2004) Old plots and new identities: ambivalent femininities in late modernity, *Discourse: Studies in the Cultural Politics of Education*, 25(2): 189–209.

Gordon, T. (2006) Girls in education: citizenship, agency and emotions, *Gender and Education*, 18(1): 1–15.

Griffin, C. (2004) Good girls, bad girls: Anglocentricism and diversity in the constitution of contemporary girlhood, in A. Harris (ed.), *All About the Girl: Culture, Power and Identity.* London: RoutledgeFalmer.

Griffin, C. (2005) Impossible Spaces? Femininity as an empty category. Paper presented at ESRC Seminar Series: New Femininities, London School of Economics, 8 July. Available at: http://www.lse.ac.uk/collections/newFemininities/Chris%20Griffin.pdf (accessed 05/03/09).

Harris, A. (2004) *Future Girl.* London: Routledge.

Hayward, K. and Yar, M. (2006) The 'chav' phenomenon: consumption, media and the construction of a new underclass, *Crime, Media and Culture* 2(1): 9–28.

Hey, V. (1997) *The Company She Keeps.* Buckingham: Open University Press.

Huk, R. (2006) *Beyond Subculture: Pop, Youth and Identity in a Postcolonial World.* London: Routledge.

Jackson, C. (2006) *Lads and Ladettes in School: Gender and a Fear of Failure.* Maidenhead: Open University Press.

Jiwani, Y., Steenbergen, C. and Mitchell, C. (2006) *Girlhood: Redefining the Limits*. Montreal: Black Rose Books.

Katz, C. (2008) Childhood as spectacle: relays of anxiety in the reconfiguration of the child, *Cultural Geographies*, 15(5): 5–17.

Lucey, H., Melody, J. and Walkerdine, V. (2003) Uneasy hybrids: psychological aspects of becoming educationally successful for working-class young women, *Gender and Education*, 15(3): 285–99.

McRobbie, A. (2007) Top Girls? *Cultural Studies*, 21(4–5): 718–37.

O'Flynn, S. and Epstein, D. (2005) Standardising sexuality: embodied knowledge, achievement and 'standards', *Social Semiotics*, 15(2): 183–208.

Osler, A. (2006) Excluded girls: interpersonal, institutional and structural violence in schooling, *Gender and Education*, 18(6): 571–91.

Reay, D. (2004) 'Mostly roughs and toughs': social class, race and representation in inner city schooling, *Sociology*, 38(5): 1005–23.

Renold, E. and Allan, A. (2006) Bright and beautiful: high-achieving girls, ambivalent femininities and the feminisation of success, *Discourse: Studies in the Cultural Politics of Education*, 27(4): 547–73.

Ringrose, J. (2006) A new universal mean girl: examining the discursive construction and social regulation of a new feminine pathology, *Feminism and Psychology*, 16(4): 405–24.

Ringrose, J. (2007) Successful girls? Complicating post-feminist, neoliberal discourses of educational achievement and gender equality, *Gender and Education*, 19(4): 471–89.

Ringrose, J. and Renold, E. (2009) Boys and girls performing normative gendered violence in schools: a critique of bully discourses, in C. Barter and D. Berridge (eds), *Children Behaving Badly? Exploring Peer Violence between Children and Young People*. London: John Wiley and Sons.

Skeggs, B. (2004) *Class, Self, Culture*. London: Routledge.

Tyler, I. (2008) 'Chav mum, chav scum': class disgust in contemporary Britain, *Feminist Media Studies*, 8(2): 17–34.

Walkerdine, V. (1990). *Schoolgirl Fictions*. London: Verso.

Walkerdine, V. (2007) *Children, Gender, Video Games: Towards a Relational Approach to Multi-Media*. London: Palgrave Macmillan.

Walkerdine, V., Lucey, H. and Melody, J. (2001) *Growing Up Girl: Psychosocial Explorations of Gender and Class*. London: Palgrave.

Youdell, D. (2006) *Impossible Bodies, Impossible Selves: Exclusions and Student Subjectivities*. Dordrecht: Springer.

Part 2

Girls' experiences in the schooling system

6　Inner city girls: choosing schools and negotiating friendships

Rosalyn George

Introduction

This chapter arises out of a longitudinal study of the emotional and social dynamics of pre-adolescent girls' friendship groups as they relocate
from their inner city state primary school to their secondary schools
(George and Browne 2000; George 2004, 2007; Pratt and George 2005). I
consider how two of the girls, Leila and Shumi, who are of African and
African-Caribbean heritage respectively, select their secondary schools and
how they manage and negotiate their friendships across ethnic divisions
after school transfer has taken place. I focus on the girls' productions of
their versions of an appropriate femininity in navigating the culture of
the school and how they produce discourses of success, achievement conformity and resistance. The importance of their mothers' involvement
in ensuring their success, both in terms of academic credentials but also
in the construction of their daughters as confident, self-assured young
women, proud of their cultural heritage, is also explored.

Context

The assumed universality of friendship, lacking differentiation and context, has resulted in very few studies of either African-Caribbean or
Asian girls' friendships. Indeed, 'generalizations about "girls culture" come
primarily from research done with girls who are class-privileged and
white; the experiences of girls of other class, "race" and ethnic backgrounds tend to be marginalized' (Thorne 1993:102). The few studies of
African-Caribbean girls' friendships have focused on academic achievement rather than on school transfer. These studies suggest that girls of
African-Caribbean heritage can find ways of achieving academic success
without conforming to many of the goals and values of the school (Fuller
1980; Mac an Ghaill 1988; Gillborn 1990; Mirza 1992). One of the groups
of girls in Shain's (2003) research on the schooling and identity of Asian

girls formed an all-Asian friendship group which became involved in activities which ran counter to the dominant values and culture of the school, while another group prioritized educational advancement and sought to avoid trouble at all costs. Shain's work resonates with the way the African-Caribbean and African girls discussed in this paper responded to school and underlines the importance, not only of comparing the differences between ethnically diverse groups, but exploring difference within them as well.

More recent research (Renold 2005; Archer et al. 2007; George 2007; Ringrose 2007) suggests that discussion of girls and their experience of schooling has to acknowledge and recognize the multiple layers and intersectionality of their lives. Furthermore, with regard to Shumi and Leila, it could also be argued that it is insufficient to think of 'race' as a unifying concept, and that we must recognize that the cultural spaces they inhabit are not fixed but are historically variable and shaped by religion, family and economic circumstances. Indeed, Shain's chapter (this collection) explores the extent to which young Asian women, who are positioned by dominant discourses of passivity, are able to conform or transform the cultural spaces they inhabit, including those of education (Sangster 2009). The challenges of class, 'race', gender and cultural hegemony, could impede the pursuit of such transformation, but for Leila and Shumi these challenges served to assist them in developing a critical consciousness (hooks 1990), which became vital in supporting the girls developing successful coping strategies. These coping strategies manifested themselves in different ways and they constructed individual approaches for coping with the contradictory needs of family, school and friends, while at the same time challenging the oppressive and offensive boundaries arising from their 'race', class, gender and cultural position (Pastor et al. 1996).

The Study

Data for this chapter are drawn from semi-structured interviews conducted with the two girls and their mothers while at secondary school and also from the journals kept by the girls during this time. The girls had attended the same primary school and were part of the same core group of friends while at primary school. Both were high achievers who had conformed to the construction of the 'ideal girl' who puts others first. Friendship held certain shared meanings for them, reflecting the socially agreed practices of their larger group of friends, practices that they maintained were anchored in a basis of intimacy and trust.

The girls in the group prioritized care for their relationships to each other over independence and competition. They idealized their friendship and through affirming their solidarity to each other, articulated an egalitarian ethos to outsiders (George 2007). When Shumi and Leila transferred to different secondary schools at age 11, however, they produced differing accounts of how their ethnicity had impacted on their choice of secondary school and their friendship patterns. Their relationship to their existing friends and to each other changed and they were placed in a position of having to negotiate new friendships in their new schools. These developed during the first and second year of secondary school and, as a consequence, primary school friendships began to fracture and new alliances formed. For Shumi, her new friendship group, unlike her ethnically mixed friendship group from primary school, was made up exclusively of girls of the same cultural heritage, while Leila's new friendship group was characterized by White high-achieving hard-working girls.

In contrast to the girls, neither mother placed a particularly high premium on the importance of friendship as a factor when choosing a secondary school for their daughter. However, the impact of their daughter's ethnicity in the choice process was high on their individual agendas, with both mothers approaching this very differently. Shumi's mother placed the responsibility of her daughter's development as an independent, autonomous young 'Black' woman equally between the school and the family, while Leila's mother felt the school's responsibility was to ensure that her daughter's life chances were maximized through the acquisition of credentials via the examination system.

The Girls

Shumi, who would describe herself as Black, and of Jamaican background, was a member of the inner circle within her group of friends at primary school. She lives with her mum and her 'grown up' older brother in a less economically advantaged area of South East London. Shumi is academically able and pursues school success. After transferring to Foresters High, Shumi began to invest heavily in her identity as a Black student.

Leila, who was born in Nigeria, currently lives in one of the poorer parts of South London. Her mother brought her and her younger brother to England when Leila was six years old. She invests everything in her children's education and Leila is perceived by her teachers and friends to be 'very bright'.

Choosing Schools

In the last decade, the focus on primary/secondary transfer has shifted to a concern regarding school choice within an increasingly marketized education system (O'Brien 2003). Research (Ball et al. 1996; Reay and Ball

1998) suggests that choosing a school and gaining a place at that school is circumscribed by social class as well as 'race' and gender, and that those with economic, cultural and other forms of capital (Reay and Ball 1998) use them to secure the best schools for their children at secondary school transfer.

Both mothers were very clear about the reasons for their choice of secondary school for their daughters, with the most critical factor being the likely impact their daughter's ethnicity would have on the schooling process. For Gloria, Shumi's mother, her daughter's identity as a young Black girl was as important, if not more important, than the dominant values and academic demands of the school system. It was also more important than any concerns that Shumi may have expressed regarding friendship. From my interviews with Gloria, it was very apparent that she knows the value of education but has problems with schooling. Her disenchantment with her daughter's primary school, despite Keith, the school's Black head teacher, had led her to ensure that her daughter's secondary school was one where the espoused vision of the school placed inclusivity as the core of its philosophy:

> I think Kington was probably the worst school. I mean, I couldn't wait to get her to secondary school . . . and Kington has got all the trappings of looking like a really wicked[1] school – I think on the surface it looks really wicked . . . The thing is, Shumi had . . . Keith was the deputy and he's now the head . . . it's not very multi-racial in its staff make up, so Keith being there was a real plus, but he's actually not, that's not his agenda at all . . . I think I personally did a lot of talking to the school. Do you know what? I think if it was left up to Kington, Shumi would just been kind of left, really . . . I think they were aware of her because I made them aware. (Gloria)

Gloria's observations suggest that although the head of Kington primary is Black, he did not necessarily value diversity, and 'race', among a predominantly White staff, was rendered invisible. Gloria's comments also challenge the assumption that, because Keith is Black, he would therefore have an understanding of 'race' and be equipped to tackle issues to do with racism within the context of the school.

Gloria was aware that Foresters High Secondary School had worked hard on its equal opportunities policy and that it was implemented effectively. She was also aware that one of the keys to the school's success was the very good provision for the personal development of students. The production of a confident, assertive young woman who knows her rights was a major consideration in Gloria's choice of secondary school for her daughter, as was the local community which the school served: 'the community is important and I was so focused on not finding a school for Shumi out of our area, because I wanted this community feel to continue. I do think it's important to put roots down' (Gloria).

Although the girls' friendship was not a prime concern for either Gloria or Jean, Leila's mother, it was the acquisition of credentials (which would open doors to a career in medicine for Leila) that was the determining factor in Jean's choice of secondary school. Jean was fully aware of the process of marginalization of many minority ethnic children and students in school and also that a 'selective', suburban school would privilege examination success above other kinds of self-development: 'I was so pleased when she got to Park Avenue . . . because you know she is so bright I didn't want her to waste it' (Jean). Jean recognized that high achievement, both academically and professionally, is not only connected to class position but also to racial values and resources and that membership of the cultural majority in terms of schooling is a significant factor in achieving educational success. Jean, therefore, felt her choice of Park Avenue, a selective school, would provide the most beneficial schooling experience for Leila in terms of academic success and that issues to do with the development of a strong racial awareness could be supported from the home and the community. For Jean, school is not the site for contesting identity formation, but for maximizing her daughter's academic credentials and life chances.

Changing Schools and Changing Friends

Moving from one phase of schooling to the next was a highly significant step for all the girls in the larger study. While at primary school they had maintained close friendships across ethnic divisions. This friendship group had coalesced around Isobel (a girl from the larger study), the leader of the friendship group, and all had accepted her direction with silence.

The shift in the power relations that followed at the point of secondary school transfer, found many of the girls stronger and more assertive. This was particularly so for those whose difference was defined by their ethnicity. For Shumi, her resistance to the oppressive structures of her new school, which valued conformity, discouraged assertiveness and subscribed to conventional understandings of femininity, became articulated through a seemingly stronger and more assertive sense of self. Despite transferring to secondary school with two of her close White friends from primary school, by the end of Year 7 Shumi had disassociated herself from them and become a member of a new set of friends who were exclusively from the same cultural heritage:

RG: So how are things now?

Shumi: They're different. Em, I'm closer to different people now . . . I'm closer to my friend Nadine and other people in my class as well.

RG: What happened to Danielle?

Shumi: Well, me and Danielle are still friends, it's that we're not as close anymore . . . because I don't really think like me and Danielle are the same type of level and that. But me and Nadine are. We [Danielle and Shumi] don't really understand each other. We see each other but we don't understand each other. We don't really . . . now it's more me, Maxine and Nadine and sometimes Tasha.

Shumi's responses could suggest that her new group of friends provide her with the confidence for articulating and living out her identity as a Black African-Caribbean girl (Way 1995).

The American Association of University Women's (1991) report on girls found that Black girls scored highest on self-esteem measures throughout adolescence. These findings are supported by Way's research, which suggests that urban adolescents of African-American descent, have a 'unique tendency to speak "one's mind" in relationships' (1995:178), and saw their relationships strengthened, not dissolved, by conflict. Certainly Shumi and her new friendship group show evidence of this, for they were at ease with telling me 'the truth' about their relationships with each other and with their teachers: 'I hate her, she's horrible, so horrible, she's just rude to people for no reason . . . I don't think you need to be rude to people for no reason and Miss Norris is. She'll come in the class and start being rude . . . she's horrible' (Shumi).

In describing her feelings towards her Year Head, Shumi clearly felt no compunction about concealing her sense of outrage. Furthermore, she and her friends were proud of their honesty and chose not to acknowledge any other way of behaving:

Maxine: I just say what I feel, I can't hold back my feelings.

RG: Do you ever think 'Oh I wish I hadn't said that'?

Maxine: No, not really . . . I just say it. 'Cos if I keep it on my chest then it would like haunt me.

RG: And do you worry that you might upset people?

Maxine: A bit, but then I say sorry to them. (Maxine, Shumi's friend)

In the culture of this friendship group which valued truth and honesty, the impact that such truth telling had on the group's relationships with other girls in the class was quite devastating. Shumi and her friends found their attempts at speaking honestly were either punished by the teachers or rebuffed by their classmates. As Lauren, who was one of Shumi's friends from Primary School, pointed out,

> Well, she's black and she's a bit of a racist . . . she hangs out with black people mainly. And she's always telling people what she thinks of them, banging on and stuff like that. She kind of classes herself in a whole different class and she and her friends, who are all black, live in their own little world. (Lauren)

During these first two years at secondary school the shifting and constantly changing nature of Shumi's identity contributed to a more heightened awareness of her position as a Black girl within the institution of the school. Shumi and her friends claimed that they were no longer able to be 'just individuals' but now subscribed to a collective embracing of their 'Black identity'.

For Shumi and her friends, identity politics often took precedence over friendship, with their friendship group functioning to support each other in achieving academic success within an environment they perceived as hostile. Like Shain's 'Gang Girls' (this volume), the girls valued assertiveness and direct conflict, and this resistance to conventional understandings of femininity was misunderstood and misrepresented as an anti-school orientation by the girls' classmates and teachers.

Ward (1996), researching the role of truth telling in the psychological development of African American girls, observed that African-American mothers showed a determination 'to mould their daughters into whole and self-actualising persons in a society that devalues black women' (quoted in Simmons 2002: 185). She found that many mothers socialize their daughters to use independence and self-confidence to resist the oppression they are likely to experience as a result of their ethnicity. Ward's observations suggest that 'parents provide their children with ways of thinking, seeing and doing' that is 'transmitted inter-generationally and intended to empower their offspring' (Simmons 2002: 185). Shumi's mother was aware that Shumi was learning to walk a fine line between fitting in with the school system and speaking up. This was evident from the several visits she made to Shumi's secondary school. For Shumi, growing up in a country where the dominant values and discourses exclude and disenfranchise her, the pursuance of success at the cost of her identity as a Black African-Caribbean girl was not a position she or her mother was prepared to engage in.

Shumi's mother's intervention fulfilled three roles. First, it acted as a check and counterbalance to Shumi's behaviour; second, it ensured that

Shumi's chances in terms of credentialism were not jeopardized; and third, it empowered her daughter against racism. Moreover, Gloria's choice of Foresters High, an inner city urban school, enabled both Shumi and Gloria to engage in a discourse of resistance to the dominant values of the school, while at the same time accommodating certain rules and regulations, thus ensuring the acquisition of potential credentials are not compromised. For Shumi, her mother's actions signified resistance, resolve and challenge and resulted in her being given a fair hearing so that social injustices could be actively resisted. Had they chosen a different school, for example Park Avenue, with its orientation to academic success, Shumi's challenge and resistance to the school values may not have stood up against its highly regulated structures, leading to her possible exclusion.

bell hooks (1996) warns against essentializing the experience of Black American girls. She reminds us that 'there is no one story of black girlhood' and that to imagine that there is a universal minority female experience would be to repeat exclusive patterns of research that at one time privileged the white middle class experience. Leila's experience lends support to hooks' view. Leila, rather than being confrontational in her relationships to teachers and school, evolved a more complex response, which involved keeping a low profile, subscribing to the values of the school and being detached from her resistant peers:

> *Leila:* The school's very kind of multi-cultural.
> *RG:* ... in your group of friends is it culturally mixed?
> *Leila:* No, it's not really, actually. But I don't know why that is. I think it's just 'cos, we, I think we just became friends because we all care about work a bit more.

Fordham's (1988) research into the conflict that high-achieving Black students' experience between 'making it' in school and identification with Black culture, resonates with Leila's case. Fordham found that the characteristics required for success within the school system contradicted those of solidarity with Black culture, resulting in the high-achieving Black female students perceiving 'making it' as being consistent with the dominant values and attitudes of the institution of the school. The dominant narrative of how to 'make it' emphasizes the importance of hard work, individual effort and education. This strategy of compliance is evident in Leila's commitment to the 'values and norms' condoned in the school context, as well as her rejection of the features of the Black community which run contrary to the values of the school, such as speaking non-standard English and commitment to group advancement rather than individualism. Fordham (1988: 83) suggests that the female students in her study: 'do not believe – nor does their experience support – the idea that they can be truly bi-cultural'. She argues that

despite the growing acceptance of ethnicity and strong ethnic
identification in the larger American society, school officials appear to disapprove of a strong ethnic identity amongst Black adolescents, and these contradictory messages produce conflict and
ambivalence in the adolescents, both toward developing strong
racial and ethnic identities and towards performing well

(1988: 55)

Thus the individualism necessary for achievement in school resulted in
Fordham's students putting a distance between themselves and their black
peers and entering into friendships which would maximize their social
and academic mobility. Leila's rather pragmatic approach to her friends
has resonance with that of Fordham's students:

> I don't need to talk much. Sarah likes to talk to Alice . . . and Alice
> talks to Cheranne and stuff like that. I don't really talk to
> them about my problems very much; I'm more, quiet . . . I have
> a friend who is really quiet, she doesn't actually talk to people
> too much . . . I see her in the library, sometimes working on her
> homework and I come and sit with her and say 'hi'. (Leila)

Leila's self-containment ensures her place in this high-achieving friendship group and, as at her primary school, Leila remains comfortably on the
margins of the group. Nevertheless, she continues to be a popular member
with all her peers as well as her teacher: 'In the elections for form captain,
Leila has come second, three terms running . . . she is very well respected'
(Miss Robson, Leila's form tutor).

Fordham's (1988) work reflects powerfully with the position adopted
by Leila in school. Leila's mother provides her with strong support for her
academic success and has encouraged Leila to internalize the values and
beliefs taught in school in order to succeed. Like the female students in
Fordham's study, Leila vacillates between modesty among her successful
peers and a carefully constructed compliance in front of her teacher and
other school officials: 'Leila and her friends are like a little intelligentsia.
They're the group that are more middle class, more intelligent, more committed to school' (Miss Robson). Leila clearly acknowledges that resistance
to the school structures might endanger herself and her future and compromise her mother's position within her community: 'I'm a very quiet
person anyway and I work hard and you know, my mum has given up
a lot so that me and Omar (her brother) have a good education' (Leila).
It could be argued that a greater danger to Leila could be that she may
become even more silent as she moves into mainstream White academic
culture in an attempt to avoid conflict and disharmony and avoid caus-
ing the animosity of others, who may resent her success. Instead, her

experiences both in and out of school lead both Leila and her mother to support an achievement ideology. For Leila, while her commitment to the 'values' and 'norms' of the school led her to adopt a low and compliant profile to the dominant values of the school, which Fordham describes, this strategy was only evident in school and amongst her school friends. Within her own black community, Leila and her family were actively involved through the church, the family and relatives and local community projects.

Conclusion

It is unsurprising that Black girls, with their different history and heritage rooted in past racism, as well as different futures dictated by institutional racism, will make friends with girls who share similar backgrounds. These girls carry the dual yoke of sexism and racism (hooks 1982). The production of Shumi and her friends' version of the feminine through 'truth telling' demonstrated how difficult it is to cross the boundaries of what are the acceptable and dominant ways of being a girl and being a friend. The school's response to Shumi's 'truth telling' 'serves to underscore feminist theory' (Davies 1979) which points to the way in which female deviance is 'individualized and responded to on the basis of inappropriate femininity' (Wright et al. 2000: 305).

Shumi and her mother are both engaged in the process of shaping schooling to facilitate Shumi in developing her own sense of identity. Gloria is also encouraging Foresters High School as an institution to engage in the politics of identity, as played out in a highly urbanized, multi-cultural and multi-ethnic globalized world. Leila and her mother, however, are choosing the school for providing them with a currency to negotiate choices that would enhance individual worth. The extent, however, to which Leila consciously or unconsciously has given up aspects of her identity and indigenous cultural system in order to achieve success, is difficult to gauge. For while Leila's mother places great store on Leila achieving academically in order to enhance life chances and facilitate social mobility, she and Leila remain firmly connected to her community and, unlike Shumi, Leila is able to express her cultural identity and have it affirmed in many other cultural contexts.

The differences in the way Shumi and Leila deal with their marginal positions within school due to their 'race' may stem from their specific cultural locations and community expectations. Both girls, however, know that they are expected to work hard and to use education as a means of enhancing their life chances. It could be argued that both girls are partially subverting the dominant discursive positions of teacher and successful

'White' student, so central to the school, by challenging and repositioning their ways of knowing and understanding who or what is a successful student (Walkerdine 1981).

While the research presented in this chapter contributes to the developing work on 'girls' and 'failing girls' (Archer et al. 2007), it also highlights the need to seek out a more authentic reading of the 'real' experiences of girls from minority ethnic backgrounds living in poor urban communities. There is a need to identify the factors that contribute to the different outcomes, with respect to groups of girls who represent different ethnicities. We need to unlock, question and subvert the ways in which the discourses of resilience, strength and assertiveness, associated with African and African-Caribbean women, challenge understandings of 'acceptable femininities' (Renold 2005; George 2007; Ringose 2007) and confront the way in which these discourses mediate and shape 'Black' urban girls dis/engagement with education and schooling (Archer et al. 2007).

Note

1. Wicked in this context means 'wonderful', 'great', 'cool'.

References

American Association of University Women (AAUW) (1991) *Shortchanging Girls, Shortchanging America: A Call to Action*. Washington, DC: AAUW.

Archer, L., Halsall, A. and Hollingsworth, S. (2007) Inner city femininities and education: race, class and gender and schooling in young women's lives, *Gender and Education*, 19(5): 549–68.

Ball, S.J., Bowe, R. and Gewirtz, S. (1996) School choice, social class and distinction: the realisation of social advantage in education, *Journal of Education Policy*, 11(1): 89–112.

Davies, L. (1979) Deadlier than the male? Girls, conformity and deviance in schools, in L. Barton and R. Meighan (eds), *Schools, Pupils and Deviance*. Driffield: Nafferton Books.

Fordham, S. (1988) Black students success: pragmatic strategy or pyrrhic victory? *Harvard Educational Review*, 58: 54–84.

Fuller, M. (1980) Black girls in a London comprehensive school, in R. Deem (ed.), *Schooling for Women's Work*. London: Routledge and Kegan Paul.

George, R. (2004) The importance of friendship during primary to secondary school transfer, in M. Benn and C. Chitty (eds), *A Tribute to Caroline Benn, Education and Democracy*. London: Continuum.

George, R. (2007) *Girls in a Goldfish Bowl: Moral Regulation, Ritual and the Use of Power amongst Inner City Girls*. Rotterdam: Sense.

George, R. and Browne, N. (2000) Are you in or are you out? A study of girls' friendships in the primary phase of schooling, *The International Journal of Inclusive Education*, 4(4): 289–300.

Gillborn, D. (1990) *'Race', Ethnicity and Education: Teaching and Learning in Multi-ethnic Schools*. London: Routledge.

hooks, b. (1982) *Ain't I a Woman: Black Women and Feminism*. London: Pluto Press.

hooks, b. (1990) *Yearning: Race, Gender and Cultural Politics*. Boston, MA: South End Press.

hooks, b. (1996) *Bone Black: Memories of Girlhood*. New York: Henry Holt & Co.

Mac an Ghaill, M. (1988) *Young, Gifted and Black*. Milton Keynes: Open University Press.

Mirza, H. (1992) *Young Female and Black*. Buckingham: Open University Press.

O'Brien, M. (2003) Girls and transition to second-level schooling in Ireland: 'moving on' and 'moving out', *Gender and Education*, 15(3): 249–66.

Pastor, J., McCormick, J. and Fine, M. (1996) Makin' homes: an urban girl thing, in B.J. Ross Leadbeater and N. Way (eds), *Urban Girls Resisting Stereotypes, Creating Identities*. New York: New York University Press.

Pratt, S. and George, R. (2005) Girls' and boys' friendships in the transition from primary to secondary school, *Children and Society*, 19(1): 16–26.

Reay, D. and Ball, S.J. (1998) 'Spoilt for choice': the working classes and education markets, *Oxford Review of Education*, 23(1): 89–101.

Renold, E. (2005) *Girls, Boys and Junior Sexualities*. London: RoutledgeFalmer.

Ringrose, J. (2007) Successful girls? Complicating post-feminist, neo feminist discourses of educational achievement and gender equality, *Gender and Education*, 19(4): 471–89.

Sangster, D. (2009) Factors that support achievement amongst African-Caribbean girls. Paper presented at Identities and Social Justice Research Group. Goldsmiths, University of London.

Shain, F. (2003) *The Schooling and Identity of Asian Girls*. Stoke-on-Trent: Trentham Books.

Simmons, R. (2002) *Odd Girl Out: The Hidden Culture of Aggression in Girls*. New York: Harcourt.

Thorne, B. (1993) *Gender Play: Girls and Boys in School*. Buckingham: Open University Press.

Walkerdine, V. (1981) Sex, power and pedagogy, *Screen Education*, 38: 14–24.

Ward, J.V. (1996) Raising resistors: the role of truth telling in the psychological development of African American girls, in B.J. Ross Leadbeater and N.Way (eds), *Urban Girls: Resisting Stereotypes,Creating Identities.* New York: New York University Press.

Way, N. (1995) 'Can't you see the courage, the strength that I have?': listening to urban adolescent girls speak about their relationships, *Psychology of Women Quarterly*, 19(1): 107–28.

Wright, C., Weekes, D. and McGlaughlin, A. (2000) *'Race', Class and Gender in Exclusion from School*. London: Falmer.

7 'Even the people you know turn their back on you': the influence of friendships and social networks on girls' experiences of physical education

Laura Hills

Introduction

Physical education (PE) has been identified as an integral component of education and as a space in schools where young people can develop skills and knowledge that may form a basis for lifelong participation in physical activity. It represents a distinctive school experience in its focus on the body and the unique opportunities for interaction between peers. PE has been viewed as a borderline and even risky activity for girls as they must negotiate the terrain of sport and its associations with masculinity (Satina et al. 1998; Williams and Bedward 2002). Furthermore, many researchers have found that girls are often dissatisfied with their PE lessons and have identified a range of factors that influence their experiences such as the curriculum, clothing, mixed-gender contexts, personal experiences of embarrassment, and broader social discourses around gender, ethnicity, class and sexuality (Flintoff and Scraton 2001; Cockburn and Clarke 2002). These are often linked to the challenging relationships between sport, embodiment, and femininity.

This chapter explores the inter-relationship between girls' experiences of PE and their management of friendship and peer relations. In particular, it investigates the ways that girls engaged with processes involved in the scaling of bodies that occurred within their social networks and their PE lessons. Contrary to other research, it focuses on overlaps as well as inconsistencies between girls' experiences and the discourses and practices of PE. Normative practices such as getting changed, choosing teams and partners, competing, and teamwork provided a context where girls reinforced, created and contested their own social networks, friendship groups, and relationships as well as their understandings of the characteristics, demands, and constraints of femininity. These informal social dynamics and power relations proved to be emotionally charged, potentially distressing, highly influential, and consistently central to girls' experiences. Bourdieu's conceptual tools are used to explore the ways that girls negotiated and managed PE and the forms of capital associated with differing social fields.

The Scaling of Bodies

Bodies are central to the organization, structure, and experience of PE in a way that differs from other parts of schooling. In previous work Hills (2007) drew upon Young's (1990) conceptualization of the 'scaling of bodies' in order to explain some of the ways that particular forms of embodiment are privileged in PE. The term 'scaling of bodies' is drawn from 19th-century discourses in which 'the gaze of the scientific observer was applied to bodies, weighing, measuring, and classifying them according to a normative hierarchy' with white male bourgeoisie bodies bearing 'intellectual, aesthetic, and moral superiority' (Young 1990: 128). Young argued that the scaling of bodies can be applied to modern discourses in order to capture the persistence of oppression and the ways that differences such as ethnicity or sexuality are marked as 'The Other' in relation to dominant visions of embodiment. Within the context of PE, particular bodies are imbued with value in accordance with recognized forms of success that incorporate both academic/schooling priorities and the demands of sport. This idealization of bodies occurs through both overt and hidden curricula that circulate within schools. For example, although the value of participatory sport may be a stated priority, PE teachers tend to privilege students who are skilled, well-behaved, and capable (Hunter 2004).

The scaling of bodies that occurs within the organization and structure of PE may also be present in other forms within girls' own social networks and frameworks. Hey's (1997) study of girls' friendship groups demonstrated that girls employed their own 'unofficial prestige systems' to identify peer acceptability and the capacity to embody successful femininity. These prestige systems involved girls' 'co-appraisals' in ongoing considerations of appearance, disposition and behaviour. Peer-group norms and evaluations may conform to and diverge from the frameworks, expectations and knowledge that underpin academic success and exist in other domains that they encounter away from school (Hey 1997; Kenway and McLeod 2004).

Bourdieu's concepts can be employed to explore the ways that the scaling of bodies operates within official and unofficial practices and discourses in PE and the ways that girls draw on these with respect to their own social networks. Hunter (2004) argued that PE can be viewed as a social field, in Bourdieu's terms, where bodies are valued by their proximity to ideal sporting bodies and how they are constituted and reflected in varying forms of available capital (see also Gorely et al. 2003). The scaling of bodies in PE, therefore, is dominated by the ability to present a skilled and competent sporting body. In particular, there is a valuing of bodies that are viewed as successful in team sports and games and other culturally and socially valued activities (Lake 2001; Hunter 2004).

For Bourdieu the concept of capital refers to the 'range of scarce goods and resources which lie at the heart of social relations...Acquisition of...capital enables individuals to gain power and status within society' (Connolly 1998: 20). Bourdieu (1980) identified four forms of capital: economic, social, cultural, and symbolic. In addition, Shilling (1993: 127) discussed the concept of physical capital which he referred to as 'the development of bodies in ways which are recognized as possessing value in social fields'. Connolly (1998) asserted that there are as many types of capital as there are social fields and suggested that feminine peer relations constituted a social field where girls informally construct and prioritize forms of capital within their own social frameworks and codes. Every social field has particular forms of power relations, logic, and normative practices and discourses (McNay 2000). Forms of capital, therefore, may cohere and contradict in different social fields yielding possibilities for change as well as the potential for an 'awakening of consciousness' as individuals reflect on the inconsistencies and differences they encounter (McNay 2000).

Several researchers have suggested that female bodies gain physical capital most readily within the context of ideas of emphasized femininity (Connolly 1998; Gorely et al. 2003; Hunter 2004; Shilling 2004). From this perspective, the associations of PE with traditional forms of sporting masculinity make it difficult for girls to utilize their capital within this context (Flintoff and Scraton 2001; Cockburn and Clarke 2002; Garrett 2004). For example, Gorely et al. (2003) found that 'muscularity' in girls was only perceived as acceptable for skilled sportswomen. There is also evidence of changing understandings and representations of female sporting bodies and a revisioning of the relationship between femininity and physicality (Hills 2006). These slippages in representation and experience require an appreciation of differences between girls and an exploration of the ways that they invest in forms of sport-related capital.

An Ethnography of Girls in PE

This chapter presents data from a year-long ethnographic study with 12- and 13-year-old girls in an inner city mixed comprehensive school. Within ethnographic research emphasis is placed on understanding the meanings

of the culture for its participants: 'Ethnographic description seeks to identify the subjective meanings people attribute to events rather than the
"objective" character of the events' (Emerson 1983: 23). The design was
influenced by feminist research in relation to the following general tenets:
to centralize girls' and women's experiences while acknowledging the diversity of the categories; to situate gender as a site of social power relations;
and to aspire to social change for girls and women. One of the overall goals
of the project was, therefore, to help understand ways that PE practices
may be improved to enhance girls' experiences.

The broader study entailed exploring girls' perceptions and experiences
of physical activity, gender and physicality with a focus on the context
of PE. This chapter focuses on data collected in relation to the ways that
girls' friendships and social networks influenced and were influenced by
the organization, discourses and practices of PE. These data included individual and group interviews and observations of lessons throughout a
school year. The overall data collection involved 28 individual interviews,
6 focus groups (3 to 10 girls in each and 33 girls in total) that met once or
twice, and 41 observations of two-hour lessons in PE.

A narrative analysis was employed to gain understanding of how girls
interpreted their experiences of PE and physicality. This allows the researcher to gain insights into process and context as it explores the cultural strategies through which people make sense of events, feelings, and
issues (Cortazzi 2001). An emerging story within the PE lessons was the
importance of friendship and the interworkings of social networks within
lessons.

Making Distinctions: Girls' Social and Physical Capital

Girls' understandings of embodiment and subjectivity were constituted
within their social networks as well as through normative practices occurring within PE. In particular, certain themes emerged from the data that
illuminated the ways that girls experienced, resisted, and recreated meanings and practices according to the frameworks of their own friendship
norms and codes of acceptability. Key issues were clothing, choosing part-
ners/teams, having a feel for the game, teasing, and peer evaluation. The
following discussion highlights some of the tensions and challenges that
girls experienced in PE as well as pointing to aspects that were enjoyable
and motivating.

Status, Style and Clothing

While previous research has asserted that girls have a problem with the
clothing policy in PE, the girls in this study generally approved of their

PE kit. They were allowed to wear black shorts, leggings, or jogging bottoms along with an 'appropriate' white top. During interviews, nine girls described the kit positively, saying it was 'fine', 'comfortable', and 'easy to move around in'. The primary complaints were expressed by seven girls who felt that there should be more choice. Some commented that 'you should wear whatever you want' or 'wear your own stuff' while four girls expressed a desire for a choice of colours beyond black and white. In this circumstance most of the girls did not articulate a particular reason for wanting more variety, but increasing choice for some may be compatible with girls' desires for independence, status, and adult female appearance (Hey 1997).

The key clothing issue for the girls in this study was the relationship between labels and status. Amy stated, 'There's one thing I hate about this school, if you don't wear top name stuff then you're just out of this world'. PE was perceived as particularly salient as the homogeneity offered by uniforms did not extend to this lesson: 'you're allowed to wear logos and things like that' (Rachel).

> *Hilary:* If you don't have good names then you get teased. And then if you're constantly getting teased it makes you feel down, makes you feel low that you're different from everybody else.
> *LH:* What's it mean to have a good name?
> *Hilary:* Well, your clothes, like Nike, if you've got Nike then people [say] 'yea, she's got Nike, she's good, she's got good clothes. I'd like to hang around with her'. If a person's got Hi-Tec [people] would be 'I'm not going to hang around with that tramp'.

Within this framework having a good name literally translated into wearing the right label and students who did not conform to peer norms were subject to teasing. 'Lisa, she wears a black and white t-shirt, ordinary t-shirt and . . . people take the micky out of her, like and say that she's a tramp an all 'cause she doesn't wear designer makes. But she wears what she's supposed to wear . . .' (Rachel).

PE clothing imposed social status in the cultural currency of student life. As Wilson (1993: 51) wrote, 'Clothing and other kinds of ornamentation make the human body culturally visible . . . clothing draws the body so it can be culturally seen, and articulates it in a meaningful form'. The association of sporting clothing and acceptable female fashion deviates from previous work identifying kit as 'babyish' and a key barrier to girls' enjoyment of PE (Williams and Bedward 2002). While acknowledging the unfairness of the system, Rachel, Hilary and Amy can still recognize themselves as being part of it, as one of the girls who wears designer labels.

Girls' acceptance of sporting gear illustrates more than just a fashion statement. The popularity of trainers, jogging bottoms, and t-shirts increases girls' comfort in PE lessons as well as their ability to move about with ease. From the perspective of participating in physical activity, the kit policy was considered effective. Girls' concerns with labels and status, however, tap into the hierarchical 'scaling of bodies' within PE that can marginalize and oppress girls who may be unable or unwilling to conform to the standards of their peers.

Picking Teams and Choosing Partners

Girls differ in their sporting skills, knowledge, interests and experience. Previous research indicates that students must manage discourses and practices related to competitive sport, many of which highlight bodily prowess and proficiency (Lake 2001; Hunter 2004). Winning represents the most overt and clear form of sporting success and lessons were often centred on games where clear winners and losers emerged (Hills 2007).

Choosing teams and partners are common practices where the scaling of bodies occurs in an overt and public way. An ethos of fairness underpins the practice requiring that teams must be seen to have equal chances to win in order to have a good game. In practice this means that individuals are positioned on an acknowledged and, within PE terms, accepted hierarchy of ability: 'If I choose teams I know which [girls] are the best' (Jo). The process of choosing teams conflates ability-based choices with peer-related concerns. Amy discusses the complications of choosing teams and the bargaining for bodies that occurs:

> *Amy:* I think teachers should choose [teams] because if kids choose all their mates they would end up falling out wouldn't they because like if … the two captains are both mates and three girls who were best mates and two of them were captains and one of them was out there, one would say 'I want so and so' and the other would go 'Yeah but I wanted her' and then they would all start arguing … plus then all the ones who haven't got many friends get in the team as well because people all choose their mates and like Lisa and Asma always get left out don't they? … [the captains go] 'Oh no I don't want her', 'you have her' 'I don't want her', 'you have her' and that makes you feel upset because you feel like you are not wanted.
> *Lin:* Even the people you know turn their back on you. They go 'ah, you're not good enough for us'.

Choosing teams or partners, therefore, has significance that goes beyond the hierarchy of skill and enters the realm of social relationships – highlighting who is in and out. The guise of impartiality and equity implicit within this form of scaling of bodies masks the needs and experiences of girls who may be excluded or marginalized (Young 1990; Talbot 1993). Choosing teams can also create conflict within friendships as captains and teammates may appear to privilege skill and competition over friendship.

Choosing may become even more intense when it involves selecting a partner. This can be stressful when girls operate in a friendship group with three people, or when they have to choose between someone who is their friend and someone who is equally skilled. Some girls prepare by agreeing to be partners prior to lessons:

> In the changing room, Jo calls Latifa over to her and says, 'are you my friend?' in a baby voice. Latifa comes over to her and Jo says, 'you be my partner'. Latifa agrees and they call each other friends. Then, Latifa and Stacy do the same. They hug each other.
>
> (Fieldnotes)

Having partners assigned by the teacher does not necessarily alleviate problems. Girls who are paired with someone they do not like may try to secretly switch partners or make it clear that they are unhappy with the person they are with: 'Nakeesha screams to Miss Davis "Miss, I want to change partners; I'm not doing it with her"'. Choosing teams and partners are processes through which girls form alliances and identify whom they wish to be with. These practices involve the public evaluation of bodies according to the physical dictates of sport and the social demands of friendship and status. While girls enjoy being with their friends the need to choose or wait to be chosen by their peers can create anxiety and stress.

A Feel for the Game

One of the elements of PE that girls enjoyed was the chance to play and socialize with other girls in a setting that allowed more interaction than other lessons:

> *LH:* What do you like about netball?
> *Mary:* It's something you enjoy with other girls.
> *Kirinjit:* It's good [basketball]. Get it down and score... You enjoy it. It's just good fun to be with all my friends and everything like that.

The activities within games such as passing or playing together in badminton were often viewed positively. In addition, girls enjoyed opportunities for success, the excitement of performing well, and the thrill of being cheered on:

> *Mitzi:* I feel good when I get a goal or basket or home run.
> *Rene:* Same for me as well.

> *Jo:* I feel good when everyone cheers me on...Like if you're the last person on in rounders or something. Or, you keep getting them goals.

PE can be a space where girls socialize, have fun, and learn skills. However, it can also be a space where girls tease, ostracize, exclude and belittle each other, often drawing on discourses and practices related to sporting skills. For example, not everyone experienced the joys of being passed to in games. Tracy ran over to the bench during a basketball game saying, 'What am I, a ghost? No one's passing to me' and, during an interview, Asma stated, 'I like basketball, but no one will pass it to me'. Girls do exhibit awareness of an ethos of inclusion. While observing a basketball game, Lucy said, 'Why don't people pass to Rachel? I pass to everyone. I even pass to Asma' (fieldnotes). Her comments, however, acknowledged both the presence of exclusionary strategies and the possibilities of alternative practices. The demands of competition and status often meant that girls prioritized sporting and/or social success over practices of inclusion and cooperation.

In addition, girls with sufficient physical capital could also help to ensure that less skilled friends were included in games. The following description of rounders demonstrates the limited allowance provided for some girls in the lessons as well as the ways that friends could protect each other:

> Latifa drops a ball and responds to the teasing 'Sorry, at least I tried'. Katie is removed from playing a base after missing a ball as someone says, 'She can't catch'. Jen is moved to home, misses one and Jo takes over moving Jen as well as Shamura to the field. Jo stands with her arms crossed talking to Stacy 'they can't catch'. Stacy on third misses a number of balls and stands talking not watching the game, however she is not removed.
>
> (Fieldnotes from rounders – girls only)

The social dynamics of rounders in this context resulted in Latifa and Jo taking over the game and assigning positions. Some girls who missed a catch were immediately removed or removed themselves from playing key positions while Stacy, who was part of a dominant social network, could make mistakes without fear of consequences.

The marginalization of some girls in games included teasing. There were numerous instances of teasing and harassment in relation to sporting skills. Some girls reflected on the competitive discourses and practices that occurred within PE and the concomitant teasing:

> Latifa she thinks it all a competition that, that's what I hate. And then shouts at you for doing something wrong. (Suffina)

Rachel: If you're on a team with good people, like, if you lose points for them they get right mad with you. But if you're on a team, like, with people who can't do it, they're all like it doesn't matter, we'll try again next time. So, sometimes I don't like being with my friends because they're all good at it.

Jenna pushes Lin 'You're not doing anything'.

(Fieldnotes)

Not all teasing about skill was perceived as harmful, however. Close friends teased each other in a more light-hearted manner or bantering style: 'Davia yells to her partner Keri "you're useless"...She can't throw she can't hit, she can't run' (Fieldnotes). Sporting competence, however, still formed a basis for some of this more friendly style of teasing. Many of the negative interactions between girls in lessons took place with respect to normative practices and discourses relating to the activities in PE. This form of teasing centred on girls not being 'good' enough. Girls drew on hierarchical thinking and notions of success that characterized the logic of the social field of PE to marginalize particular girls and reinforce their own social networks and status.

Each of these themes links to girls' awareness of peer evaluation and a sense of 'being watched' (Hilary). While girls could enjoy positive affirmation from other girls for their skills, appearance, adornment, and status, they also identified feelings of embarrassment, self-consciousness, anxiety, and rejection. Girls did not necessarily accept the practices associated with the scaling of bodies at face value. Some girls were aware that their own efforts to maintain status and identity perpetuated practices that could result in marginalization and exclusion. There was, however, limited support for alternative visions and practices of care or emotional protection that may have prevailed in other social fields. As Rachel stated, 'They just put you in front of loads of people and put you under stress'. Girls who were able to dominate the lessons drew on their physical and social capital which afforded them the ability to control team selection, positions in games, and also help their friends. The ability to dominate was facilitated by the legitimacy afforded to displays of skill and active engagement in lessons. In Bourdieu's terms the dominant can maintain their power through misrecognition of the dominated and a 'refusal to...recognise them other than on the terms of the dominant culture on which their own claims to distinction are based' (Lovell 2007: 71). The hierarchy of the 'scaling of bodies' is (re)created in the tension between the normalized practices and codes of success operating within PE and girls' more informal social networks. Understanding power relations between girls, therefore, necessitated exploring how they constructed their experiences and identified and legitimated desirable subject positions and forms of capital.

Conclusions and Implications

Bourdieu's concepts can be used to explore the ways that the social fields of female peer relations and PE overlap and provide opportunities for girls to access and use forms of capital. Rather than focusing on conflicts between the norms of femininity and PE to explain girls' experiences, this chapter shows how girls do have a 'feel for the game' and engage with the organization and practices in PE to further their own social agendas and consolidate friendship groups and social status. For example, PE-related physical capital incorporates sporting skills and fitness and success is characterized by displays of prowess that can be acknowledged by peers and teachers. Some girls are able to use their physical capital to consolidate social capital by choosing who to include and exclude on teams and within activities. These practices are legitimized through the ethos of the scaling of bodies that permeates PE. In addition, girls positioned clothing as an additional component of physical capital according to their own frameworks of acceptable style. Within lessons, students have myriad opportunities to differentiate hierarchically between classmates. This can be a painful or at best stressful component of PE for those who are left out and, for those who feel compelled to choose one friend over another. Girls with limited access to valued forms of capital, therefore, have many ways to lose and lose out within PE; they risk being unsuccessful socially as well as physically.

The implications for practice centre on strategies that minimize the scaling of bodies in both social and educational practices. This, in part, entails refocusing discourses away from competitive norms that legitimize hierarchies, public evaluation, and the privileging of particular bodies to an emphasis on participation, inclusion, learning, and enjoyment. Research indicates that normative practices in PE continue to reinforce competition over cooperation and elitism over participation (Dodds 1993; Donovan 2003; Lake 2001). These characteristics may also be found within other educational domains. For example, Jackson's (2006) work on laddish behaviours indicated that the privileging of competence and competition over effort and the process of learning in educational strategies can reinforce students' hierarchies and exacerbate their 'defensive behaviours' as they strive to avoid demonstrations of failure. The interconnection between students' social negotiations and academic practices has implications for the ways that educational settings are organized. Providing opportunities for participation and achievement without fear of embarrassment or teasing can help to reduce feelings of failure and enable young people to become more active and motivated subjects within and beyond PE. The challenges, however, are complex and the constraints on educators who wish to introduce change include time, numbers of students, access to equipment and facilities, and resistance to revisioning the traditional delivery of sport and other academic subjects.

Girls' social networks and interactions and they way they are legitimized within PE are an influential component of how girls view their experiences within lessons. Educators may benefit from capitalizing on the strength of girls' networks to enhance enjoyment and involvement in lessons. However, it is important not to assume that girl-only spaces are necessarily emotionally safe. While girls cooperate, support each other, and enjoy being teammates, they also tease, marginalize and exclude their peers (Hey 1997). Some evidenced a desire to resist exclusionary discourses and practices; however, they had limited capacity to introduce change. Support from teachers may be required to facilitate inclusion, cooperation, and motivation to participate. Involvement in sport and physical activity can be a rewarding, fun, and even empowering, experience; however, many challenges remain for (physical) educators hoping to provide students with meaningful lessons as well as a desire for lifelong participation.

References

Bourdieu, P. (1980) *The Logic of Practice*. Stanford, CA: Stanford University Press.

Cockburn, C. and Clarke, G. (2002) 'Everybody's looking at you!': girls negotiating the 'femininity deficit' they incur in physical education, *Women's Studies International Forum*, 25(6): 651–65.

Connolly, P. (1998) *Racism, Gender Identities and Young Children: Social Relations in a Multi-ethnic Inner-city Primary School*. London: Routledge.

Cortazzi, M. (2001) Narrative analysis in ethnography, in P. Atkinson, A. Coffey, S. Delamont, J. Lofland and L. Lofland (eds), *Handbook of Ethnography*. London: Sage.

Davis, K. (1997) *Embodied Practices: Feminist Perspectives on the Body*. London: Sage.

Dodds, P. (1993) Removing the ugly 'isms' in your gym: thoughts for teachers on equity, in J. Evans (ed.), *Equality, Education and Physical Education*. London: Falmer Press.

Donovan, T. (2003) A changing culture? Interrogating the dynamics of peer affiliations over the course of a sport education season, *European Physical Education Review*, 9(3): 237–51.

Emerson, R.M. (ed.) (1983) *Contemporary Field Research: A Collection of Readings*. Prospect Heights, IL: Waveland Press.

Flintoff, A. and Scraton, S. (2001) Stepping into active leisure? Young women's perceptions of active lifestyles and their experiences of school physical education, *Sport, Education and Society*, 6(1): 5–21.

Garrett, R. (2004) Negotiating a physical identity: girls, bodies and physical education, *Sport, Education and Society*, 9(2): 223–37.

Gorely, T., Holroyd, R. and Kirk, D. (2003) Muscularity, the habitus and the social construction of gender: towards a gender-relevant physical education, *British Journal of Sociology of Education*, 24(4): 429–48.

Hey, V. (1997) *The Company She Keeps: An Ethnography of Girls' Friendships*. Buckingham: Open University Press.

Hills, L. (2006) Playing the field(s): an exploration of change, conformity and conflict in girls' understandings of gendered physicality in physical education, *Gender and Education*, 18(5): 539–56.

Hills, L. (2007) Friendship, physicality, and physical education: an exploration of the social and embodied dynamics of girls' physical education experiences, *Sport, Education and Society*, 12(3): 335–54.

Hunter, L. (2004) Bourdieu and the social space of the PE class: reproduction of doxa through practice, *Sport, Education and Society*, 9(2): 176–92.

Jackson, C. (2006) *Lads and Ladettes in School: Gender and a Fear of Failure*. Maidenhead: Open University Press.

Kenway, J. and McLeod, J. (2004) Bourdieu's reflexive sociology and 'spaces of points of view': whose reflexivity, which perspective? *British Journal of Sociology of Education*, 25(4): 525–44.

Kenway, J., Willis, S., Blackmore, J. and Rennie, L. (1994) Making 'hope practical' rather than 'despair convincing': feminist post-structuralism, gender reform and educational change, *British Journal of Sociology of Education*, 15(2): 187–210.

Lake, J. (2001) Young people's conceptualisations of sport, physical education and exercise: implications for physical education and the promotion of health-related exercise, *European Physical Education Review*, 7(1): 80–91.

Lovell, T. (ed.) (2007) *(Mis)Recognition, Social Inequality, and Social Justice*. London: Routledge.

McNay, L. (2000) *Gender and Agency: Reconfiguring the Subject in Feminist and Social Theory*. Cambridge: Polity Press.

Satina, B., Solman, M., Donetta, J.C., Loftus, S.J. and Stockin-Davidson, K. (1998) Patriarchal consciousness: middle school students' and teachers' perspectives of motivational practices, *Sport, Education and Society*, 3(2): 181–200.

Shilling, C. (1993) *The Body and Social Theory*. London: Sage.

Shilling, C. (2004) Physical capital and situated action: a new direction for corporeal sociology, *British Journal of Sociology of Education*, 25(4): 473–87.

Talbot, M. (1993) A gendered physical education: equality and sexism, in J. Evans (ed.), *Equality, Education and Physical Education*. London: Falmer Press.

Williams, A. and Bedward, J. (2002) Understanding girls' experience of physical education: relational and situated learning, in D. Penney (ed.), *Gender and Physical Education: Contemporary Issues and Future Directions*. London: Routledge.

Wilson, E. (1993) Deviance, dress, and desire, in S. Fisher and K. Davis (eds), *Negotiating at the Margins: The Gendered Discourses of Power and Resistance*. London: Rutgers University Press.

Young, I. (1990) *Justice and the Politics of Difference*. Princeton, NJ: Princeton University Press.

8 Schoolgirls and power/ knowledge economies: using knowledge to mobilize social power

Carrie Paechter and Sheryl Clark

Introduction

This chapter is about how economies of knowledge are used by girls to mobilize power within and between friendship groups. We examine the forms of knowledge that the girls employ, and how these intersect with power relations. Through this we illuminate how power/knowledge relations among girls of primary school age enable and restrict the possibilities of friendship, social success and failure.

Previous studies have considered the complexities of social groupings among primary school girls. Kehily et al. (2002) note that girls' gendered identities are constructed and regulated within such groups. Girls have been shown to form themselves into hierarchically based groupings whose borders are policed in various ways and which encapsulate different levels of social status and forms of femininity (Hey 1997; George and Browne 2000; Reay 2001; Renold 2001; Kehily et al. 2002; Renold 2005). Researchers point to the importance of talk and other forms of verbal communication, such as note-writing, in this regard (Hey 1997; Kehily et al. 2002). Relatively little attention, however, has been given to the ways in which knowledge that arises from and contributes to these interactions can itself act to mobilize power in relationships between girls.

We understand power as having a capillary operation, located within mobile relations and fundamentally bound up with knowledge (Foucault 1980). It is both a relational effect, produced through social interaction, and concerned with the mobilization of resources (Allen 2003). In the social world of the playground and classroom the resources mobilized are forms of knowledge that children construct, develop and amass about the world and each other. These can be understood as forming an 'economy of knowledge' that underpins social hierarchies.

Context and Background

Our data come from a one-year study of tomboy identities, carried out in one class of 9–11 year olds in each of two schools in London.[1] Here we concentrate on the girls at Holly Bank,[2] a predominantly White, highly competitive, middle-class school in a leafy suburb. Sheryl spent two days a week in the school for two terms, observing the children in class and in the playground, and conducting interviews with children (singly and in groups), school staff and some parents.

Several competing and hierarchically organized groupings were evident in the children's friendships. This was the case for both boys and girls, but it was in the girls' groups that the mobilization of knowledge within power relations was particularly evident. There were three main female friendship groups,[3] with alliances shifting through the year and some girls floating between groups and 'best friend' pairs. The most dominant group, 'the cool girls', comprised Kelly, Chelsea, Bridget, Pippa, Joanna and Holly, and seemed to be led by Kelly, though the other girls within the group were reluctant to admit this. Group membership shifted: by the end of the fieldwork period, Joanna had left the 'cool girls' for other friendships. The group that she 'defected to', the 'achievers', was originally a threesome of middle status, high-achieving, sporty girls: Leafy Blue, Nirvana and Spirit. The third main group of girls in the class – the 'nice girls' (sometimes referred to by higher-status children as 'goody goodies') consisted of Maria, Charlotte, Melissa, Athena and Lucy. While, in common with girls in other studies (Hey 1997; Reay 2001; Kehily et al. 2002) they prided themselves on being 'nice', 'niceness' sometimes meant that they could not stand up to bullying, especially by higher-status boys. Two further girls, Monica and Britney, who originally formed a 'best friend' pairing, eventually became caught up in the politics of the class, moving into separate friendship groups. Finally, Mia was the lowest-status girl in the class and the others frequently and vehemently complained about her. At the same time, she was remarkably mobile and omnipresent in the various groups and was a crucial part of the social dynamics. Her on/off friendship with Kelly brought Mia both considerable personal hurt as well as relative, occasional, tastes of power.

The hierarchy of the class operated so that those at the bottom supposedly aspired to join the 'cool girls' and those at the top had the option of 'dropping down a level' if they needed to. The value of the 'cool girls', position meant that they spent a great deal of time upholding their status, vying for power within their own clique and attempting to protect themselves from other 'wannabes'. A great deal of this maintenance was undertaken through participation in, and manipulation of, the economies of knowledge operating within the classroom.

Power/Knowledge Formations and Interactions

Various interacting knowledge forms were used to mobilize power relations, constructing a significant power/knowledge nexus through which the girls negotiated their positions within the hierarchy of individuals and groups. Three broad forms of knowledge were mobilized by girls in different positions in the hierarchy, in order to maintain status, challenge the status of others, and construct and maintain subject positions within the overall social relations of the classroom and playground. These were: hierarchical knowledge; knowledge as capital; and knowledge as performance. Finally, we will discuss the position of the researcher in this knowledge/power nexus, exploring how the researcher and the research process can themselves be used by those being researched to underpin and undercut the very power/knowledge relationships being studied.

Hierarchical Knowledge

Hierarchical knowledge, in this context, is knowledge about who is where in the social hierarchy, and why. It is also the knowledges that are used to make claims to particular positions, or to position others. Knowledge of one's own place in the social hierarchy of the playground is particularly important, as mistakes risk public ostracism: it does not pay to try to join a group to which one has no 'legitimate claim' to membership. The micro-political manoeuvrings involved in the holding and withholding of hierarchical knowledge were subtle and complex but could cause enormous disruption and pain.

One form of knowledge available only to the social élite concerned how the school uniform was worn. The reconfiguration of school uniform to mark various degrees of 'coolness' has been remarked upon elsewhere (Epstein and Johnson 1998), and this was very apparent at Holly Bank. The children had elaborated a number of unspoken rules relating to dress, specifying what was and was not socially acceptable (Renold 2001, 2005). For the girls, skirt length was highly regulated and policed by the peer group. Those with 'too short' skirts were labelled 'tarts' and those with skirts considered to be too long were accused of being 'neeks' (a colloquial term combining geek and nerd). Other rules such as how to wear your socks (rolled up or down) also applied:

> Britney and Monica sit with me on the picnic table. Both have their knee length socks rolled down to their ankles. Monica teases Britney that she used to wear her socks up, and I notice that Charlotte [one of the 'nice girls'] still does.
>
> (Fieldnotes, 12/09/05)

Regulations concerning proper skirt length and sock style may seem trivial and inconsequential, but this is precisely why they were so important to governing 'coolness'. The 'cool girls', awareness of these minutiae allowed them to set themselves apart from other children (especially other girls), permitting them to distinguish between who was clued in and who was not. Awareness of these rules, however, often served as an internal form of regulation which kept the 'cool girls' constantly aware of their own appearance and its conformity to mutable ideals. It also prevented them from taking any risks that might possibly receive a negative interpretation.

This happened when the girls were permitted to wear trousers. At the start of the fieldwork the school insisted on skirts or dresses for girls. Halfway through, the policy changed, allowing girls to wear trousers. Although this was a result of lobbying from children and parents, only one girl in the class took up this possibility, despite claims in our interviews by several girls that they hated skirts. Nirvana wore trousers on the first day, but quickly abandoned them. Her teacher commented,

> It would have been interesting to see, had more girls in my class worn trousers, whether she would have continued to. And I don't think, you know, Nirvana isn't a strong enough character in the class to think, 'I'm going to do what I want, I'm going to wear my trousers and I don't care what other people think'. 'Cause I don't think lots of children aspire to be Nirvana.

The one girl who did continue to wear trousers was Charlotte, a low-status girl who seemed unaware of the other children's inhibitions. Her lack of knowledge seemed to grant her a degree of freedom, which neither the 'cool girls' nor the 'achievers' had access to.

Hierarchical struggles were particularly common among the 'cool girls', who spent a lot of time jostling for the favour of the central figure, Kelly. These favours were frequently bought by supporting the exclusion of another girl in the group. During the fieldwork period both Chelsea and Holly were banished for periods of varying length, to the enormous distress of each, but the knowledge of why they had been ousted was never vouchsafed to them, or to Sheryl: 'Kelly tells me that Chelsea took the friendship test and Bridget adds that she failed. Joanna chides her, "you weren't supposed to tell" and then they tell me not to tell Chelsea' (Fieldnotes, 03/10/2005). Similarly, the 'cool girls' would consolidate their power through petty bullying, and then banding together to withhold information about the precise perpetrator, making their group solidarity (usually against someone temporarily ousted) extremely evident. Their teacher reports one incident in which Chelsea had sellotape deliberately stuck in her hair:

And instantly the Kellys of this world were saying 'Oh I didn't do it'. Well I didn't ask any of the group 'Did you do it?' I was just like, 'Well, Chelsea, I'm just trying to get this out of your hair'. And she sort of looked around the group as if to say, 'I wonder who's done that to me?' but she didn't say anything.

Chelsea's exclusion from the rest of the 'cool girl' group's knowledge of who had put the sellotape in her hair thus served to underline her marginality and tenuous position within the group.

The withholding of knowledge as a means of claiming and mobilizing of power also operated with respect to the school staff and, in the case of the 'cool girls', Sheryl. Within the class there was a strong taboo on 'grassing', or informing adults about anything from minor misdemeanours to serious bullying. This allowed the higher-status children to get away with much of their more problematic behaviour, such as bullying and exclusion. The 'cool girls' were particularly self-policing in this regard. For example, both Holly and Chelsea were seriously distressed by periods of seemingly inexplicable ousting from the group (Chelsea cried herself to sleep for several nights and Holly took the next day off school sick) but neither discussed their unhappiness either with Sheryl or with the school staff.

Retaining knowledge within the child group seemed to be an important way of claiming power *vis-à-vis* adults, which in turn supported individuals' positions of power among their peers. It demonstrated independence, (supposed) resilience, and a primary loyalty to the group. Telling an adult about bullying or other misbehaviour (such as looking at pictures of naked women in class) was essentially a surrendering of communally held knowledge and so a betrayal of the group. It also underlined one's own personal lack of power. Having to tell a teacher about something that was done to one (as the weaker, 'nice girls' did) was an indication of one's lack of power within the peer group. Thus 'grassing' was seen as a strategy of the less powerful, and completely out of the question for those near the top of the hierarchy.

Knowledge as Capital

In understanding knowledge as a form of capital we are treating it as a commodity, as something that can be accumulated, traded or given away. The functioning of knowledge as capital in these circumstances is connected with the circulatory and capillary aspects of power/knowledge: what really matters with respect to the capitalist accumulation of knowledge is not accumulation as such, but the possibility that it can be mobilized in power/knowledge relations. Knowledge, when mobilized effectively, is thus seen here as a form of social capital (Bourdieu 1987) which some children are able to use to their advantage.

In its relationship to power, knowledge as capital functions similarly to commodity capital, in that those who have most also find it easier to acquire more, and this is related to the powerful positioning that the knowledge gives them. This is not altogether straightforward, however. In the complex dynamic of classroom and playground, knowledge is indeed power, but only if it is husbanded in particular ways. Some children are extremely adept at using their knowledge, both to bring them more knowledge, and to enhance their position in wider power/knowledge structures. Others are not so canny, and distribute their knowledge unprofitably and with profligacy.

Although the knowledge economy operated largely through the medium of talk, generally the province of the girls, the child with the greatest amount of knowledge at his disposal was a boy. Humphrey was easily the most powerful child in the class, able to manipulate others and admired and feared in equal degrees. He satisfied the criterion for male popularity of overt athletic prowess but was also extremely adept at collecting and disseminating knowledge. This combination of skills made him supremely powerful, and his influence was felt throughout the class (and, arguably, the school).

Thus, when knowledge was being exchanged within the classroom, it was with Humphrey that most children wanted to trade, and he maintained his position within these power/knowledge relations by the judicious releasing and withholding of knowledge. One day Humphrey had got into trouble and was in the hall being reprimanded by the headteacher; while the class could not hear what was going on, Sheryl could. Afterwards, Kelly (next one down in the knowledge-accumulation hierarchy) asked Sheryl whether she had heard anything. Sheryl replied that she could not tell Kelly what had happened, but surely Kelly could ask Humphrey himself when he came in. 'Humphrey never tells us anything,' Kelly despaired. Despite Kelly's considerable influence in the classroom, Humphrey remained one step beyond her.

Although Kelly was unable to gain information directly from Humphrey (unless he felt that it was in his interest to pass it on), she acquired a huge amount from other children due to her perceived importance. When Dave looked up the word 'masturbation' in his dictionary, he reported the definition to a select group of boys around him, and to Kelly. Similarly when Mia was called a 'chav'[4] by Hedgehog [a boy], she strategically reported this to Kelly, highlighting Hedgehog's ignorance over the 'true' definition of chav and bringing Kelly's derision upon him. Other children also preferentially reported their knowledge to the most powerful individuals in the hierarchy of exchange. When Charlotte came across an image of a naked couple in bed during a Google search for a class project, she immediately reported this to Humphrey, who displayed his disdain for her excitement by remarking, 'That's it? They're not even having sex'. Humphrey and the 'cool girls' were both careful to maintain the impression that knowledge passed on from other children was of questionable value, while the information they themselves held was particularly important. This was often an illusion, since the information was usually trivial or inconsequential, yet by refusing to disclose it, and by publicly announcing its existence while withholding its content, the illusion remained intact.

A significant amount of the knowledge accumulated by the 'cool girls' was of the confessional variety, conferring upon them a degree of pastoral power (Foucault 1982), which was rarely used benevolently. The tendency throughout the class was for the less powerful to confess to the more powerful, thus augmenting the latter's power, particularly through the potential for betrayal. This was especially the case with regard to the spreading of rumours about classroom romances. Knowledge of who liked whom was a highly valuable commodity and often exchanged only between best friends. Leaked information about crushes[5] was usually very painful and had ended or damaged many a friendship. Frances (from a parallel class) reported that she and Leafy Blue [a girl] had not spoken for a week, after Leafy Blue told everyone about Frances's crush on Humphrey. Secrets concerning whom one 'fancied' were often treated as the highest form of trust or giving, which made them especially useful in the mobilization of power/knowledge. Consequently, lower-status children sometimes tried to use the confession of such secrets as a means to gain recognition or acceptance from those of higher status.

Another significant action in the power/knowledge economy of the classroom was the disclosure of one's MSN password. This was of equivalent importance to confession of whom one 'fancied', because it had similar potential for mortification: having someone else's password meant that one could alter their online identity, wreck their mailbox setup, or send embarrassing messages in their name. An extract from Sheryl's fieldnotes demonstrates how serious and far-reaching the effects of this could be, and how, because of the precious and rarely traded nature of such information, using it both identified the user and made clear the deliberately malicious nature of the act:

> I've noticed that Monica and Britney are no longer playing together and seem to have split off into separate groups . . . I get a chance to ask Britney about it in class and she tells me that they got in a fight about MSN. Allegedly, Monica changed Britney's username to 'I love Humphrey' on a computer at school

that they were both using. Then later Britney says her emoticons were removed from her account and this must have been Monica 'because she's the only one with my password'.

(Fieldnotes, 14/11/05)

Of course the most adept manipulators of power/knowledge relations are not naïve enough to use such information immediately; having persuaded someone to buy friendship with the coveted MSN password, they hoard it carefully until it can be used with less likelihood of detection. Joanna, one of the 'cool girls', told Sheryl that 'she convinced Mia to exchange MSN passwords with her. She told Mia a fake password and got Mia's in return. She doesn't know yet what she'll do with it' (Fieldnotes, 26/09/05).

Mia was a particularly naïve and vulnerable, yet constantly active, participant in the knowledge-exchange system of the class. As an outsider who sold her knowledge cheaply for temporary favours, she was at the same time a ubiquitous go-between and intermediary in knowledge trading, in particular keeping Kelly's knowledge supply at as high a level as possible. While she understood the importance of knowledge sufficiently to involve herself heavily in knowledge exchange, she seemed unable to mobilize what she had effectively in power/knowledge relations, or to retain any to herself for long enough for it to accumulate high value. Consequently, she was able only to buy a brief illusion of friendship. She acted as a go-between in (and stirrer-up of) disputes both within the 'cool girls' group and between this group and other children, for example by passing on insults or betraying confidences from one group to another. In a constant attempt to be included, Mia also told Kelly enormous amounts of highly personal information, for example about her father's critical illness, only to be rejected as soon as her usefulness was over.

Performing Knowledge

It was often not the actual possession of knowledge that mattered within the power/knowledge structures of the classroom, but rather the appearance of having it. The performance of knowledge ownership and exchange was central to power/knowledge relations in the class as a whole. The 'cool girls' in particular regularly performed the exchange of secrets, through public and exclusive whispering between themselves. Their claimed monopoly over whispers (and therefore over information) was made particularly clear one day at lunch after an altercation with Mia in which she had been excluded from the group. In response, Mia began chatting with another group of girls not far away:

Maria, Melissa, Mia and some others have sat down on the ledge near the popular girls' spot and they glance over at them often enough to suggest that what Kelly's group is doing is 'important' and worthy of interest. When Mia begins whispering to Maria and Melissa, Pippa calls out to her 'What you whispering about?' as though to question her permission to do so. Kelly's group then begin whispering conspicuously to one another, flaunting their 'knowledge' to the others.

(Fieldnotes, 20/10/05)

Since neither group had anything particularly important to say, the process of conspicuous exchange suggests that it is not the content of the whispers that matters but their exclusiveness and presumed impact. The fact that others do not know, yet wonder about, their content, makes the whispers (and the whisperer) powerful. When Pippa called out to Mia and then started her own set of whispers, she was both denying the importance of Mia's knowledge and enforcing the importance of her own and that of her friends.

Conspicuous whispering was also used by the 'cool girls' to exclude one of their number. One day at lunch, Kelly noticed a small bubble of hair in Bridget's otherwise perfect ponytail. Turning away from Bridget, Kelly covered her mouth and whispered this to Pippa, who passed it on to Chelsea. Bridget quickly caught on and demanded to know what they were talking about, becoming increasingly desperate to know as the girls continued to smile and withhold any clues. When she was finally told of her 'crime', Bridget frantically felt at her hair, then rushed to the lavatories to fix it. Kelly's secret was not particularly damning, or even interesting, yet her ability to withhold it from Bridget, and to make Bridget squirm, conveyed a considerable degree of control.

Mobilizing the Researcher in the Knowledge/ Power Nexus

As a researcher regularly spending playtimes and lunchtimes with the class, who observed but did not comment on behaviour that other adults would punish, Sheryl was in an anomalous position. Part of this anomaly consisted in her ability, as an adult, to move between the different groups of girls without overt challenge, although the 'cool girls' did have a number of strategies to resist her presence. At the same time, she was considered an honorary girl to the extent that attempts were made to co-opt her into the various groups. For example, when Sheryl left Britney and Monica to talk to the 'cool girls' one lunchtime, Monica expressed their concern that she might show the contents of her notebook with 'I thought you were our friend'. The 'cool girls' in particular wanted to have most of Sheryl's attention and, when they did not get it, attempted to manipulate her in a number of ways that did not differ significantly from their power/knowledge manoeuvres with respect to their peers, including conspicuously excluding her from their knowledge exchange: 'Bridget says she wonders something about me and whispers it around the group. Sadly, this is how they treat each other (or those in marginal standing, at least), and I am made to stand and pretend not to care' (Fieldnotes, 13/10/05).

Sheryl was also used much more overtly within the power/knowledge relations in the class. Her notebook was a source of fascination to many of the children, and there were several attempts to read it or write in it. Several of the lower-status girls were concerned that writing about them should not be shown to those in the 'cool girls' group. The 'cool girls', on the other hand, despite their usual resistance to her taking notes of their conversations, exploited Sheryl's interest in what they had to say as part of their mobilization of power relations within the class, using the fact of her notetaking to enhance the power of their claimed knowledge:

> Kelly and Pippa run over to me (with their friends behind them) and ask me to write down that Holly likes Hedgehog. They say this loudly in front of everyone (including Hedgehog) and Holly looks upset. I ask her if that's right, and she says no. When I try to write down subtly that they asked me to write this down, Kelly reads [what I wrote] and excitedly announces, 'She wrote it down!' as though this makes it official. Holly is upset despite my explanation to her and she runs away.
>
> (Fieldnotes, 10/11/05)

Conclusion

Knowledge forms a vital aspect of power relations between groups of girls in the latter years of primary school. We have analysed and documented the precise workings of these power/knowledge relations as they were mobilized by girls at different levels of the class hierarchy. The complexities of the ways in which knowledge may be traded, accumulated, used and performed, are important for understanding the operation of competing friendship groups among girls at this age.

The fascination with and mobilization of the knowledge economy of the class group has different effects on different girls. For those of lowest status, being excluded from knowledge exchange was relatively unimportant. Their knowledge was not considered significant but, on the other hand, these girls were not competing for power to the same degree as those higher up the social pecking-order. For girls further up the ladder, there were possibilities both for the mobilization of knowledge to improve one's position, and for knowledge that one had entrusted to others to be used against one. This resulted in times of acute embarrassment when a secret was relayed to the rest of the class, but also times of recognition, when one could temporarily bask in the glory of being the person from whom new information emanated. The degree to which such knowledge could be mobilized varied, however. Mia, in particular, was not able to use her frequently acquired knowledge to improve her outsider status. She sold her secrets too cheap, and they and she were valued accordingly.

For the girls at the top of the social hierarchy, the power/knowledge nexus operated as a two-edged sword. While much of the time the 'cool girls' were collectively able to mobilize knowledge, or the appearance of having it, to maintain and consolidate their power, as individuals most of them were subject to a mutual coercive gaze, checking for any infraction of dress and behaviour codes. A real or imagined breach of the unwritten rules governing membership of the 'cool girls' group could make one an object, rather than a possessor, of knowledge. Girls might whisper about each other, exclude someone without saying why, or broadcast their secrets to lower-status classmates, and the victim would have no easy means of redress. Prevented by the unwritten rules of the economy of knowledge, they would be unable to tell an adult of their plight, and, without the added value of group membership, any knowledge that they took with them into exclusion would automatically be devalued.

At a time when the wider knowledge economy is being transformed through the proliferation of multiple means of communication, it is salient that power/knowledge configurations within and between girl groups operate at the level both of face-to-face and online communication. Already in this study we found that instant messaging was a fertile site for the development of complex power/knowledge practices: we anticipate that the increasing use of new communications technologies will add further to the complexities of power/knowledge configurations between girls. Furthermore, we expect the reach of the local, mutually coercive gaze will be much extended through the increased use of social networking sites by girls of this age group and above (cf. Ringrose, this volume).

Power/knowledge relations in and between girl groups have complex and multiple effects on girls' friendships, their social standing, and their happiness at school. Talk between girls can be seriously destructive, holding girls in a power/knowledge nexus in which they may be objectified and humiliated, even as they continue to consolidate their position in the hierarchy by objectifying and humiliating others.

Notes

1. 'Tomboy identities: the construction and maintenance of active girl-hoods.' ESRC number RES-00-22-1032, 2005-6, Goldsmiths College, London. Carrie Paechter was the grant-holder and Sheryl Clark the fieldworker.
2. Pseudonyms were chosen for the school and children, in the latter case by the children themselves.
3. The names of these groups are a combination of those the girls used themselves and those given by us.
4. 'Chav' is a term of abuse used by middle-class people to impute and deride a working-class habitus.
5. Intense, usually unreciprocated, infatuations.

References

Allen, J. (2003) *Lost Geographies of Power*. Oxford: Basil Blackwell.

Bourdieu, P. (1987) What makes a social class? On the theoretical and practical existence of groups, *Berkeley Journal of Sociology*, 32: 1–17.

Epstein, D. and Johnson, R. (1998) *Schooling Sexualities*. Buckingham: Open University Press.

Foucault, M. (1980) *Power/Knowledge: Selected Interviews and other Writings 1972–1977*. Hemel Hempstead: Harvester Press.

Foucault, M. (1982) The subject and power, in H.L. Dreyfus and P. Rabinov (eds), *Michel Foucault: Beyond Structuralism and Hermeneutics*. Brighton: Harvester Press.

George, R. and Browne, N. (2000) 'Are you in or are you out?': an exploration of girl friendship groups in the primary phase of schooling, *International Journal of Inclusive Education,* 4(4): 289–300.

Hey, V. (1997) *The Company She Keeps: An Ethnography of Girls' Friendship*. Buckingham: Open University Press.

Kehily, M., Epstein, D., Mac an Ghaill, M. and Redman, P. (2002) Private girls and public worlds: producing femininities in the primary school, *Discourse*, 23(2): 167–77.

Reay, D. (2001) 'Spice girls', 'nice girls', 'girlies' and 'tomboys': gender discourses, girls' cultures and femininities in the primary classroom, *Gender and Education*, 13(2): 153–66.

Renold, E. (2001) 'Square-girls', femininity and the negotiation of academic success in the primary school, *British Educational Research Journal*, 27(5): 577–88.

Renold, E. (2005) *Girls, Boys and Junior Sexualities: Exploring Children's Gender and Sexual Relations in the Primary School*. London: Routledge.

9   'You've got to have the pink one because you're a girl!': exploring young girls' understanding of femininities and masculinities in preschool

Barbara Martin

Introduction

> Nina is choosing toy pictures with me. She matches the pink of
> her skirt to the pink picture of the magic castle and smiles at me.
> Nina to me: 'I want that girl one!'

This extract from my fieldnotes shows how Nina, aged three, newly arrived in nursery, is learning to identify pink as a marker of femininity. She
is learning that she is a girl and that girls wear pink and play with pink
toys. In this chapter I show how young girls in a nursery class learn about
the complex significance of 'pink' as a symbolic and material marker of
femininity. I explore how young girls are positioned within regulatory
hegemonic discourses of femininity, and how they position themselves as
active agents within discursive practices. As Harris (2004) and Robinson
and Jones Diaz (2006) argue, girls' choices need to be understood in the
context of dominant neo-liberal discourses of individualism that suggest
people are responsible for their own success, as rational, unitary selves.
This has implications for early childhood educators, who are expected to
adhere to principles of 'developmentally appropriate practice', privileging
individual autonomy, independence skills and 'free play'. Emphasizing individual child development and ignoring gendered power relations results
in the perpetuation of inequalities and reproduction of oppressive hegemonic practices (MacNaughton 2005; Robinson and Jones Diaz 2006). As
MacNaughton (2005) argues, practitioners need to ask what children in
their setting are 'free' to do, which children are able to make choices,
and who is excluded from various activities. I examine power/knowledge

relations involved in everyday play practices in a nursery class to show how girls are constrained by the discourses to which they have access.

I draw upon Foucault's (1978) understandings of power and knowledge in my analysis of young children's gender constructs. Foucault emphasizes that power is exercised in micro-situations, in interactions between individuals, and argues that where there is power, there is also resistance. Practices are not simply reproduced, they are reinterpreted and recreated and sometimes modified and changed. Herein lies the potential for shifts in power relations and moves towards equity (MacNaughton 2005). Young children are actively involved in the construction of their own gender identities, as they position themselves within discursive practices, but as MacNaughton (2005) emphasizes, young children's development of gender identity takes place through interaction with others, and the constructs they can develop are limited to the alternatives that are available to them. Davies (1989) shows how important it is for young children to position themselves as 'correctly' gendered within contradictory discourses of gender dualism, for social and emotional survival. Davies demonstrates that young girls' choices are constrained by the gender narratives available to them, and shows how they enact gender through differentiated cultural practices within power relations. Individual children can, and do, deviate from these dualistic gender positions, but this provokes category-maintenance work around gender boundaries (Thorne 1993). Teasing, ridicule and policing make it clear to children when they have got their behaviour 'wrong' (Davies 1989).

Feminist ethnographic research has produced complex analyses of children's play practices and relations with each other, showing that children often construct gender as oppositional (Francis 1998; Lowe 1998; Reay 2001; Blaise 2005; Renold 2005). Researchers including Lloyd and Duveen (1992) and Browne (2004) have shown how young children choose same-sex playmates. Drawing on Paechter (2007), I argue that children learn what it is to be masculine and feminine through legitimate peripheral participation in communities of femininity and masculinity of older children and adults, while taking part in communities of practice of girls and boys of a similar age to themselves, as full participants (Paechter 2007). Children learn to engage in practices that become central to their sense of self, through participation in a shared repertoire with others.

Research Setting

This chapter is based on analysis of data obtained during my two years of fieldwork in an urban state primary school in England where I followed cohorts of children as they joined the Nursery class. The children were aged

3 and 4 years during this phase of my research. The children came from 16 different ethnic groupings, and 13 different languages were spoken in addition to English in the nursery where I conducted my research. The children came from families who lived in rented accommodation on the adjacent council estate. Two-thirds were in receipt of free school meals, an indicator of poverty. Children came from a variety of class backgrounds, and many of their families were recently arrived refugees in England. I used methods of participant observation, semi-structured interviews based on stories, drawing and roleplay activities, and discussion with children and adults in the setting. The advantage of these methods is that they produced rich data on individual children's interactions with others, and enabled me to focus on ways in which young children are active agents in their own learning (Connolly 1998; Mayall 2002).

'Pink for Girls': Embodying Femininity

Wenger (1998) uses the term 'reification' to refer to the process by which certain objects and practices are taken as markers of community member-ship or points of focus for organizing the negotiation of meanings within communities of practice. Within my research setting 'pink for girls' was used in play practices by both girls and boys as an important symbolic reified marker of femininity. In the following fieldnote, Lan is distressed until she is offered a pink sticker, because she 'knows' pink is the one for girls:

> All the girls pick a pink sticker. When Lan comes to choose, there
>   are no pink ones left.
> *BM:* Do you want to choose one Lan?
> *Chloe:* She wants a girl one.
> *BM:* Is the one you want not there Lan?
> *Lan:* No.
> I get out a spare sheet of stickers. Lan immediately points to the
>   pink dolls' house and says 'I want that one'.

Young children learn to enact an embodied gender identity as they find out that certain ways of moving, speaking and behaving will enable them to participate in the local communities of practice to which they belong (Paechter 2007). Gleeson and Frith (2004) argue that pink has become a symbolic representation of normative immature femininity, and it has been a symbolic marker of young femininities in the UK for several decades. When they come into nursery girls have already learnt from the clothes they have been dressed in and the toys they have been given at home that 'pink is for girls'. Even though children at this age do not choose and buy their own clothes, they are very aware of the importance of having girls' clothes and accessories (Blaise 2005). There are variations in style, for example African girls often have braids and hair extensions, but wearing pink is a common marker of girlhood. The norm of 'pink for girls' is embodied by individual girls, in their clothing, hair ornaments, jewellery, toys, lunch boxes, school bags, and fashion items. Girls often make remarks to each other about their clothes, as overtures of friendship: 'Sara to Hong "I like your skirt. I like your pink shoes." Hong smiles, two girls sitting close, lots of eye contact'.

Some girls expressed considerable interest, preferences and concern about clothes, hairstyles and shoes. Here, Yomi draws on her home experience, in conversation with a female member of the nursery staff:

> *Yomi to Mrs M:* 'I like doing fashion'.
> *Mrs M:* 'Does your sister like fashion?'
> *Yomi:* 'My sister like fashion. She likes to do, she likes to, shows off, she wears Nigeria clothes. My sister wear high heels'.
> *Mrs M:* 'That's nice'.
> *Yomi:* 'She got red hair and black hair'.
> *Mrs M:* 'Yes. Your sister has textured hair. She uses dye'.

Davies (1989) shows how girls experiment with fantasies, inserting themselves into discourses of heterosexual romance. The majority of girls in my research setting frequently drew on discourses of female fashion, and positioned themselves within heteronormative scripts in role play and drawings. Many girls drew elaborate pictures of themselves in princess costumes, party and wedding dresses and often portrayed their faces with bright lipstick, exaggerated eyelashes, and 'big' hairdos. These pictures were in marked contrast to boys' self-portraits, usually showing them playing ball, eating, or running. Below, I have been talking to Zuhre about what she likes to do. She told me she likes playing football and jumping on the blocks, but her picture of herself shows her in a 'grown-up' feminine outfit: 'Zuhre's picture shows her in a long dress with highheeled shoes. Zuhre (to me): "My shoes have heels with spikes, go tap tap tap on the floor"'.

As Harris (2004) argues, girls are positioned within discourses of neo-liberalism and individualism that often construct 'choice' as the expression of desire through consumerism. Pleasure is shaped by consumer structures, so that young girls' desires to have pink clothes and objects are framed by advertising and marketing that create the desires. Young girls in my research nursery were learning that status and recognition can be gained through having certain items of feminine clothing and accessories (George 2007). Below, Lan's desire to own Barbie Princess t-shirts is constructed within discourses of femininity that position her as a consumer.

She uses the t-shirt to claim status within the community of practice of femininity in nursery:

> Lan showing her Barbie Dancing Princesses t-shirt to Sammie and
>   Sara, they name the princesses, very animated . . .
> *Sara:* I be the Cinderella . . .
> *Lan:* I be Jasmine.
> [. . .]
> *Lan: I'm* Cinderella.
> *Sammie:* I'm Sleeping Beauty.
> *Lan:* Tomorrow my Mum going to get me Little Mermaid.

My research findings support Blaise's (2005) work showing how children in a US preschool construct gender in relation to practices of hegemonic masculinity. She documents girls expressing diverse femininities through the clothes they wear, knowledge and use of make-up, range of body movements, enactment of 'being beautiful', and fashion talk. She shows how these central practices are situated within a heteronormative framework, as girls engage in performative discursive practices that reproduce discourses of gender dualism. Blaise explores how girls frequently position themselves within discourses of emphasized femininity, enacting narratives where they dress up and 'make themselves beautiful' for princes and imaginary 'boyfriends'.

My findings add to Blaise's (2005) and Renold's (2005) work showing how educators regulate girls' appearances and girls police their own appearances within discourses of normative (hetero)sexuality, subject to the heterosexual male gaze. The episode below in nursery illustrates Nina's and Madia's preoccupation with their appearances:

> *11.00am Storytime*
> Mrs M (in front of everybody, reprovingly) 'Nina, pull your skirt
> down!' (Nina looks embarrassed and tugs her skirt down. There
> is a fashion for girls to be dressed in very short tight skirts over
> leggings or tights at the moment. The skirts tend to ride up.)
> [. . .]
> *11.45am TV time*
> Nina to Madia, gesturing to her legs, in concerned voice 'Look,
> dere [there]!'
>   Leans across and touches Madia's trousers, pointing out that
> there is a muddy mark on her white trousers.
> Madia: 'Oh my goodness!' (Looks in consternation at the muddy
>   stains, then at Nina, eyes wide in horror, then starts to scrub
>   ineffectually at her muddy trousers.)

It is possible that Nina noticed and commented on Madia's 'problem' with her clothes partly because Mrs M had just commented on Nina's. Mrs M is policing Nina, and Nina is policing Madia, to make sure girls are neat, clean and modest in their attire. Furthermore, 'My goodness', or more often, 'goodness me,' is a phrase used by teachers to convey disapproval. Here Madia is using the same phrase to criticize herself for having got her white clothes dirty playing in the garden. Nina and Madia are learning that it is their responsibility, as girls, to adapt their behaviours to accommodate their clothing. I observed many similar instances, where young girls were learning to pay close attention to their appearance, monitoring how they look to others (Foucault 1984).

Objects of Knowledge

Within my research nursery, art and collage activities; knowledge about fashion; play centring on families and home; Disney princess stories; Barbies; the colour pink; and dance were markers of femininity, seen by the children as 'things for girls'. Construction; 'fighting' games; ball games; and knowledge of sport were markers of masculinity, seen by the children as 'things for boys'. New girls often watched older girls, sometimes for long periods of time, and then copied an aspect of play. As older children in the nursery usually played in same-sex groups, new children observed that this is what is done, and often re-enacted similar practices, frequently gaining the approval of Nursery staff:

> Tagan and Oni go into the playhouse, get dolls, put them in buggies and push them round the area outside the play house. Fifi goes into the playhouse, puts a doll in a buggy and follows Oni and Tagan round, pushing her buggy.
> *Mrs O:* Oh very good Fifi, you've got a baby in your buggy.
> Fifi smiles.

Fifi is learning that adults in nursery approve of girls who push dolls round in buggies. She embodies feminine 'girl' behaviour: by pushing the doll in the pram with other girls she enacts a central practice of girls in this nursery community of femininity. When Fifi pushes the pram she enacts a hegemonic anticipatory practice of femininity, anticipating her future roles as mother and child carer. Fifi gains pleasure from engaging in the practice partly because it positions her as correctly gendered, but in so doing, she 'gives up' attempts to engage in other pleasurable activities such as kicking a football. The gender divide in terms of objects of knowledge often positions girls as less powerful than boys, because masculine objects of knowledge such as construction, superhero and football games give greater access to space and resources.

Pink as a Pollutant

New boys in nursery learn from 'oldtimers' that 'pink is for girls' and that they should avoid anything coloured pink as if it were a pollutant. Below, Mani offers to share his sand bucket with another boy, Ravi, to save Ravi from being contaminated with a pink girls' bucket:

> Sand tray
> Ravi starts to fill a pink bucket with sand.
> Mani (to Ravi, urgent voice): 'No! You can't have that. That's for girls. Pink! You can share my one'.

For many boys, pink is a pollutant, to be avoided at all costs (Ivinson and Murphy 2007). Douglas (1966) argues that although pollution can be committed intentionally, intention is irrelevant to its effect, and pollution is more usually unintentional. The result of becoming polluted is that a polluting person unleashes danger for others because they have crossed some line or developed a 'wrong' condition. This is what happens when some young boys treat pink objects as pollutants in nursery, as 'pink' is understood to feminize and therefore weaken boys: 'Kumi (disgusted voice): That a girl pen. (He does not use it – it is pink and has some little flowers on it. He takes the tub of assorted felt pens.)' This labelling of pink as a symbol of pollution reflects boys' awareness that they are potentially positioned as more powerful than girls, but that they have to struggle to enact superior positions, in the face of individual real-life girls who often give articulate and skilful performances.

There is a long history of 'pink' as a dominant symbolic marker in the making and marking of young femininities (Ivinson and Murphy 2007). As a symbol, 'pink' can be constructed variously as powerful, powerless, or even polluting. It can be used to reinforce hegemonic masculinities, for if 'pink is for girls', potentially everything else can be claimed 'for boys'. In the following episode, Harrison uses 'pink for girls' in a symbolic way to gain the upper hand in small world play with Chloe:

> Dinosaur table
> Chloe and Harrison
> Chloe to Harrison, (advancing a dinosaur to attack his dinosaur, roaring fiercely): 'Rah, rhah'
> Harrison to Chloe (scornful): 'You don't even scare me.' Gives her a pink dinosaur: 'You gotta have this one. It's a girl one'. Attacks her dinosaur 'Mrrr, rrh' (fierce sounds).

Chloe (high-pitched voice): 'Help!'
Shona comes and sits next to Chloe, they do not play with the
   dinosaurs, talk together, leaning towards each other, giggles,
   eye contact.

Harrison extends the category of 'pink for girls' into dinosaur play, in an
attempt to exercise power over Chloe. His performance is successful because she changes her position from performing fierce dinosaur to female
in need of protection, and abandons the game.

   When young boys categorize things 'for girls' or 'for boys' they are
doing more than making simple classifications. They are learning to dis-
associate themselves from 'feminine' things, as they learn that 'masculine'
things carry more power and pleasure for themselves, within communities
of practice of boys and men (Paechter 2007). For many boys, understanding pink as a pollutant is an important way of keeping boundaries in place,
of policing boundaries, and denying power to girls. This includes instances
of generalizing 'pink for girls' in ways that deny girls access to resources
and prevent them from taking part in activities, as in the dinosaur episode
above.

Pink for 'Girl Power'

Advertising, manufacturers and media play a large role in promoting the
cult of pink for girls. Taft (2004) discusses the ways that the discourse
of 'girl power' has been used by elements of popular culture and media
to construct girlhood as powerful through the ability to purchase goods.
This emphasis sees 'girl power' as a cultural phenomenon, centred on fashion and sport, and suggests that feminism is no longer necessary, as girls
can and do 'have it all'. This depoliticizes 'girl power', undermines ways
that girls might act collectively, and reduces the possibilities for critical
thinking and political analysis. The construction of girls as a homogenous
group obscures the diversity of experiences and differences of 'race', class,
sexuality and ethnicity. Harris (2004) argues that a central message of neo-
liberal ideology is that people, as individuals, are responsible for their own
success, and that 'good' choices and strategic effort will result in success.
This conceals the socioeconomic structures that shape and regulate people's possibilities. Agency is constructed as an individual responsibility
and choice, rather than constrained by relations of power.

   I recognize that the term 'girl power' is a contested one, and I use it here
to describe how young girls in my research nursery acted collectively, using
pink as a powerful symbol of feminine solidarity. Some girls recognized
that some boys used practices of hegemonic masculinity to exclude them

from spaces and resources and claimed 'pink' as a powerful symbol of shared femininity. The climbing frame in the nursery garden is an area where girls sometimes seized power. In the following episode, Ayo declares that the climbing frame is 'pink' and boys are not allowed in. She is using 'pink' in a symbolic, not literal sense, as the climbing frame is yellow not pink. She uses 'pink' as a rallying cry to other girls, as a symbol of collective girl power:

> Ayo, Yomi, Ayla, Molly on the climbing frame.
>
> Ayo (standing on the climbing frame, speaking loudly, as if making an announcement): 'This is girls pink house, boys not allowed to come in'.
>
> More girls run over and get on to the climbing frame, total seven.
>
> Yomi: 'This is a secret place'.
>
> Girls chanting loudly, rhythmically, together, hugging close together 'Her, hay, her, hay'.
>
> Daniel and Kumi run over together, in attacking postures, at base of climbing frame, both wearing caps, making loud combative sounds 'Rah, rah', punching air with their fists.

When the girls chant together, they link arms and hug, and their physical closeness emphasizes their group membership as girls. Ayo and Yomi were often leaders in these ritual 'girl power' bids, and they derived a lot of pleasure from leading a group of girls and taking over territory on the climbing frame. Younger girls often watched them, and then joined them, and a great sense of drama and excitement developed as more girls joined and the volume of the chanting increased. Some of the boys enjoyed grouping together and attacking the girls' stronghold, as in the episode above. There is a ritual public quality to these encounters between girls and boys, enacting gender difference and symbolizing gender as not only different but oppositional (Thorne 1993). These 'girl power' bids on the climbing frame were a regular feature, and staff disapproved of them. I understand the episodes as taking place in the context of the nursery where girls had to struggle to gain access to resources. Some of the boys took up more space than girls, took equipment and resources from girls on a regular basis, and dominated activities indoors and outdoors in all construction areas and garden areas. The 'pink' girl power bids are successful attempts by some girls to gain space and control over activities. They also provide a way for girls to demonstrate publicly that they are members of the community of practice of girls within the nursery. All girls can join these episodes. Girls often had difficulties accessing the climbing frames at other times.

Some boys attempted to keep girls off the climbing frames, sometimes using physical force, sometimes trying to make girls take the role of spectator. Consequently some girls had few opportunities to develop their climbing skills. This was compounded by the nursery rule that children may not climb if they are wearing jewellery:

> Climbing frame
> Ryan shows Mrs R his socks, pulling up his trouser legs.
> Mrs R: 'Very nice Ryan. They look like men's socks'.
> Ryan, very pleased face, grinning: 'Yeah, they're football socks'.
> [...]
> Tagan goes to climb.
> Mrs M: No Tagan, you can't climb today you are wearing jewellery. Tell Mummy.
> Tagan goes over to Mrs M, taking off her ring.
> Mrs M: No, don't take it off Tagan, you have got to leave it on. You've got to tell Mummy.

Here, Tagan is not allowed to go on the climbing frame because she is wearing a ring. She tries to resolve the problem by taking off her jewellery, but is not allowed to do this. Ryan gains Mrs R's attention and approval with his request that she look at his socks. Mrs R compliments Ryan's appearance, telling him his socks are 'like men's socks', which he takes as a great compliment, as it positions him within the adult community of practice of men who wear football socks. Teacher approval consolidates Ryan's position as a central member of a community of masculinity. In contrast, teacher disapproval emphasizes problematic aspects of femininity practice for Tagan. Mrs M says to Tagan that she must tell her mother not to let her wear jewellery, thus making her responsible for her mother's behaviour. The rule of no jewellery in theory applies to boys and girls, but I never saw a boy wearing anything that resulted in him being forbidden to climb. This emphasizes how femininity is often constructed as problematic and lacking, within dualistic gender discourses that position girls as less powerful and their needs and desires as less important than boys'.

Conclusion: Thinking Ahead

Young children in my research were actively involved in constructing 'pink' as a central symbol in nursery play practices. Girls in my research study were positioned as powerless by boys in discourses of 'pink as a pollutant', but sometimes they used 'pink' as a powerful symbol of collective femininity, resisting boys' hegemonic practices of masculinity. If early years educators can support young girls in their struggles to use empowering symbols, such as 'pink', as a symbol of resistance and strong femininity, this could be an important way to shift the Symbolic. It is

very difficult for young children to resist heteronormative regulatory practices and to cross gender boundaries within the communities of practice of boys and girls in school (Davies 1989; MacNaughton 2000; Blaise
2005; Renold 2005; Paechter 2007). Pleasure and recognition for young
children is often bound up with demonstrating that they know how to
perform their gender 'correctly' and this involves reproducing normative
gender behaviours, rather than queering or bending gender (Blaise 2005;
Renold 2005). We need to intervene to help children explore their ideas
and feelings about gender and provide young girls with experiences that
empower them and give them pleasure, without endorsing stereotypes or
positioning girls as weaker or inferior in relation to boys (Browne 2004;
MacNaughton 2005).

Children do attempt to position themselves in ways that challenge gender stereotyped behaviours. They can sometimes do this successfully by
embodying what appears to be a contradiction, for example, a girl who
plays football, or makes model cars, in a culture that says these activities
are only for boys. Nursery staff often told me that they tried to provide
girls and boys with equal access to all activities, but that they could not
influence the children's gendered choices because children must be allowed 'free choice'. My research demonstrates that young children do
not have 'free choice' over activities because they learn what is acceptable
and valued within nursery communities of practice to which they belong.
They learn that some 'masculine' marked objects carry more power and
status than 'feminine' marked objects. Discourses of individualism and
'developmentally appropriate practice' focus on individual child development and ignore gendered power relations. This allows some young boys
to enact practices of hegemonic masculinity that perpetuate inequitable
relationships to the detriment of all children (MacNaughton 2005).

Children position themselves in different ways, depending on the op-
tions available to them, and are motivated by desire for pleasure, and desire to gain recognition and praise from other children and adults. There
is often a tension between desires to fit in and belong within communities
of practice, and desires to experiment and take up adventurous positions.
Boys often learn that they can experience power through enacting practices of hegemonic masculinity. Girls often gain pleasure from conforming to dominant norms of femininity but also want to experiment with
other positions. As Davies (1989) shows, it is through negotiating these
conflicts and contradictions that individual identities are developed, and
young children can attempt to subvert gender norms if they are able to
challenge discourses of gender dualism. Blaise (2005) documents ways
in which Madison, an Anglo-American girl in pre-school is able to use
her competence, confidence and skills to engage in Lego building and
how she encourages other girls to participate with her. A crucial aspect of

Madison's success is the support of her teacher, as a group of boys are used to dominating and controlling play with Lego.

There is a need for more research into gendered power relations in early years settings (Browne 2004; MacNaughton 2005). By exploring what gives children gender security and pleasure, we can appreciate the emotional investments they make in enacting particular practices of femininity and masculinity, and we can gain insights into the difficulties children face when they cross gender boundaries. Imaginative play opportunities and storytelling can enable young girls to access alternative gender discourses and position themselves in powerful roles (Davies 1989; Marsh 2000). Children in my study policed roleplay clothes very strictly, insisting that girls were not allowed to wear firefighters', footballers' or builders' outfits, and boys were not to wear dresses or anything pink. When I introduced an assortment of capes for imaginative play, children sometimes allowed each other to be more experimental and flexible in what they wore and roles they took. Through experiences like these we can help children gain access to alternative discourses that enable them to gain pleasure and empowerment beyond gender dualism.

References

Blaise, M. (2005) *Playing It Straight*. London: Routledge.

Browne, N. (2004) *Gender Equity in the Early Years*. Buckingham: Open University Press.

Connolly, P. (1998) *Racism, Gender Identities and Young Children*. London: Routledge.

Davies, B. (1989) *Frogs and Snails and Feminist Tales*. London: Allen and Unwin.

Douglas, M. (1966) *Purity and Danger*. London: Routledge.

Foucault, M. (1978) *The History of Sexuality Vol.1: An Introduction*. New York: Vintage Books.

Foucault, M. (1984) *The History of Sexuality Vol.3: The Care of the Self*. London: Penguin.

Francis, B. (1998) *Power Plays*. Stoke-on-Trent: Trentham Books.

George, R. (2007) *Girls in a Goldfish Bowl*. Rotterdam: Sense.

Harris, A. (2004) *Future Girl*. London: Routledge.

Ivinson, G. and Murphy, P. (2007) *Rethinking Single-sex Teaching*. Oxford: Oxford University Press.

Lowe, K. (1998) Gendermaps, in N. Yelland (ed.), *Gender in Early Childhood*. London: Routledge.

MacNaughton, G. (2005) *Doing Foucault in Early Childhood Studies*. London: Routledge.

Marsh, J. (2000) 'But I want to fly too!': girls and superhero play in the infant classroom, *Gender and Education,* 12(2): 209–20.

Mayall, B. (2002) *Towards a Sociology of Childhood.* Oxford: Oxford University Press.

Paechter, C. (2007) *Being Boys, Being Girls: Learning Masculinities and Femininities.* Buckingham: Open University Press.

Reay, D. (2001) 'Spice girls', 'nice girls', 'girlies', and 'tomboys': gender discourses, girls' cultures and femininities in the primary classroom, *Gender and Education,* 13(2): 153–66.

Renold, E. (2005) *Girls, Boys and Junior Sexualities.* London: RoutledgeFalmer.

Robinson, K. and Jones Diaz, C. (2006) *Diversity and Difference in Early Childhood Education.* Oxford: Oxford University Press.

Taft, J.K. (2004) Girl power politics: pop-culture barriers and organizational resistance, in A. Harris (ed.), *All About the Girl: Culture, Power and Identity.* London: RoutledgeFalmer.

Thorne, B. (1993) *Gender Play.* Buckingham: Open University Press.

Wenger, E. (1998) *Communities of Practice: Learning, Meaning and Identity.* Cambridge: Cambridge University Press.

10 Gender and the new discipline agenda in Scottish schools

Sheila Riddell, Jean Kane, Gwynedd Lloyd, Gillean McCluskey, Joan Stead and Elisabet Weedon

Introduction: School Discipline and the Construction of Gender

The way in which schools manage pupil behaviour plays a key part in the construction of dominant discourses of masculinity and femininity, which in turn provide the backdrop against which individual pupils negotiate their gender identities (Mills 2001; Osler 2003). Since the passage of sex discrimination legislation in the 1970s (Sex Discrimination Act 1975), most schools in Britain, including comprehensive co-educational schools in Scotland, ostensibly offer the same curriculum to boys and girls and subject their pupils, regardless of sex, to the same discipline, or behaviour-management, systems. At the same time as the official discourse of gender neutrality holds sway, it is evident that much of what goes on in schools, including the ways in which men and women interact with boys and girls in different subject areas, reflects teachers' perceptions of gender differences. For example, the advent of single-sex classes in some mixed comprehensive schools appears to have been informed by the view that, in certain circumstances, boys and girls require separate education either as a temporary measure to redress existing inequality, or to take greater account of their inherently different characteristics and dispositions (Ivinson and Murphy 2007). Another strategy which has attracted some attention recently is the practice of sitting boys next to girls in classrooms (gendered seating), which, according to Ivinson and Murphy (2007: 5), is based on 'assumptions about girls' passivity and conformity, which are seen as a civilising influence on boys, perpetuating an ancient cultural view whose source can be traced to Greek and early pagan philosophies'.

In this chapter, we first describe changes in Scottish policy on behaviour management over the past 40 years, drawing attention to the way in which supposed gender neutrality has actually produced very different experiences of the school discipline system for girls and boys from different social class backgrounds. We then focus on restorative practices as an example of a new approach to school discipline, whereby pupils are encouraged to take far more responsibility for their own and other pupils' conduct, and teachers and pupils are also encouraged to resolve tensions through negotiation rather than confrontation. While restorative practices are recognized in education and in wider social contexts as offering a new agenda for conflict resolution, a number of intrinsic dangers are also recognized. In particular, there are ongoing debates about the types of situations where restorative practices may be used legitimately. It has been argued, for example, that in cases of sexual or racial abuse mediated solutions may be inappropriate because of the danger of amplifying existing power differentials. There is the additional danger that the resources of women and girls may be marshalled to contain the socially destructive behaviour of men and boys, thus, possibly inadvertently, underlining the assumptions of innate differences between women and men which have ancient origins but which still constitute a powerful element of our cultural narrative. To explore these issues we draw on case study material from two schools which featured in an evaluation of restorative practices funded by the Scottish Executive (Kane et al. 2007). The primary and secondary case study schools exemplify very different types of institutions in terms of their approaches to restorative practices, linked to wider differences in the schools' cultural understandings of gender. Finally, we discuss the implications of new disciplinary regimes for the social construction of pupils' gender identities.

Discipline and Gender in Scottish Schools

Corporal punishment was formally abolished in Scottish schools in 1986, although in some parts of the country, such as Strathclyde Region, it was prohibited in 1982. While the tawse (a leather strap, manufactured in Lochgelly) was used to control the behaviour of both boys and girls, the victims were predominantly boys from socially disadvantaged backgrounds. Such practices were very clearly based on a display of power by the teacher through the use of ritual humiliation of pupils they regarded as the most threatening, and provided an extremely vivid illustration to pupils of the school's underlying understandings of masculinity and femininity, since girls, particularly as they got older, were spared such sanctions.

Since the abolition of the belt, efforts have been made to manage behaviour through 'pervasive patterns of surveillance and regulation' (Slee 1995: 3) which lend themselves to Foucauldian analyses (Thomas and Loxley 2001) but which, as we demonstrate later, are still applied and experienced differently by boys and girls and contain strong elements of control and humiliation. For example, systems based on 'assertive discipline' (Canter and Canter 1992), sometimes referred to as 'zero tolerance', entail totting up offences perpetrated by pupils in classrooms and administering fixed penalties such as being sent to 'time-out' rooms for a period of isolation. In Scotland, the ideas of assertive discipline are reflected in the Discipline for Learning (DfL) programme, which was described as less prescriptive than some approaches used in the USA (Down 2002), and also in the *Framework for Intervention* (FfI). http://www.betterbehaviourscotland. gov.uk/initiatives/staged/accessforall/framework.aspx

Most of the approaches already described have behaviourist underpinnings and little to say about the social characteristics of the pupils who are most likely to fall foul of school discipline systems, making little or no mention of gender, disability or social class. However, just as most violent crime is committed by men under 25 years old, statistics on violence, and school discipline more widely, reveal that the vast majority of recorded incidents involve boys rather than girls. For example, statistics collected between 1998 and 2003 (Scottish Executive 2004) reveal almost a four-fold increase in recorded incidents of violence against staff in school, rising from 1898 in 1998/99 to 6899 in 2002/03. There were strong associations between gender, additional support needs and violent or anti-social behaviour; 83 per cent of incidents involved boys and 65 per cent involved pupils with special educational needs.

Scottish Government (2008) school exclusion data show that, apart from a slight fall in exclusions between 2000 and 2003 when targets for reductions in exclusions were imposed by government, there has been a steady rise in the number of children excluded from school (38,656 in 2000/01, rising to 44,794 in 2006/07). Again, patterns are gendered, with boys accounting for 78 per cent of all exclusions. Other social divisions are also apparent, for example, children who are entitled to free school meals, who are looked after by the local authority and who have been identified as having additional support needs are 13 times more likely to be excluded than others. Age and stage are also significant, with most pupils being excluded at age 14, around the middle of their secondary school career.

Recent surveys of teachers' views of school discipline (Munn et al. 2004) also confirm that, at both primary and secondary levels, boys' behaviour is seen as much more problematic than that of girls. Overwhelmingly, therefore, boys are identified not only as the major perpetrators of the most serious disciplinary transgressions, but also of daily acts of transgression. They are also the recipients of the most punitive disciplinary sanctions. Recently, there has been a reaction to the focus on masculinity and deviance, and writers such as Lloyd (2005) and Osler (2003) have drawn attention to the fact that, while girls' behaviours might be less challenging than boys', girls may also be 'troubled and troublesome'. There is also some evidence of an increase in girls' offending behaviour. For example, recently published figures from the Scottish Children's Reporters Administration (SCRA 2007) show that between 2000–01 and 2005–06 there was a 40 per cent increase in the proportion of girls referred to Scotland's children's hearing system, although boys continued to outnumber girls by three to one. While it is clear that the relationship between gender and deviance shifts over time, it is still the case that boys are regarded as the major source of problematic behaviour in schools.

The New Agenda in School Discipline: Restorative Practices

As noted earlier traditional systems of discipline and punishment tend to reinforce social inequalities and, as a result, a number of developed countries such as Canada, the USA and Australia have imported new systems of restorative justice into their existing criminal justice system, with the aim of repairing damaged social relationships and reintegrating 'wrongdoers' (Braithwaite 1989). In education, restorative practices have been enthusiastically championed in the USA by people such as McCold and Wachtel (2003), who have run demonstration projects at the International Institute for Restorative Practices.

In the UK, enthusiastic proponents such as Hopkins (2003) have developed restorative practices further, emphasizing their transformative potential. Many different strategies are seen as contributing to a restorative school environment, such as circle time (Mosley 2001), peer mediation (Tyrell 2002) and more formal practices such as family group conferencing (Hayden 2004). The growing popularity of such practices was indicated by the commissioning of an evaluation of school-based restorative justice in England and Wales (Youth Justice Board 2005). The report pointed to the success of a number of innovations, such as restorative conferences, but also highlighted the need for a whole-school approach supported by strong leadership to achieve cultural change.

A striking feature of the literature on restorative practices is that, even though serious infringements of school discipline are highly gendered, discussion of the theory and practice of restorative practices is almost entirely gender-free. It is also evident that methods of restorative practices, such as the defusion of conflict and the encouragement of individuals to take responsibility for their own actions, tend to reflect traditional ways of disciplining girls, rather than boys. As we will argue, despite their social decontextualization, restorative practices have implications for the negotiation of gender relations in schools, in particular, in relation to the work assigned to girls and women in taking responsibility for the behaviour of boys and men.

Restorative Practices in Scottish Schools: Implications for Girls

In 2003 the Scottish Executive Education Department launched a pilot project on restorative practices in three local authorities. A research team at Edinburgh University (the authors of this chapter) was commissioned to undertake a formative evaluation of the initiative over two years. The researchers conducted questionnaire surveys with pupils and staff in 18 schools (six in each authority drawn from primary, secondary and special sectors), analysed statistics (particularly relating to school exclusion trends), and gathered qualitative data to explore the ways in which restorative practices were understood and implemented.

As the work progressed, it became evident that the understanding and implementation of restorative practices was strongly influenced by the gender regime of the particular school and sector. Survey findings showed that there was greater support for the principles and practices of restorative practices in the primary sector, where 93 per cent of teachers are women, compared with secondary schools, where women make up just over 60 per cent of teaching staff. In general, survey findings indicated that men tended to have more punitive attitudes than women to pupil discipline (see Kane et al. 2007 for further details). Secondary school teachers were much more likely to agree with the survey statement that sometimes pupils needed to be punished (77 per cent of secondary teachers, compared with 55 per cent of primary teachers, definitely agreed with the statement 'It is sometimes necessary to punish pupils'), and when the responses of men and women in the secondary sector were compared, men were significantly more likely to agree with this statement.

Women played a major role in implementing the pilot projects, making up 14 out of the 18 school-based co-ordinators. They were responsible for setting up training projects for staff, pupils and parents, and generally enthusing people about the innovative approach to managing behaviour. By way of contrast, at local authority level, co-ordinators of the restorative practices initiative tended to be men and were often educational psychologists. At the end of the first phase of the pilot, the Scottish Executive appointed 12 individuals to form a national co-ordinating team. These were all seconded from schools and about half were men. So whereas the day-to-day responsibility for implementation of restorative practices at school level rested with women, the more prestigious and higher paid co-ordinating roles at local authority level were filled by men. In the following section we present brief case studies of a primary and a secondary school to illustrate some contrasts in the implementation of restorative practices and their implications for the formation of gender regimes. The schools are selected to exemplify differences between school ethos and disciplinary regimes in primary and secondary schools, which tended to be more child centred and restorative in the former and more subject centred and punitive in the latter, possibly reflecting the different gender balance of the staff in the two sectors. All names have been changed, and precise statistics have not been presented to preserve anonymity.

Fiarach Primary School

Context and Ethos

Fiarach Primary was a large school (over 400 pupils) housed in a Victorian building near the centre of the city. Within the school, children's backgrounds ranged from very advantaged to fairly disadvantaged. Exclusion was a rarely used sanction, with only three exclusions over the past three years. The head teacher emphasized the school's child-centred focus and staff described the atmosphere as 'friendly and welcoming'. There had been a concerted effort to improve the ethos of the school over a period of time, with an emphasis on communication and mutual respect. In the past, school discipline policy had been more punitive, with a telling-off by the head teacher regarded as the ultimate sanction. This created a daily log-jam outside the head teacher's office, and a new system was instituted whereby teachers were encouraged to deal with behavioural issues in their own classroom, with children only being sent to the head teacher for praise. Circle time (where children sit down together to recount experiences and practise speaking and listening skills) and buddying systems (where children are paired up to help each other deal with difficult situations) were in place well before the advent of restorative practices.

Classroom assistants, almost all women, were seen as key members of the team. The head teacher was aware of the danger of exploiting the goodwill of this group, but felt it was better to give them responsibility and respect rather than leaving them as marginalized and insecure workers. Two women classroom assistants attended the four-day externally run training course on restorative practices, and were allocated a lead role in raising staff awareness. While most staff were enthusiastic about restorative practices, some degree of dissent remained. For example, in a feedback session on training, the only male classroom assistant objected to the use of circle time with adults as infantilizing. During this session, the facilitators demonstrated active listening practices by requesting that only those holding the bean bag should speak, and should otherwise listen attentively. A male classroom assistant commented, 'It's OK for kids, but adults should be able to talk about things without waiting for a bean bag'.

Discipline Policy

Despite the focus on restorative practices, elements of earlier discipline systems persisted. For example, as recommended by the *Framework for Intervention*, the school kept logs of children's behaviour which were stored in the child's progress record. Some disciplinary methods, such as making a pupil kneel in a corner, were clearly somewhat out of line with the official rejection of punishment: 'Usually in my class if you are bad you either get to kneel in the corner and do your work or that night you have to write a letter to the teacher to say you are sorry for what you did and bring it in the next day' (Morag).

Teachers (all women) were aware of changing practices in the school, and were generally comfortable with the shift away from punishment, although they were aware that being asked to reflect on bad behaviour could be construed as a psychological punishment. Children were encouraged by teachers to control their own behaviour, using techniques such as anger management in extreme cases. They were also seen as having a role in helping to control other children (mainly boys) with significant behavioural difficulties: 'They are very good at ignoring [bad behaviour] and in fact they are good at encouraging them to work and do their best' (Teacher).

Girls and Restorative Practices

Peer mediation was a particularly strong feature of the way in which the school encouraged pupils to take responsibility for their own and other children's actions. About 20 pupils, aged 10–11, acted as peer mediators, the majority of whom were girls. A group of girls explained how the system worked:

> *Laura:* There is usually three peer mediators, one for writing, one for listening and one for back-up to go to the teacher and tell them if the pupil is late because of peer mediation.
> *Deirdre:* . . . or watch if something gets out of hand.
> *Laura:* The third person tends to be there if someone gets all wound up. Then they'll take them away. If your friends are in trouble, you are not allowed to mediate them in case you take sides.
> *Jennifer:* We have got like teachers, so that, if we do have problems or we have a complaint or anything, we just go to them. And we normally do it once a week. Sometimes if there is not enough of us we have to cover for someone. Sometimes the Gaelic boys and girls go away for a trip or something so we have to cover for them.

Alice: Usually it is two girls and a boy because there is more girls than boys.

[...]

Laura: Out of seven [groups], there is only one with two boys in it.

Interviewer: So boys were less keen to be peer mediators?

Laura: We got voted by our classmates and the girls were chosen more than boys.

Alice: Or if they never wanted to be chosen at all there was no point in voting. I think that most of the boys didn't want to do it.

Deirdre: They wanted to play football.

It was also evident that the boys who were chosen as peer mediators had sometimes taken the task less seriously than the girls. A learning support assistant reported that at one point peer mediators wore sashes to identify them, and the boys ran round the playground using the sashes as whips.

Girls rather than boys tended to volunteer to be peer mediators, which involved staying indoors to deal with other pupils' emotional upsets. It was difficult to know whether more disputes between boys or girls were dealt with, but during our periods of observation, mediation in classrooms and other areas of the school tended to involve boys, who were seen as the major rule-breakers. The resolution of disputes described by the pupils involved the adoption of an adult or parenting role, using techniques such as distraction and the encouragement of self-awareness. On the one hand, this might be seen as children being co-opted into adult roles as enforcers of discipline, but it could equally well be seen as a welcome democratization of disciplinary procedures. However, the fact that it was girls rather than boys who were developing these techniques for the management of behaviour and emotions might be seen as problematic.

Millfore High School

Context and Ethos

Millfore High School was a city school whose roll had fallen from over 1500 to less than 500 over a 20-year period. At the time of the research the roll was rising, but the school had experienced a net loss of pupils with about 25 per cent of its potential intake choosing to place requests for other schools. A high proportion of children were entitled to free school meals and the exclusion rate was considerably higher than the average for secondary schools in that authority. Attainment in the school was low, although slowly improving. Virtually no pupils entered higher education but a relatively high proportion moved into employment on leaving school.

Although the school had been chosen by the local authority to participate in the restorative practices pilot, there was considerable ambivalence about the initiative. Following a negative report by Her Majesty's Inspectorate of Education (HMIe), school staff believed that the priority was to improve pupil attainment rather than introduce a new discipline strategy. Overall, there was a strong sense of grievance in the school, with resentment of the parallel pressures to raise attainment, improve discipline and be socially inclusive. It was pointed out that the school had to accept children who had been excluded from other schools and a high number of pupils had a diagnosis of ADHD and autistic spectrum disorder. A guidance teacher expressed the view that, since the implementation of school choice policies in the early 1980s, the school had suffered badly, having lost about a quarter of catchment area pupils to more affluent neighbouring schools. Almost all the parents who had used their right to choose schools were middle class, so the remaining pupils tended to be from more disadvantaged social backgrounds.

Discipline Policy

Prior to the advent of restorative practices, the school had invested in training on Discipline for Learning (DfL) and during an in-service session on restorative practices, major disagreements arose about the relationship between the two initiatives. There was a strong gender dimension to the debate, with the woman deputy head arguing strongly in favour of restorative practices, and a number of men defending the existing approach. An angry objection was made by a male teacher, who argued that there was insufficient time to deal with each misdemeanour in a restorative way in a class of 30, and that discipline problems should be the responsibility of management: 'the people who have the time and the training'. In general, men on the staff rallied to defend the existing system and questioned whether culture change in the school was really required:

> *John:* The impression I'm getting is DfL is a bad system and it's out.
> *Louise:* No, I'm just saying it could be more restorative.
> *Pat:* But we should improve and have it so that it's something we can all buy into; that's something we always wanted.

By the end of the training session, a decision had not been made about the extent to which the restorative approach should be developed further in the school. However, the head teacher failed to appoint a new restorative practices co-ordinator, thus effectively signalling the end of the initiative. The attachment of male members of staff to the DfL approach appeared to have been a major factor in his decision.

Pupils' Views of School Discipline Policy

Although pupils interviewed were reasonably positive about their experience of secondary school, it was evident that they regarded school discipline policy as punitive and ineffective. The 'time-out' room was organized as a series of carrels, creating a panoptican effect so that the member of staff in charge could see all the pupils, but pupils could not see each other. Staff referred to these as 'the byres', and they were generally occupied by boys, some of whom regularly met their mates there. The following exchange indicates pupil awareness of how staff viewed the time-out facility, but also their ability to subvert its intentions:

> *Gary:* My French teacher is like, 'Right, your name is up, your name is down and if you get two ticks you might be going to prison'. You don't go to prison, but she thinks time out is like prison.
> [...]
> *Interviewer:* Overall, do you think the discipline system works or it doesn't work?
> *Linda:* It doesn't work for some people because they are smart and when their friends aren't there they act all nice, and when they get an orange slip and go to time out they just come back and act the same.

While girls were much less likely than boys to be sent to the time-out room, there was a sense from the interviews that they were somewhat at sea in the more hostile secondary school environment. They reflected nostalgically on practices like buddying which had existed at their primary school:

> *Linda:* I really miss my buddy. She was so sweet. I really liked her.
> *Katie:* My friend loved hers. If it is her birthday or Easter or anything she always goes to her old school and gives her buddy something. I am like 'You are not in that school now, you don't have to'.
> [...]
> *Jenny:* We used to go back in second year, we used to go back to Fiarach because it is just round the corner and see our buddies, but now we are not allowed into the playground.

In general, it seemed that girls learned to operate within the more punitive regime of the secondary school, but they were aware of the contrast with the more benign and gentle regime of the primary school.

Conclusion

In this chapter, we began by drawing attention to the evidence that serious infringements of school discipline are largely carried out by boys, often from socially disadvantaged backgrounds, reflecting a wider link between masculinity and violence in late capitalist society (Mills 2001). However, much writing about school discipline, including advice for teachers on best practice, is rooted in behaviourism and ignores the salience of social factors such as social class, disability and gender. Restorative practices may be seen as a new approach to behaviour management, based on consensual approaches to the defusion of conflict, but its proponents are also strangely silent on the salience of social class and gender in social interaction. Evidence from our research suggests that girls and women are largely taking responsibility for the implementation of restorative practices at school level, and some of the activities involved are rooted in traditional assumptions about women's moral superiority and their responsibility for the management of anti-social male behaviour. For example, girls at the primary school acting as peer mediators spent their break time indoors defusing arguments between their peers. In the secondary school, women teachers attempted to implement a system which was treated with great suspicion, if not contempt, by most of their male colleagues, and the women were expected to absorb and defuse this antagonism. It is also significant that the initiative was incorporated into primary school practice relatively easily, particularly where a child-centred and non-punitive ethos was deeply embedded. Interestingly, the only voice of dissent heard in the case study primary school was that of one of the few male staff members, a classroom assistant, who saw attempts to train teachers in restorative interactions as infantilizing. In the secondary case study school, male members of staff were highly resistant to restorative practices, much preferring a system with a clearly defined structure of punishment. While this school was an outlier in our study (most secondary schools were at least willing to pay lip service to restorative practices), survey data revealed that men in secondary schools were generally less accepting of restorative practices than their women colleagues.

Overall, the new agenda of reparation rather than punishment in school has many positive features, but it is important to recognize that much of the associated emotional labour is being conducted by girls and women, with some degree of resistance from boys and men, who are, somewhat ironically, likely to be the main beneficiaries of more humane approaches to school discipline. Ancient but persistent cultural narratives about the peacefulness and moral superiority of girls and women, and their responsibility for managing the potentially destructive behaviour of boys and men, are being used in the implementation of restorative practices, although such assumptions generally remain tacit. Nonetheless, they are likely to have a powerful impact on the social context in which girls and boys negotiate their gender identities, and therefore need to be acknowledged. For restorative practices to be a genuinely disruptive force in the gendered balance of power within schools, as advocated by Mills et al. (2004), much greater engagement of boys and men in the difficult processes of negotiation and mediation will be required.

References

Braithwaite, J. (1989) *Crime, Shame and Reintegration*. Cambridge: Cambridge University Press.

Canter, L. and Canter, M. (1992) *Assertive Discipline* (revised edition). Santa Monica, CA: Lee Canter Associates.

Down, H. (2002) Towards inclusion: a whole school approach that incorporates the principles of 'Discipline for Learning' and its effect on three Year Ten pupils, *Pastoral Care*, 20(3): 29–35.

Hayden, C. (2004) *Family Group Conferences in Education: Evaluating Early Outcomes*. Portsmouth: ICJS, University of Portsmouth.

Hopkins, B. (2003) *Just Schools: A Whole School Approach to Restorative Justice*. London: Jessica Kingsley.

Ivinson, G. and Murphy, P. (2007) *Re-thinking Single-sex Teaching: Gender, School Subjects and Learning*. Maidenhead: Open University Press.

Kane, J., Lloyd, G., McCluskey, G., Riddell, S., Stead, J. and Weedon, E. (2007) An Evaluation of *Restorative Practices in Schools: Issues in Implementation*, Research Report. Edinburgh: Scottish Executive Education Department.

Lloyd, G. (ed.) (2005) *Problem Girls: Understanding and Supporting Troubled and Troublesome Girls and Young Women*. London: RoutledgeFalmer.

McCold, P. and Watchel, T. (2003) *In Pursuit of Paradigm: A Theory of Restorative Justice*. Available at: http://www.restorativepractices.org/library/paradigm.html.

Mills, M. (2001) *Challenging Violence in Schools: An Issue of Masculinities*. Buckingham: Open University Press.

Mills, M., Martino, W. and Lingard, B. (2004) Attracting, recruiting and retaining male teachers: policy issues in the male teacher debate, *British Journal of Sociology of Education*, 25(3): 355–69.

Mosley, J. (2001) *Working towards a Whole School Policy on Self-esteem and Positive Behaviour.* London: Positive Press.

Munn, P., Johnstone, M. and Sharp, S. (2004) *Teachers' Perceptions of Discipline in Scottish Schools, Insight 15.* Edinburgh: Scottish Executive Education Department.

Osler, A. (2003) *Girls and Exclusion: Rethinking the Agenda.* London: RoutledgeFalmer.

Scottish Executive (2004) *Incidents of Violence and Anti-social Acts Against Local Authority School Staff in 2002/03.* Edinburgh: Scottish Executive.

Scottish Government (2008) *Exclusions from Schools 2006/07.* Edinburgh: Scottish Executive.

Scottish Children's Reporters Administration (SCRA) (2007) *Annual Report 2005–06.* Edinburgh: SCRA.

Slee, R. (1995) *Changing Theories and Practices of School Discipline.* London: RoutledgeFalmer.

Thomas, G. and Loxley, A. (2001) *Deconstructing Special Education and Constructing Inclusion.* Buckingham: Open University Press.

Tyrell, G. (2002) *Peer Mediation: A Process for Primary Schools.* London: Souvenir Press.

Youth Justice Board (2005) *Restorative Justice in Schools: Summary of the National Evaluation of the Restorative Justice in Schools Programme.* London: Youth Justice Board.

Part 3

Relationships between girls' out-of-school experiences and school life

11 Demanding time: balancing school and out-of-school demands

Carolyn Jackson

Introduction

Displays of academic labour are regarded as 'uncool' within many secondary schools. Although government ministers and some researchers (Osler and Vincent 2003; Power et al. 2003; Francis and Skelton 2005) have suggested that the 'uncool to work' discourse applies only to boys, my research suggests that it is also dominant for girls (Jackson 2006). Yet there is a requirement in contemporary society for girls and boys to acquire 'good' academic credentials to enhance their chances in the competition for a 'good' career. This requirement is now well documented, and is a product of the broader 'neoliberal ethos of individualization, competition and marketization' (Ringrose 2007: 484). Given pressures on students to work for good academic credentials, the 'uncool to work' discourse can pose problems for them: how can they be 'cool' and popular, but also academically successful? Although some researchers have explored this and related questions in relation to boys (Frosh et al. 2002; Younger and Warrington 2005), girls have received very little attention in this regard, although there are signs that this is changing (Renold and Allan 2006; Francis this collection). This chapter explores how, given the contradictory 'uncool to work' and credentials discourses, secondary school girls in my research organized key aspects of their in- and out-of-school lives. Most girls attempted to balance academic and social (cool) demands, so I explore how they did this, and which girls were most able to achieve both academic and social 'success'.

I draw upon data from an ESRC funded project[1] that explored 'laddishness' among Year 9 pupils (13–14 years old; see Jackson 2006). The study generated questionnaire data from approximately 800 pupils and interview data from 153 pupils (75 girls) and 30 teachers. Six secondary schools in the north of England were involved: four co-educational (Beechwood, Elmwood, Firtrees, Oakfield), one girls' (Hollydale) and one boys'

(Ashgrove). The schools were selected to ensure a mix of pupils in terms of social class, 'race' and ethnicity, and a mix of schools in terms of examination results, and gender of intake (single-sex and co-educational). This chapter draws mainly upon data from interviews with girls (from the five schools where there were girls), although occasional references are made to questionnaire, and teacher interview, data.

Pupils were interviewed individually in spring–summer 2004, during the school day, in school, for approximately 30 minutes. Interviews were semi-structured and covered several topics including attitudes and approaches to school work; tests; pressures in school; friends and popularity; out-of-school activities. They were audio-taped and transcribed in full. Transcripts were analysed using the computer package Nud*ist Vivo, in which responses were coded thematically (see Jackson 2006 for more details). Names in this chapter are pseudonyms.

Constructing Popular, Cool Femininities: Negotiating the 'Credentials' and 'Uncool to Work' Discourses

The importance of popularity and friendship in girls' school lives is well recognized and documented (e.g. Hey 1997; Osler and Vincent 2003; Girlguiding UK and the Mental Health Foundation 2008). Not all girls aspire to be 'popular' because, as Paechter (2007) notes, being in the popular group often indicates more about how much social power a girl has rather than how much she is liked or respected. However, few, if any, girls want to be at the unpopular end of the 'popularity continuum' because of the negative consequences that ensue from being unpopular and not 'fitting in' (Hey 1997; Paechter 1998; Kehily 2001; Renold 2005).

Most of the girls I interviewed identified, without difficulty, features of popular femininity within their schools. They also recognized that popular girls had the most social power and were most able to influence and police 'acceptable' ways of 'doing girl' within their (heteronormative) school communities. Popular girls were usually regarded as (a) pretty, which involved being thin; (b) fashionable – they wore trendy clothes, make-up and had the latest mobile phones; and (c) sociable – they 'hung out' with friends inside and outside school, and were 'interested in', and attractive to, popular boys. In addition, and importantly, a recurring theme was that to be popular (or at least to avoid being unpopular) girls, like their male counterparts, generally had to avoid overt hard work and exhibit an air of indifference about academic endeavours. This finding challenges other work that suggests working hard is acceptable for girls, but uncool and unacceptable for boys (Osler and Vincent 2003; Power et al. 2003;

Francis and Skelton 2005). Popular girls were also commonly portrayed as loud, and sometimes as smokers and/or drinkers. The following examples illustrate how girls depicted popular femininity:

Sarah (Firtrees)
So what makes them [group of girls] popular?
...it's like the clothes they wear and the way they never do any work...smoking and drinking on Friday nights and everything, and like shouting at teachers and not doing as they [teachers] say.

Nassima (Oakfield)
What sorts of things make girls popular in school, do you think?
...Well now, it's who's got the best shoes I think, the best pointy shoes. And the best hairdos, best coats, bags, shoes, everything, make-up, best looks, who's with the best guy or who can pull the most.

Clara (Hollydale)
They [popular girls] go out with the popular boys and get drunk and stuff...They just dress like in all the latest stuff and they like all the latest phones and stuff. So everyone wants to be seen with them.

Jenny (Firtrees)
Most of the popular girls you see walking in groups together and they've all got the same hairstyle and their hair is perfectly straight. Like [they've got] the same coats and they're all dead skinny and there's all these little chubby girls walking behind them going 'oh I want to be like that'.

Gail (Elmwood)
I wouldn't say they're popular because they're hard workers, I'd say it's maybe more of the opposite: some people might say it's because they're not [hard workers].

As flagged earlier, the centrality of the 'uncool to work' discourse in the construction of popular femininity created problems for girls because of the dominance of the counter, 'credentials' discourse. Pressures to succeed – to gain credentials – were reported regularly by schoolgirls in the interviews, and these were frequently transmuted into pressures not to fail. For example, girls spoke of teachers and parents emphasizing the need to work hard and succeed in school in order to avoid 'dead-end' jobs and a bleak future (see also Reay and Wiliam 1999). Almost all students had taken this message on board. For example, on a questionnaire 72 per cent of pupils (girls and boys) chose 'very true' and 18 per cent chose 'mostly true' in response to the statement 'doing well in school is important in order to get a good job in later life' (points 5 and 4 on a 5-point scale).

The credentials discourse is dominant in schools. However, the 'uncool to work' pupil discourse is an equally dominant, yet contradictory, discourse. Given this, how do students navigate these discourses?

All interviewees spoke of the value of academic credentials, and none rejected academic work completely. However, some suggested that they prioritized social rather than academic goals because it was uncool to work. Sandy (Hollydale), for example, suggested she did not work hard because it was not cool to do so:

> *If it was really cool to work hard in school and you got status from working hard, would you work hard?*
> Yes I would, I would if it was [cool]. But because at the moment it's not, I just don't [work hard]. I don't try and I don't intend to.

By contrast, a minority rejected the 'uncool to work' discourse and instead subscribed to the credentials one. Within their groups these girls attempted to redefine school work as cool. This attempted redefinition was not, though, accepted by the majority. Generally, the price girls paid for overtly prioritizing school work over 'cool work' was being labelled as unpopular and mocked by their 'popular' peers.

While the 'uncool to work' pupil discourse was accepted by a small minority, and challenged by a small minority, the majority attempted to balance school work and 'cool work'. Frosh et al. (2002) reported similar findings from their study of 11–14-year-old boys. They argued that most boys attempted to negotiate what Frosh et al. call a 'middle way'. In other words, they tried to undertake school work in ways that avoided attracting the label 'swot'. For most girls in my research the tension between wanting to appear relatively 'cool' and popular in school, and also wanting to do well academically and attain good exam results, was difficult to manage. Not surprisingly, some were more adept at managing this than others. The next sections explore how some girls managed both academic and social 'success', and which girls were most likely to accomplish these.

Strategies for Balancing Social and Academic Demands

Whether or not a girl was successful at balancing academic and social demands depended, to a large extent, on the strategies she adopted and the resources at her disposal.[2] Strategies for 'getting away with' undertaking academic work without being cast as uncool operated on two levels, which I term 'direct' and 'indirect'. Time was central to both.

Direct strategies were those that girls employed deliberately to *hide* their work and effort. Girls hid or downplayed their effort because although academic achievement *per se* is not uncool, working hard to achieve is.[3] Such strategies included, for example, girls pretending they were not listening in class when they were, and working at home but hiding it. The latter frequently involved girls claiming to their peers that they had spent much less effort and time on their work than they actually had (see Jackson 2006 for more detail).

Indirect strategies were those that enabled students to *offset* the negative implications of school work, to negotiate more time and/or space for academic work without becoming unpopular. After-school socializing was one such indirect strategy; by ensuring they were sufficiently sociable outside of lessons and school, girls could 'get away with' some work. For example, Jane (Firtrees) explained how girls can work hard and still be popular if they balance their time:

> *Could a girl who worked hard and did really well be popular?*
> Yes
>
> *How would she manage that?*
> 'Cause you do your work and you try hard but you still have time for your friends. You don't just ignore your friends and [you] hang about with them as well as revising. Like you do your revising three days a week and go out with your friends the other three, or leave your work all the week and then do it at weekends.

Jane stressed the importance of making time for friends. Time was a big issue for most girls, and it arose in almost all of the interviews. Time is central to our lives, yet is often an invisible and taken-for-granted aspect. But lessons about time are an important part of the school's 'hidden curriculum'. Hughes (2002: 135) argues that

> Schooling is a key site where time discipline is instilled. . . . The organization of schooling is fixed according to age and calendar. The days are divided into periods and lesson activities are also planned to linear time. The length of examinations is set to specific hours and minutes. Teaching time of lessons is set aside from play time and home time. Children learn that if they have not finished their work they are taking too long or if they finish early they have not done enough. Accurately gauging the appropriate level of input in relation to the time available is a key skill.

The school system is premised on the assumption that pupils invest a lot of time and effort outside of school on their school work in order to be academically successful (see also Frosh et al. 2002). Yet, as we have seen, this is not straightforward for girls. Furthermore, in addition to the time demands of homework and socializing with friends, some girls reported having to perform domestic duties such as looking after family members or undertaking household chores (which no boys reported having to do) (see also O'Brien 2003). Overall, the ways in which time is used, presented and negotiated by students is central to their academic lives *and* the activities that enable them to acquire 'popular' status, or at least avoid being 'unpopular'.

Strategies for hiding work and effort and balancing social and academic demands depended on pupils having the wherewithal to be able to pull them off. The remainder of this chapter explores how access to resources shaped the ways in which girls were able to balance the social and academic demands of schooling.

Resources for Balancing Social and Academic Demands

In his study of 10–11-year-old boys, Swain (2004: 171) argues that the boys' 'position in the peer group is determined by the array of social, cultural, physical, intellectual and economic resources that each boy is able to draw on and accumulate'. This applies to secondary school girls too. Furthermore, not only does access to these resources shape the pupils' position in their peer group, but crucially, it shapes how well they are able to *balance* the different demands of their lives.

Resources are inextricably linked to time. As O'Brien (2003: 265) argues, 'as the demand for more time on school work done at home increases through second level [schooling], working-class girls may not have the resources to meet this demand'. When the demands on time are viewed not only in terms of academic ones, but also in terms of social ones, access to resources becomes even more salient. In my research, access to resources that facilitated quick and effective home study practices left girls with more time to socialize with friends and undertake activities that could earn them peer approval. For example, some girls said that having a computer at home helped them to organize their school work and to work efficiently (see also Valentine et al. 2005). Computer technology also enabled some girls to undertake social activities without them leaving their homes, and to socialize while also (privately) doing their homework. For example, Steph (Hollydale) who attained scores of 6, 7, 6 in her SATs[4] spoke about how, using the internet, she did her homework and socialized with friends simultaneously:

> I always make sure that I've done my work because that's one of the most important things. But I like, when I've done it, I always try and do it quickly so then I have time to 'talk' [on the internet]. Or you can 'talk' to your friends when you're doing it or something. And then it's like, if I'm on the internet at home doing my

research I can 'talk' to my friends at the same time, so I can get both things done at the same time.

It was clear from Steph's comments that she had long periods of uninterrupted internet access at home. It was also clear that girls who did not have internet access would be excluded from the regular socializing that occurred online between Steph and her friends. While online social networks did not replace face-to-face ones (Steph went out with friends at weekends), it meant that she could balance social and academic demands with relatively little effort (see also Gannon 2008). Contrast that with girls who do not have access to online social lives, and who have to meet up physically to socialize, the time demands are markedly different. So are the opportunities for combining work and social time. Steph could work while socializing and hide her work and effort; it is much harder to do homework in the park without being noticed.

While access to computers seemed to offer those who had them numerous advantages over those who did not, it was not only in terms of technology that resource differences were apparent. Zoe (Elmwood) for example, who got 7, 7, 6 in her SATs spoke proudly of having more resources at home than at school:

> When you're doing projects and things, at home you've got like an art box, and you've got all erm, like lollypop sticks and erm, sequins and cards and buttons and things. So when you're doing your work you can tend to do like little fancy borders. And I tend to do it on the computer because I think the more I write, the more my handwriting gets scruffier and my spelling gets a bit careless. So I think that's the facilities I've got there and I've not got at school.

Girls' access to resources differed markedly; while Zoe boasted of having more facilities at home than at school, finding space to study was an issue for some students (see O'Brien 2003; Ridge 2005). For example, Helen (Beechwood), who got 3, 3 and a score below test level in her SATs told me, 'I have like a cabin bed upstairs with't table and that underneath, and we don't have a table or owt downstairs, we just have a like, a breakfast bar'.

Overall, while many students talked about pressures of time and the difficulties of fitting in the demands of school and of being cool and popular, some had the resources to make this balancing act easier.

'They've Got It All': Image and Class in the Balance

So far I have discussed the ways in which access to certain resources enables pupils to undertake school work relatively quickly (and privately) thus providing them with more time for the requisite 'cool work' (direct strategies). Resources also help in a second way: certain resources help to offset the negative implications of school work. In other words, pupils were more likely to 'get away with' working if they were cool in other ways (indirect strategies) and, to an extent, cool could be purchased. It was easier for girls to be cool and popular if they wore the 'right sorts' of clothes and had the 'right sorts' of fashion accessories. Although there were some differences between the schools regarding fashion, the 'right sorts' of clothes and accessories were almost always very expensive (see also Swain 2002):

> Aisha (Oakfield)
> *So what are the cool things to wear?*
> ...right now for girls it's pointy shoes, and cropped jeans...I mean, the more expensive you look, the more cool you look.
>
> Ruth (Elmwood)
> *So who defines what's cool? I mean how do you decide what's cool and what's not cool?*
> It's probably clothes or something. Or the way you look....I think it's more makes than anything...They have to wear make [branded] clothes or you look like a scruff or summat.
> *So the scruffy ones aren't cool?*
> No. I think they're sectioned into three, you know, there's swots, cool and scrubbers, as they call them.
>
> Alice (Hollydale)
> We like to wear nice clothes and everything. Some people just look like tramps and everything but most of my friends and everything have nice clothes because we don't really want to be seen walking around with somebody who looks a tramp. But most people, it's not because of the clothes that they wear that we're not friends with them, it's just we don't really get on with them if you know what I mean.

Ruth and Alice's comments both convey downward social comparisons in terms of class. They talk about 'scruffs', 'scrubbers' or 'tramps' and both reveal the negative values attached to such labels. Alice's comment that 'it's not because of the clothes that they wear that we're not friends with them, it's just we don't really get on with them', conveys that it's not only clothes that make them 'Other' but also their ways of being. 'Swots' too were placed as 'Other': while they were not 'scrubbers', neither were they cool. This was partly because 'swots' did not wear 'fashionable' versions of school uniform and, crucially, they wore their uniform in an uncool way, which usually meant they wore it in accordance with school rules. For example, at Beechwood students who wore their ties in line with school rules were called 'swotknots'. Undoubtedly, wearing the 'right sorts' of clothes in the 'right sorts of ways' and having appropriate accessories (for example, the latest mobile phones) enabled students to jump several rungs up the 'cool ladder' as it contributed to a cool image. Swain's (2002: 66) work in junior schools demonstrated how clothes act as 'a powerful signifier of the pupils' worth as people, and were an essential ingredient of social acceptability (or rejection) within their specific peer group culture'. In addition to the ways students dressed and adorned their bodies to portray an air of coolness, the body itself was central to the performance. Here again, some were given a head start. It was reported time and again during the interviews with pupils and teachers that girls could 'get away with' spending time working academically if they were heterosexually attractive. Many girls invested a lot of time in their appearance; this was conveyed by Ms Walters (Hollydale):

> I quietly laugh at my Year 9 because they have a little contingent that we refer to as 'the Barbies', which is a lovely expression.
> *It's one that the girls used as well.*
> Did they? Well we [teachers] refer to them as that and it's no reflection of their ability because some of them are the most able girls. And they're very nice natured girls and also very pretty girls and they've got everything going for them. But they do spend a tremendously long time grooming themselves and it's that sort of, you know, everything has to be just so and it's as though you can't start the day until everything is in order and in place.

According to Ms Walters this group of popular Year 9 girls have 'got it all. They're talented, they've got the looks, they've got the personality and I look at one or two of these charming young women and I think well, you're a hard act to follow love'. According to teachers and students at Hollydale these girls balanced academic and social demands very well: 'they're quite clever even though they're still always going out. They're really clever' (Iram). Appearance was central to the image of this group, an image that reflected traditional models of white, heterosexual femininity. Like Ms Walters, some pupils described them as having 'everything': 'They always like, they've always got the lip-gloss and the pink shoes and they're quite rich. They always get designer clothes and [are] the ones with everything. Like, most of them have got long blonde hair and blue eyes and [are] like tall and they're all slim and they all get all the lads from [the local boys' school] and everything' (Faya).

Without a doubt the social class position of these girls underpins and is central to their image of 'got it all'. It is their class position that facilitates their balancing of social and academic realms. The admiration of their teacher about their ability to balance academic and social demands in an apparently effortless way, and their lifestyles in general, was clear:

> They're quite cool because they've got it all. They can do it but they're not the ones that are constantly, you know, the teacher's pet…They can be told off for inappropriate comments in the same way as somebody sitting on the front row deliberately chatting or somebody who isn't interested. That's what makes them cool, is that they're not really the swotty type. They can do it, they've got the ability, they're interested, they're well motivated, they're clever girls but they don't appear to be overly zealous when it comes to their work. Everything is done, they just quietly get on with it. They're the ones that finish their science in the double lesson, they're the ones whose books are always on the shelf on a Monday morning because they've done their homework. But they can balance it.
>
> (Ms Walters, Hollydale)

But strip away their expensive clothes and their charm, remould their tall, slim bodies, long blond hair and blue eyes, and they would have a much harder time maintaining their popularity without being regarded as swotty. Their bodies and their expensive feminine accoutrements are key to enabling them to create the time and space to undertake academic endeavours without rebuke.

Conclusion

Girls who were apparently effortlessly successful in academic and social realms were generally regarded as 'having it all'. These girls were able to acquire the necessary academic credentials while also being cool and popular. The apparent effortlessness of their academic success was very important: the dominance of the 'uncool to work' discourse in these schools meant that while academic success was accepted (and admired), overtly working hard to attain academic success was uncool.

Of course, very few girls are 'effortless achievers', but some are more adept than others at creating the impression that they are. Effort and time are inextricably linked. To be effortlessly successful academically means getting good results without (apparently) spending much time on school work. To be successful socially depends on spending time with friends. Therein lays the problem for many girls: how can they spend enough time (without showing it) on school work to succeed academically, and also spend enough time with friends to be popular?

In this chapter I have outlined some of the ways in which girls attempt to balance academic and social demands in order to be successful in both spheres. I have argued that resources play an important role in facilitating this success. Furthermore, by virtue of their range of resources, middle-class girls are more likely than their working-class counterparts to be able to balance the demands of being popular and academically successful. That is not to say that the balancing act does not take its toll on middle-class girls; other research has revealed the high emotional costs for some middle-class girls of striving to meet neo-liberal demands to be 'successful' in all domains (for example, Walkerdine et al. 2001; Renold and Allan 2006). We need to keep the demands faced by girls firmly on the research agenda, and question and challenge the popular rhetoric that girls are fine.

Notes

1. RES-000-27-0041.
2. I adopt Swain's distinction between 'strategy' and 'resource' (2004: 168): 'resources' are the capital or stock that people draw upon and 'strategies' are the processes they use to apply them.
3. Pretending not to work hard has numerous potential benefits. Not only does it earn girls 'cool points', but it also protects them if they 'fail', as failure without effort does not automatically imply low ability. Furthermore, success without effort (effortless achievement) is regarded as the ideal in schools (see Jackson 2006 for an extensive discussion about this).
4. SATs are national tests taken by pupils in England. They were introduced for 7-year-old pupils in 1991 and those aged 11 in 1995; these are ongoing. SATs were introduced in 1993 for pupils aged 14, but in October 2008 School Secretary Ed Balls announced that he was ending the requirement for schools to run national tests for 14-year-olds with immediate effect. See: http://www.dcsf.gov.uk/pns/DisplayPN.cgi?pn_id=2008_0229. At the time of the research the 'expected' or 'target' level for SATs taken at age 14 was 5, and the maximum levels were 7 for English and science and 8 for maths.

References

Francis, B. and Skelton, C. (2005) *Reassessing Gender and Achievement: Questioning Contemporary Key Debates*. London: Routledge.

Frosh, S., Phoenix, A. and Pattman, R. (2002) *Young Masculinities: Understanding Boys in Contemporary Society*. Basingstoke: Palgrave.

Gannon, S. (2008) 'Twenty-four seven on the computers': girls, ICTs and risk, *Gender and Education*, 20(4): 361–73.

Girlguiding UK and the Mental Health Foundation (2008) *A Generation Under Stress?* Available at: http://www.mentalhealth.org.uk/publications/?EntryId5=62067 (accessed 15/4/09).

Hey, V. (1997) *The Company She Keeps: An Ethnography of Girls' Friendships.* Buckingham: Open University Press.

Hughes, C. (2002) *Key Concepts in Feminist Theory and Research.* London: Sage.

Jackson, C. (2006) *'Lads' and 'Ladettes' in School: Gender and a Fear of Failure.* Maidenhead: Open University Press.

Kehily, M.J. (2001) Issues of gender and sexuality in schools, in B. Francis and C. Skelton (eds), *Investigating Gender: Contemporary Perspectives in Education.* Buckingham: Open University Press.

O'Brien, M. (2003) Girls and transition to second-level schooling in Ireland: 'moving on' and 'moving out', *Gender and Education*, 15(3): 249–67.

Osler, A. and Vincent, K. (2003) *Girls and Exclusion: Rethinking the Agenda.* London: RoutlegeFalmer.

Paechter, C. (1998) *Educating the Other: Gender, Power and Schooling.* London: Falmer Press.

Paechter, C. (2007) *Being Boys, Being Girls: Learning Masculinities and Femininities.* Maidenhead: Open University Press.

Power, S., Edwards, T., Whitty, G. and Wigfall, V. (2003) *Education and the Middle Class.* Buckingham: Open University Press.

Reay, D. and Wiliam, D. (1999) 'I'll be a nothing': structure, agency and the construction of identity through assessment, *British Educational Research Journal*, 25(3): 343–54.

Renold, E. (2005) *Girls, Boys and Junior Sexualities: Exploring Children's Gender and Sexual Relations in the Primary School.* London: RoutledgeFalmer.

Renold, E. and Allan, A. (2006) Bright and beautiful: high achieving girls, ambivalent femininities, and the feminisation of success in the primary school, *Discourse: Studies in the Cultural Politics of Education*, 27(4): 457–73.

Ridge, T. (2005) Feeling under pressure: low-income girls negotiating school life, in G. Lloyd (ed.), *Problem Girls: Understanding and Supporting Troubled and Troublesome Girls and Young Women.* London: RoutledgeFalmer.

Ringrose, J. (2007) Successful girls? Complicating post-feminist, neoliberal discourses of educational achievement and gender equality, *Gender and Education*, 19(4): 471–89.

Swain, J. (2002) The right stuff: fashioning an identity through clothing in a junior school, *Gender and Education*, 14(1): 53–69.

Swain, J. (2004) The resources and strategies that 10–11-year-old boys use to construct masculinities in the school setting, *British Educational Research Journal*, 30(1): 167–85.

Valentine, G., Marsh, J. and Pattie, C. (2005) *Children and Young People's Home Use of ICT for Educational Purposes: The Impact on Attainment at Key Stages 1–4.* Available at: http://www.dfes.gov.uk/research/data/uploadfiles/RR672.pdf

Walkerdine, V., Lucey, H. and Melody, J. (2001) *Growing Up Girl: Psychosocial Explorations of Gender and Class.* Basingstoke: Palgrave.

Younger, M. and Warrington, M. (2005) *Raising Boys' Achievement in Secondary Schools: Issues, Dilemmas and Opportunities.* Maidenhead: Open University Press.

12 Sluts, whores, fat slags and playboy bunnies: Teen girls' negotiations of 'sexy' on social networking sites and at school

Jessica Ringrose

Introduction

According to Ofcom statistics, in a survey of 5000 adults and 3000 children 49 per cent of those aged between 8 and 17 have an internet profile on social networking sites (SNSs) such as Bebo and Facebook (Waters 2008). boyd and Ellison (2007: 11) suggest that they 'constitute an important research context for scholars investigating processes of impression management, self-presentation, and friendship performance'. This is particularly true for researchers exploring issues of peer networks, friendships, intimacy and gendered and sexualized identities, subjectivities and power dynamics formed through the social context of schooling. Social networking sites are an important bridge into understanding social relationships at school, because contrary to the notion that young people are making many new contacts in cyberspace, Livingstone (2007), boyd (2008) and the research drawn on in this chapter,[1] suggest that young people are mostly communicating with their school friends online. SNSs mainly work to extend and amplify school-based relationships, as young people use them to communicate with school-based contacts when outside (but also when possible inside) the physical school space. However, schools are faced with difficulties in understanding and addressing SNSs, as many view online engagement as happening mostly outside the bounds of schooling (Selwyn 2008). Consequently, schools have also not addressed the specifically gendered and sexualized aspects of student's engagements with SNSs, nor how these impact on students' experiences at school.

In this chapter I address the relationship between the social space of online SNSs and schooling, focusing on how girls' representations online relate to their experiences in 'real life' at school. I analyse the hypersexualized and 'pornified' content of the SNSs in which young people participate. 'Pornification' is a way to theorize the normalization of pornography in everyday life (Levy 2005). I examine intensified sexual commodification of girls' and women's bodies online on young people's SNSs. Through analysis of online representations and interview narratives with girls about their sites, I examine how girls negotiate the highly sexualized content online and pressures upon them to perform as 'sexy' on their SNSs.

My theoretical approach involves discursively 'mapping' (Gonick 2003) the way 'porno-discourses', shape and construct the *discursive and visual* 'conditions of possibility' (Foucault 1982) for forging sexual subjectivity (Youdell 2005) on social networking sites. As Thomas (2004: 361) describes, 'certain moments of seeing, and particular visualities are central to how subjectivities and sexualities are formed'. I illustrate how Bebo sites create normalized visual expectations around idealized femininity. These images, which commodify girls as sexualized objects, are 'central' (Thomas 2004) to our participants' sexual subjectivities online. However, demands to present the self as 'sexy' online create discursive contradictions for girls in negotiating an acceptable sexual identity in 'real-life'. Demands around visually desirable heterosexual femininity online lead to 'real-life' anxieties, conflicts and violence in their relationships at school. The problems of hypersexualization and pornification in young people's engagements with SNSs thus constitute significant gender equity issues that should be addressed by schools.

Methodology

This chapter analyses data from a pilot study exploring how 23 students (aged 14–16) in two secondary schools use and understand social networking sites. The school is an important environment to discuss social networking since the friendship networks are typically organized around school-based peer groups (Livingstone 2007). The research team worked with students from an English/Media Studies class in Thornbury Secondary, a high-achieving rural specialist college, where the level of socioeconomic disadvantage was well below average. We also studied students from a Media Studies class in New Mills Secondary, which was, in contrast, in a Southern London borough, in an area of 'high deprivation'.

We conducted group and individual interviews with 11 boys and 12 girls. These revealed that the majority of students were using Bebo, a social networking site used 'predominantly by the 13- to 24-year-old age group' in the UK (Smithers 2008). After group interviews (where we asked for permission to view their Bebo sites) we returned for individual interviews (six girls, one boy) with students whose sites raised important issues around sexual representation and identity. We then continued to analyse the Bebo sites of our participants over a period of two months through a process of observation of changes on the sites. The hyper-sexualized images I explore were evident on the SNSs of participants from both schools, despite their different academic cultures and socio-economic intake, indicating the 'pornified' environment teens are navigating.

Signifying Practices on SNSs: Bebo and the Sexually Commodified Female Body

Virtual spaces and sites such as YouTube, Myspace and Bebo are highly commodified environments that structure the display of identity and practices of consumption through particular templates (Duncan and Leander 2000; boyd 2008). Bebo is a commercial product, a brand, which has been marketed and taken up by a specifically teen target audience. Most Bebo profiles contain some form of commercial culture including links to favourite songs, music videos, TV shows, movies, spoof advertisements, clothes, football teams, sports cars (etc.) as part of the signifying practices of representing the self online. Consumer, pop and celebrity culture is often infused with highly sexualized and increasingly 'pornified' meanings (Gill 2009) and these trends are immediately apparent on young people's Bebo sites.

One of the most important visual forms on the site is 'skin', which is the background that covers the generic site. These are downloaded off SNSs and can be googled on the internet and frequently changed. Skins are backgrounds that can only be modified with specialized technical skills, so they are not authored in the same way text or blogs are. They exist as commodities themselves that young people find online, trade or even pay someone to make through Bebo networks. Many are explicitly hyper-sexualized.

Indeed, a popular skin at New Mills High school is a background featuring a shot below the knees of a male in Adidas shoes pressed against by a female in stiletto heels with her knickers at her ankles (it is also one of the top 50 UK Bebo skins at the time of writing).[2] Another Adidas skin displays a female volleyball team clothed only in Adidas g-strings, socks and footwear, in a huddle with their butts facing outward. The playboy bunny is a popular skin used by one of our participants, Marie (16, New Mills), which represents a significant slippage of soft core pornography in the images/commodities marketed at girls (Bloom and Hepburn 2008). Jen (16, New Mills) had a skin that read 'Boom Chicka Wah Wah' which is a reference to a highly sexualized 2007 advertising campaign for Lynx male deodorant spray, featuring men attracting hundreds of (often semi-naked) women after applying the spray, but which also, according to the urban dictionary, is 'used to describe someone that is very hot'.[3] Presumably Jen used this message to signal her 'hotness' or to reference what she talked about in a group interview as being called 'sexy' online. Pamela (16, New Mills) told us in a group interview how her skin said 'hold me in your arms and tell me that I'm your baby girl'. The skin used by Daniella (14, Thornbury), whose site is discussed further below, featured a picture of a naked Marilyn Monroe in bed, with the quotations 'It's all just make believe isn't it?' and 'A wise girl kisses but doesn't love, listens but doesn't believe, and leaves before she is left'. The Bebo skin used by Sam (15, Thornbury) the boy Daniella was dating, also featured a scantily clad woman posing in platform heels beside a Ford GT exotic sports car (price approximately £100,000).

The heterosexualized dynamics prominent in advertising and pop music are appropriated and used within the visual and textual context of many of our participants' Bebo sites, to varying degrees. The specific skins I've already explored illustrate the constitution and constraining of the conditions for performing normalized and idealized forms of teen masculinity and femininity online, in ways that relate to wider dominant, globally marketed discourses of heterosexual desirability (Nayak and Kehily 2008). These specific Bebo skins represent masculinity as epitomized in buying the consumer goods (i.e. cars and shoes) with which to gain access to the sexually commodified female body. Femininity in contrast is epitomized through approximating a sexually commodified body, performing as (scantily clad) sexual object, and occupying the position of sexually desirable 'baby girl'. These online representations represent a significant degree of sexism and sexual objectification that girls must negotiate, and which necessarily impact on their experiences at school.

Also informing the highly sexualized discursive milieu of Bebo sites are game and quiz 'applications' that repeatedly circulate in the social networks of Bebo. Applications are programmes that are passed through the online community and are not authored by young people. Popular Bebo applications on our teen girl participant sites include 'make a baby', and 'Celebrity look-alikes', 'What type of kisser are you?' or 'Are You Sexy, Flirty, Or A Slut?' If you get the 'Flirty' result, as Marie (16, New Mills) did, a woman on an erotic dancing pole is featured on your Bebo site, normalizing pole dancing as a form of flirty fun. Other applications include: 'What Kind Of Lingerie Are You?', which gave another participant the result 'v-string panties', with a close up of a woman's crotch with a diamante studded 'sexy' on a yellow g-string; while 'What kind of girl are you' can generate the response 'Eye Candy'; and 'What Sexual Fantasy

Are You?' creates the image/text 'Sexy Schoolgirl' with a grown woman posing in pigtails, kilt, mini skirt and half top.

Whether or not girls using these applications identify with the results, participants were bombarded by applications: 'At the moment I've got about 31 applications sitting in my "To Do" list' (Louise, 16, New Mills). These applications are a structural process (created by adults) where the normalization of celebrity culture, hyper-sexualized representations and pornographic imagery occurs through the repeated and everyday use of these visual, interactive applications.

As outlined, then, young people's sites are replete with increasingly normalized and intensified examples of sexual commodification of the feminine body. This intensified sexual commodification is tied to a 'visual cyber culture' (Thomas 2004) organized on the sites where pornographic imagery (pole dancing and g-strings) and symbolism (playboy bunny etc.) are totally normalized in a phenomenon feminist commentators have called 'porno-chic' (McRobbie 2004; Duits and van Zooenen 2006). This is not unique to Bebo but part of a wider cultural phenomenon of 'pornification', according to Paasonen et al. (2007: 4): 'The media immerses us in the pornographic aesthetic. Now integral to popular culture, porn is part of our everyday lives. Sexual desire is commodified, pornified and the media leads the way.' The central question, however, is how this pornified environment impacts on girls' representations of themselves online and how this then affects their relationships at school.

Visual Culture: 'Slutty Girls' Who Are 'Up for Anything'

Sites are further personalized through the individual display photos, names and taglines. The display photo is the first thing one sees when looking at friends or doing a search through Bebo. This visual display is particularly important for girls:

> Daniella (14, Thornbury): Say someone took a picture of me when I just woke up in the morning, I'd never put that on Bebo. Because it would just be embarrassing. I need to feel . . . have all my hair done and my make-up done . . .
>
> Louise (16, New Mills): You can airbrush yourself . . . you can make yourself look better then, well – what can I say? – I've been doing it all the time!

Louise refers to the common practice of altering photos to attain a 'better' visual effect. A great deal of discussion also focused on how much cleavage a girl should display, from which angle, and there were significant tensions around how to display themselves sexually online in many of the group and individual interviews:

> Daniella (14, Thornbury): I think like if you've got like say a slutty girl, she'll take a picture of her body or whatever and have it as her image . . . If I came across a Bebo thats someone's got a picture of their cleavage and their body, and nothing else. And I'll think, 'Well, they obviously think too much of themselves'.
>
> Louise (16, New Mills): If you put pictures on like that people are just going to think oh look you're like a bit of a slut or you're gagging to have sex, I had to make that choice because I thought I don't want people to see me like that.
>
> Marie (16, New Mills): It's like you, if you go on some people's pictures, you go, you see pictures of girls in their bras, bikinis and all that . . . It's like putting yourself down, it's making everyone think, oh, she's a slag . . . they're trying to impress everyone. Like get all the boys thinking . . . they're up for anything . . . I could but I don't really like going round in short skirts, bikini tops and that 'cause one it's too cold and two . . . I think it makes the boys think you'll do anything if you're walking around like that . . . making yourself look desperate.

Daniella, Lousia and Marie are describing some of the complex gendered and sexualized negotiations that have to be undertaken by girls as part of self-representation on Bebo and then at school. Sexual regulation in teen peer groups, including peer rules around girls not being seen as too 'slutty', is well documented in research on girlhood and girls' friendships (Kehily 2002; Lamb 2002; White 2002; Ringrose 2008). boyd (2008) also suggests in relation to MySpace there are tensions for girls around appearing 'slutty' online. However, what I would like to suggest is that the intense visual imperative to represent the self as 'sexy' and sexually confident online creates new contradictions for girls, who appear to still need to navigate not appearing 'too slutty' in peer contexts at school. Contradictions between online representations and what the girls said in interviews in school settings were striking.

For example, after Daniella's disparaging comments about 'slutty girls' online in the group interview at school, the research team were at first surprised to view her site and find that her username was actually 'slut' (as are nearly 25,000 other Bebo usernames). Moreover, one of her closest friends Nicola (14, Thornbury) called herself 'whore'. Daniella's profile photograph also featured a plunging neckline and heavy make-up with dramatic eye-liner, and many further images on her sites featured her breasts, one of which had been put through a Bebo application to apply flashing stars to her cleavage. As mentioned, Daniella's skin featured a naked Marilyn Monroe in bed, but there were also explicit textual references to selling sex and to preferred sexual positions, since her tagline (the text immediately following her username, 'slut') was 'I like it up the bum, just like your mum, and I suck dick for £5'. Nicola, whose Bebo username was 'whore', wrote this tagline on Daniella's Bebo site as a 'joke' when they traded Bebo passwords (needed to alter one's Bebo profile) one weekend. The tagline was left up on the site for some time. Daniella's skin, photos, username and tagline illustrate the trend towards pornification (normalization of pornography in popular culture) and her use of 'porno discourses' which are reconstituted on Daniella's Bebo site through online visual and textual representations.

The differences between Daniella's condemnation of 'slutty' in the group interview at school and her online representations as 'slut' indicate, however, massive contradictions. She struggles to negotiate an appropriately sexualized identity in the group interview at school (condemning 'slutty' girls), while she tries to represent a sexually confident, knowing representation of self in the virtual space of Bebo. One interpretation of Daniella calling herself 'slut' is that this term has shifted discursive meaning and now can represent being a sexually confident, experienced and knowing feminine subject (Atwood 2007). While Daniella may use 'slut' to connote her sexual confidence online, it would be problematic, to interpret this as necessarily 'empowering'. Rather as Rosalind Gill (2008: 53) suggests in her Foucauldian analysis of increasingly normal pornified and hyper-sexualized popular culture, positioning the self as always 'up for it' and the 'performance of confident sexual agency' has shifted to become a key *regulative* dimension of idealized femininity; or a 'disciplinary technology' of performing sexy femininity across mainstream media and advertising. In this dynamic girls and women are 'required to be skilled in a variety of sexual behaviours', and to display their expertise, something evident in Daniella's online visual and textual displays. But online 'sexual confidence' does not necessarily translate into 'real-life' sexual confidence for girls in secondary school.

My research exploring relationships at school through interview narratives, *as well as* online representations, reveals the fissures in the 'sexy confident' online veneer of teen girls like Daniella. Daniella told me in her individual interview about her anxieties about her body and looking 'perfect', saying she 'hated' her legs and felt 'huge' and 'fat' compared to her friends. She spent a lot of time doing clothes and make-up to produce photos to post online with her friends, immediately deleting ones that were unflattering. She discussed the pressures informing the production of the ideal *visual* feminine to be performed online and worried about whether or not she could sustain the 'perfect' self she constructed online in her real relationships with boys:

> Daniella: popular boys in this school, you don't see them going out with girls that they would probably *see as ugly* . . . puts a lot of pressure on girls to make themselves look pretty, to make themselves just look perfect to that one boy that they really want; because, otherwise, if they don't try or make an effort they're not going to want to go out with them.

Daniella also discussed her intimate relationship with a particular teen boy at her school, Sam (15, Thornbury). Daniella worried that she could not call Sam her 'boyfriend' as he had not yet officially asked her out (despite 'seeing each other' for six weeks). It would appear that more conventional heterosexualized power dynamics of positioning the male as the one who can seek and ask out were very much alive, since Daniella positions herself as passively waiting for commitment in their real-life relationship. The pornified norms of representing the feminine self as sexually confident and in control online appear to directly contradict more conventional rules of heterosexualized romance and boys asking girls 'to go out' at school which remain 'cast in terms of binaries such as male/female, pursuer/pursued, assertive/submissive, demanding/conciliatory' (Kehily 2002: 67). This is part of the dynamic of online/offline gendered/sexualized representations and relationships young people must negotiate on a daily basis.

Playboy Bunnies and Fat Slags

The teen girls at New Mills also struggled with the difficult demands to perform as sexually desirable online and at school. Marie (16, New Mills) worried about her appearance and body, telling me, for instance:

> I used to be fat . . . not proper fat, but I used to be proper chubby, chubby cheeks, chubby belly, everything . . . And I used to try and walk round with my stomach breathed in, everything. I've never liked my stomach . . . Even now that I'm skinny I don't like my stomach.

Marie, as mentioned above, was also critical of girls who displayed themselves in their 'bra or knickers', which she said made girls look 'desperate'. But she still wanted to position herself as attractive and desirable, spending a lot of time constructing her online photos.

Indeed, Marie's site prominently featured a picture of herself in fluffy pink bunny ears which she had put through an application that allows the user to cartoonize pictures (or turn any photo into a cartoon-like image). This was in the context of her Bebo skin background which displayed the Playboy bunny symbol. When we asked Marie about the playboy bunny skin and cartoon photo of herself in bunny ears she said,

> *Marie:* And like in my pictures... there's a folder called 'Random' and it's got loads of pictures of Playboy bunny and everything like that. I was going through my skins and there was a Playboy bunny skin so I just picked that one.
>
> *Jessica:* Ok. Now, did your mum get you the Playboy stuff or?
>
> *Marie:* Yeah.
>
> *Jessica:* Yeah, and what does it mean to you, the symbol?
>
> *Marie:* To most people it means like the Playboy mansion and all the girls and that but with girls it's just the bunny and like girls like rabbits and...
>
> *Jessica:* So do you, are you thinking that about, you know, the Playboy bunny mansion or anything like that?
>
> *Marie:* No, it's just a good cartoon...
>
> *Jessica:* And do you have like the shirts and...
>
> *Marie:* Yeah I've got one, I've got two tops with the Playboy bunny on it.
>
> *Jessica:* Ok, so you know other people might think of it as like the Playboy mansion?
>
> *Marie:* Yeah.
>
> *Jessica:* And how do you, what do you think about that? The fact that you see it one way and other people might see it another way.
>
> *Marie:* It's other people's opinion, it's completely up to them, I just like it because of the picture.

As suggested earlier, the playboy bunny is a fairly obvious example of pornification in popular culture – the soft-porn symbol of the bunny has become so normalized in the domain of popular consumer culture that it is a multi-million dollar industry marketing t-shirts and pencil boxes to teen but also even younger girls (Gill 2007; Bloom and Hepburn 2008). Indeed, the Playboy bunny symbol is contradictory, it operates simultaneously as a symbol of sexiness, an escape to glamour and material wealth through the sexually commodified body, *as well as a symbol of* childhood innocence – 'rabbits', 'a bunny'. Marie's response reveals these contradictions as she is adamant it is 'just a good cartoon', despite her earlier statement that it refers to 'the Playboy mansion and all the girls' for 'most people'.

In my interpretation, the playboy bunny symbolism is used by Marie to signal herself as sexy and sexual online, as part of managing her feelings of physical inadequacy in 'real life', explored earlier. While Marie is not actually posing as a playboy bunny in a bodice, since she is clothed, the Playboy bunny as a sign is drawn upon as part of a 'chain of signifiers' (Lacan 1977) to signify her sexiness in the context of her Bebo site and Bebo network, where the playboy bunny icon is prominent. Because there is a *visual imperative* to display a sexy self on the social networking sites of many of the girls, the moment of seeing and being seen as 'sexy' is absolutely 'central' (Thomas 2004) to how *desirable* sexual subjectivities are formed within the visual culture of our teen girls' Bebo sites. Marie attempts to perform sexy visually online by drawing on the purchase of the iconic playboy bunny symbols. What is also apparent is how Bebo appears to intensify Marie's use of and relationship to the Playboy bunny symbol in 'real life'. The 'real' playboy bunny t-shirts and bunny ears products purchased by her mum, are added to by a virtual folder with a collection of playboy bunny pictures, the playboy bunny skin and the cartooning application, which Marie uses to turn herself into a Playboy bunny on her online Bebo profile.

These intensified norms of meeting the criterion of sexy online also, however, have very real, embodied effects at school. Marie is harshly critical not only of herself but also other girls. Only days before the group interview with Marie at New Mills, she called her 'friend' Louise (14, New Mills) a 'fat slag' on MSN. Louise (who was visibly overweight) was judged by Marie as failing to meet the criterion for 'sexy'. Louise confronted and then hit Marie after school the following day. While I do not have space to explore this episode in depth, it points to how girls are under particular and constant threat of failing to meet the pornified and hyper-sexualized visual ideals of 'perfect' femininity online. The violent confrontation also shores up how sexual politics online directly impact the physical spaces of schooling.

Conclusion

Recent feminist research on contemporary issues of gender equity and schooling illustrates that issues of sexism and sexualization (e.g. sexual bullying) of and among young people are positioned by policy makers as peripheral to concerns over academic literacy and performance league tables (McNeil and White 2007; Skelton and Francis 2009). Issues of hyper, (hetero)sexual commodification and objectification of girl's bodies (Duits and Van Zoonen 2006) are rendered largely invisible in relation to the dominant story of 'successful girls', measured through 'higher performance' than boys on tests at school (Ringrose 2007). Moreover, educational researchers have suggested that sexism in popular culture is not being adequately addressed in the sex education curriculum with its focus on disease and pregnancy (Alldred and David 2007); and that there is a massive gap between official sex education and the '"lived" experience of sexuality among pupils' (Kehily 2002: 71). In addition, while media studies scholars have done work in developing teaching resources for media studies sessions by exploring depictions of sex, love and relationships in the media and in advertising (Buckingham and Bragg 2004) these interventions are often piecemeal, with PSHEE and media studies sessions given low priority and status within the performance cultures of schools.

The findings in this chapter illustrate, however, the increasing normalization of pornography and sexual commodification of girls' bodies online has a direct relationship to girls' 'real-life' experiences and relationships at school. The intensified sexual commodification of girls' bodies online needs, therefore, to be positioned as a crucial gender equity issue that falls within school's requirements to meet the criterion of the new UK Gender Equality Duty (2007). Finding ways to intervene into the curriculum to help 'guide' (boyd 2008) young people around the gendered and sexualized meanings and power dynamics imbued in online representations and how this impacts experiences at school is also an important area for further educational research and policy development on gender equity in schools.

Acknowledgements

This chapter builds on: Willett, R. and Ringrose, J. (2008) 'Sharing the luv': consumers, identity and Social Networking Sites. Paper presented at the *Child and Teen Consumption Conference* 24–25 April, Trondheim, Norway. I would also like to thank Rebekah Willett for her insights and comments on this chapter.

Notes

1. 'Young People's Negotiations of Online Social Networking Sites', carried out in 2008 with Rebekah Willett, funded by Norwegian Centre for Child Research (NOSEB) and the Centre for the Study of Children, Youth and Media (Institute of Education, University of London, UK).
2. http://www.bebostation.com/top-rated-bebo-skins/, accessed11/10/08.
3. http://www.urbandictionary.com/define.php?term=Boom+chicka+Wah+Wah, accessed, 11/10/08.

References

Alldred, P. and David, M. (2007) *Get Real About Sex: The Politics and Practice of Sex Education*. Maidenhead: Open University Press.

Attwood, F. (2007) Sluts and riot grrrls: female identity and sexual agency, *Journal of Gender Studies*, 16(3): 231–45.

Bloom, A. and Hepburn, H. (2008) Danger of the bunny syndrome, *TES*, 5 December. Available at: http://www.tes.co.uk/article.aspx? storycode=6006033 (accessed 7/12/08).

boyd, D.M. (2008) Why youth social network sites: the role of networked publics in teenage social life, in D. Buckingham (ed.), *Youth, Identity, and Digital Media*. Cambridge, MA: MIT Press.

boyd, D.M. and Ellison, N.B. (2007) Social network sites: definition, history, and scholarship, *Journal of Computer-Mediated Communication*, 13(1): article 11. Available at: http://jcmc.indiana.edu/vol13/issue1/ boyd.ellison.html (accessed 06/08).

Buckingham, D. and Bragg, S. (2004) *Young People, Sex and the Media: The Facts of Life?* Basingstoke: Palgrave Macmillan.

Duits, L. and van Zoonen, M. (2006) Headscarves and porno-chic: disciplining girls' bodies in the European multicultural society, *European Journal of Women's Studies*, 13(2): 103–17.

Duncan, B. and Leander, K. (2000) Girls just wanna have fun: literacy, consumerism, and paradoxes of position on gURL.Com, *Reading Online*, 4(5). Available at: http://www.readingonline.org/electronic/elec_ index.asp?HREF=/electronic/duncan/index.html (accessed 14/04/08).

Foucault, M. (1982) The subject of power, in H. Dreyfus and P. Rabinow (eds), *Michel Foucault: Beyond Structuralism and Hermeneutics*. Brighton: Harvester.

Gill, R. (2008) Empowerment/sexism: figuring female sexual agency in contemporary advertising, *Feminism and Psychology*, 18(1): 35–60.

Gill, R. (2009) Supersexualize me! Advertising and 'the midriffs', in F. Attwood, R. Brunt and R. Cere (eds), *Mainstreaming Sex: The Sexualization of Culture*. London: I.B Tauris.

Gonick, M. (2003) *Between Femininities: Ambivalence, Identity and the Education of Girls*. New York: SUNY.

Kehily, J. (2002) *Sexuality, Gender and Schooling: Shifting Agendas in Social Learning*. London: RoutledgeFalmer.

Lacan, J. (1977/2002) *Ecrits: A Selection*. New York: Norton.

Lamb, S. (2002) *The Secret Lives of Girls: What Good Girls Really Do – Sex Play, Aggression, and Their Guilt*. New York: Simon & Schuster.

Levy, A. (2005) *Female Chauvinist Pigs: Women and the Rise of Raunch Culture*. London: Free Press.

Livingstone, S. (2007) Teenagers' use of social networking sites for intimacy, privacy and self-expression. Paper presented to the 'Poke 1.0 – Facebook social research symposium', 15 November, University of London.

McNeil, R. and White, H. (2007) Sexist bullying and teenage attitudes towards violence. Paper presented at 'Gender Equality Duty: Are Schools Ready?', Cavendish Conference Centre, London, 20 March.

McRobbie, Angela (2004) The rise and rise of porno-chic. *The Times Higher,* 1 February: 23.

Nayak, A. and Kehily, M.J. (2008) *Gender, Youth and Culture, Young Masculinities and Femininities*. Basingstoke: Palgrave.

Paasonen, S., Nikunen, P. and Saarenmaa, L. (2007) *Pornification: Sex and Sexuality in Media Culture*. Oxford: Berg.

Ringrose, J. (2007) Successful girls? Complicating post-feminist, neoliberal discourses of educational achievement and gender equality, *Gender and Education*, 19(4): 471–89.

Ringrose, J. (2008) 'Every time she bends over she pulls up her thong': Teen girls negotiating discourses of competitive, heterosexualized aggression, *Girlhood Studies: An Interdisciplinary Journal*, 1(1): 33–59.

Selwyn, N. (2008) Online social networks: friend or foe?, *Teachers TV program*. Available at: http://www.teachers.tv/video/24687 (accessed 15/7/08).

Skelton, C. and Francis, B. (2009) *Feminism and 'the Schooling Scandal'*. London: Routledge.

Smithers, R. (2008) Bebo named as best social networking site in survey, *The Guardian*, 4 January.

Thomas, A. (2004) Digital literacies of the cybergirl, *E-learning*, 1(3): 358–82.

Waters, D. (2008) Children flock to social networks, *BBC News*. Available at: http://news.bbc.co.uk/1/hi/technology/7325019.stm (accessed 10/1/09).

White, E. (2002) *Fast Girls: Teenage Tribes and the Myth of the Slut*. New York: Scribner.

Youdell, D. (2005) Sex-gender-sexuality: how sex, gender and sexuality constellations are constituted in secondary schools, *Gender and Education*, 17(3): 249–70.

13 'I was kinda paralytic': pleasure, peril and teenage girls' drinking stories

Fin Cullen

Introduction

A few months ago, during my evening commute, I noticed a large bill-board with a stark 'anti-drinking' message aimed at the female drinker. The poster depicted a middle-aged man in badly applied make-up with the slogan 'If you drink like a man, you might end up looking like one' (see Figure 13.1). This London based alcohol and drugs charity campaign links gender, drinking, vanity, and regulatory norms of (hetero)sexual feminine attractiveness. The campaign attempts to shock female drinkers about the effects of excessive drinking (i.e. 'like a man') by suggesting that such consumption practices will have a detrimental effect on 'feminine beauty'. The campaign reflects growing concerns evident in the contemporary policy arena in the UK about young people, particularly young women, and underage 'binge' drinking.

This chapter considers teenage girls' drinking cultures and is informed by feminist post-structuralist work on schoolgirls' friendships (Hey 1997; Reay 2001; Renold 2005; George 2007). I focus on anxieties about teenage girls' drinking cultures, as such a focus offers important insights into recent media panics about girls, and the pathologization of certain 'new femininities'. Interestingly, such panics are not new. As Jackson and Tinkler (2007) argue, concerns about drinking among young women were evident in the 1920s in the UK, and then, as now, young, female drinkers were represented as overstepping the boundaries of 'appropriate femininity'.

Current anxieties are reflected in recent policies and proposals. For example, in 2008, announcements by the British Home Secretary, Jacqui Smith (*Children and Young People Now* 6 February 2008: 1; *Daily Mirror* 7 February 2008), by the British Medical Association (BMA 2008), and in the Youth Alcohol Action Plan (H.M. Government 2008) included calls to: criminalize the public possession of alcohol by under 18-year-olds; issue

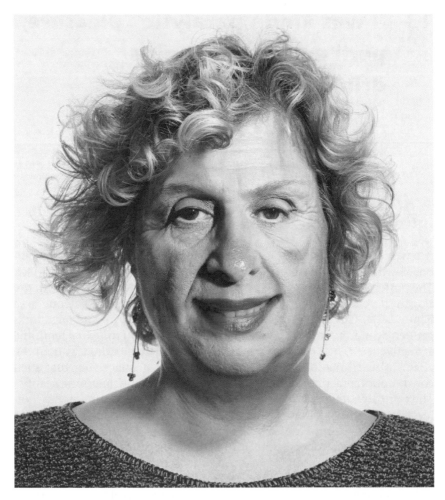

Figure 13.1 If you drink like a man you might end up looking like one. Wine doesn't just come with cheese. For women it's also accompanied by hair loss, wrinkles and obesity, plus the other problems like breast cancer, early menopause and memory loss. Reproduced with permission from TWBA\London and the Drug and Alcohol Service for London.

parenting contracts and orders for guardians of underage drinkers (*Children and Young People Now* 6 February 2008; *The Observer* 1 June 2008), ensure stricter enforcement of license legislation for commercial venues that sell alcohol to minors; and increase the revenue payable on alcoholic beverages (BMA 2008). Such alcohol control policies aim to curb underage[1] drinking by using criminal justice and education interventions to bring about a 'cultural change' in young people's use of alcohol. Such interventions include enhancing existing school-based alcohol education, and formalizing further young people's out-of-school recreational activities to deter public drinking (Youth Alcohol Strategy 2008). Yet despite input from a range of groups, policy and practice responses to curb teenage drinking remain largely ineffective. Teenage girls, in line with the rest of the UK adult population, are apparently still 'binge' drinking in commercial and non-commercial venues, in public outdoor spaces, and within the family home (Measham 2004; Coleman and Cater 2005; Plant and Plant 2006; Cullen 2007; H.M. Government 2007; Szmigin et al. 2007).

Beyond such policy concerns, new agendas emerge relating to the increasing pathologization of youth, and a growing pedagogization of the body through health education discourses. These are exemplified in the proliferation and extension of school-based pastoral care roles for teaching, guidance and welfare staff over the past decade (Watts 2002; Smith 2004). Concerns range from issues about obesity, to the reduction of teenage pregnancy, alcohol misuse and supporting pupils' emotional welfare. Indeed, such concerns may be bracketed as a new phenomenon, as part of 'risky' adolescent transitions that necessitate careful management by schools and other children's and youth services. In my study many of the young female participants articulated views about their own and others' drinking practices which reflected both 'new' versions of girl power *and* older traditional femininities. Their discourses of pleasure were constrained within social conventions of normative ways of 'doing' girl, with the assumed transition to a respectable future of 'feminine' sobriety.

Since the early 1990s, a burgeoning Girls' Studies literature has documented significant shifts in the reproductions of 'new femininities' (Ward and Cooper Benjamin 2004; Aapola et al. 2005; Mikel Brown and Chesney-Lind 2005; Jackson and Tinkler 2007). Such work highlights how the rise of post-feminist, 'new femininities' of girl power within popular discourse has simultaneously pathologized the 'mean girls' (Mikel Brown and Chesney-Lind 2005; Ringrose 2006) of contemporary youth, and celebrated new neoliberal feminine subjectivities. The *Good Girl/Bad Girl* (Griffin 2004) split endures within policy and practice debates, with girls portrayed as aggressive and excessive and/or victims of perilous appetites. I suggest in this chapter that the drinking cultures of teen girls illustrate these contradictions and tensions, as girls attempt to extend the boundaries of normative ways of doing girl successfully, yet still navigate obstacles and demands of traditional (hetero)normative femininities. I document how some of these tensions and contradictions played out for the young female drinkers in my research by examining the ways in which participants regulated their own and 'Othered' girls' drinking practices.

In general, the attention focused on girls' drinking behaviours in public discourse is far from surprising, particularly when considering recent UK media coverage about female celebrities who drink, smoke and take drugs. For example, the singers Amy Winehouse and Kerry Katona have faced much recent censure regarding their drinking and drug taking. Such celebrities form the weekly fodder of UK popular magazines (*Heat*, *Closer*, *Now*), with shots of them inebriated and falling out of nightclubs in states of distress. The public pillorying of young female celebrities provides a stark warning of the tightrope to be walked between the pleasures and perils of intoxication, where such celebrities are alternatively valorized in the press for their independent, glamorous clubbing lifestyles, yet vilified for alcohol and drug taking 'excess'. The media furore around intoxicated women explicitly depicts the social pitfalls for a woman wishing to portray herself as a party-going hedonist (Griffin, 2005; Jackson and Tinkler 2007).

The Research

The chapter draws on data from fieldwork that took place over 17 months between 2003 and 2005. The two field settings were located in an affluent suburb of a large southern English city. Despite the relative prosperity of the area, the participants came from a wide range of social, cultural and economic backgrounds. The settings were a generic youth centre, and youth provision in a large further education college. These youth centres were spaces of recreation and informal education, where young people could participate in art and music workshops, seek information and advice on welfare issues, take a lead in running youth events, and socialize with friends.

During my fieldwork I was employed as a youth worker in the youth centre and was a volunteer at the college. The local youth centre members were predominantly white British and aged 14–18 years. The college students were older (16–19 years) and were ethnically mixed as the catchment area for the college was extensive, with students often commuting large distances across the city. In this chapter I concentrate on the experiences of teenage girls up to the age of 16 who were interviewed as part of the study.

This multi-method, qualitative research involved: participant observation, group and individual interviews, bulletin board postings and visual participatory methods. The girls involved used the youth social spaces.

Participants included 36 girls who were interviewed either individually or in informal groups. This chapter draws on findings from interviews and participant observations in these settings. To ensure anonymity all names have been altered, and where possible, substituted with participants' own choices of pseudonyms.

Drinking Stories and Coping Strategies

Although here I consider girls' out-of-school drinking activities, clearly there is a temporal and spatial flow between in- and out-of- school contexts. This flow can be seen in the ways girls revisited highlights from their night-time escapades during the school day, and in the formal and informal schools-based alcohol and drugs education sessions aiming to curtail young people's alcohol use (Youth Alcohol Action Plan 2008). Prior schools-based studies into schoolgirl friendships, most notably work by Valerie Hey (1997) and Rosalyn George (2007), have been highly influential in shaping my thinking.

As in earlier research, purposefully 'getting drunk' was a central part of participants' nocturnal and weekend leisure pursuits (Blackman 1998; Sweeting and West 2003; Coleman and Cater 2005), and was viewed as a fun activity which 'facilitated social bonding', and provided a 'release' from the multiple pressures and constraints of school and family life (Szmigin et al. 2007). Underage drinking at weekends and at night was commonplace, with under 18s consuming alcohol in outdoor locations such as parks, (known locally by the young people as 'cotches'), at home, at parties, and at commercial venues such as pubs and nightclubs. Although the bulk of drinking took place with friends and siblings, some girls spoke about consuming alcohol with their parents. For example, one 14-year-old girl said she shared a bottle of tequila with her mother which she felt indicated their close bond.

Alcohol was acquired via older friends and family or by purchasing it illegally at various lenient retail venues by 'passing' for 18 using fake identification. A range of products were reportedly consumed, although cheap alcopops and Lambrini – described by several young people as 'bitch piss' – were largely subordinated as the favoured tipples of less sophisticated, pre-teen and early-teen female drinkers. The favoured choices of many of the girls were red wine, lager, and especially vodka.[2] To 'do girl' successfully in this context required a careful construction and monitoring of one's drinking identity within the highly competitive scene of teenagers' friendship groups. While portraying a sassy, party-girl persona was important, the continuing dominance of certain traditional versions of 'emphasised femininity' (Connell 1987) demanded that girls were not too 'slutty' or drunken, reflecting the 'controlled loss of control' identified in earlier work on drug-taking women (Measham 2002: 349). The theme of 'control' reoccurred in many of the interviews, often in relation to girls seeking to claim autonomy from their parents.

For these teenage girls, excessive drinking enabled a public performance of a 'fun', sexually desirable, autonomous, in-control, 'cool', drinking femininity. But such performances were highly regulated for fear of risking censure from others in their social network. While there were girls who could tell tall tales of weekend excess, to do so *too* often resulted in them being admonished by other girls, who remained eager to maintain an 'elastic' mantle of situated feminine respectability. By 'elastic' here I mean that the kudos and value placed on such versions of feminine 'calculated hedonism' (Brain 2000: 8) was highly dependent on space and time and the micro power dynamics of the peer network. As a result, drinking stories shared by the girls were highly malleable with regard to the content and the 'moral take' on a night's events. The depictions within these drinking tales of a 'respectable' gendered identity were also highly contextual, and varied between times, places and audiences. Girls' drinking stories therefore conveyed a complex mix of youthful hedonistic fun, a sense of personal agency, and a quest for a traditional, classed feminine 'respectability' (Skeggs 1997).

A move towards 'respectability' underpins many of the girls' descriptions of their alcohol use. The quest for heterosexual desirability *and* respectability for the girls creates a series of difficult negotiations in constructing and performing the potentially contradictory position of 're-spectable female drinker', particularly for girls who were Othered through factors such as (younger) age and social class. Indeed, girls took great care in their self-portrayals in such stories, because a misreading or misrepresentation could have dire social consequences in the intricate and shifting social hierarchies of their friendship groups. For example, there were tensions about how girls might perform an 'up for it' persona if they transgressed the localized normative versions of drinking femininities.

For instance, Andi was a 14-year-old White British girl who attended the youth club weekly. She rarely performed the glamorous femininities of popular older girls at the club who had carefully lacquered hair, tight clothes and make-up. Andi would appear with her straight brown hair loosely tied back, no make-up, and her usual uniform of hooded top and sweat pants. However, Andi's wish to perform a kind of 'tough', laddish, drinking femininity meant that her drinking stories could often face censure rather than validation from the other females at the centre. For example, one evening Andi was happily recounting a story about the previous weekend when she had visited the riverside with friends. She told how she had drunkenly befriended a much older man and accepted a bottle of cider from him. The female audience expressed outrage, not at Andi's drinking story per se, but because she had transgressed the boundaries of acceptable, respectable femininity by talking to an unknown, older man. Echoing the widespread health education campaigns aimed at female drinkers, they pointed out vehemently the risks of sexual violence and 'date rape' from the potentially drugged bottle of cider. Andi was left red-faced as the audience united to chide her about her reckless behaviour. Unlike in another recent study (Szmigin et al. 2007), these girls drew on discourses of harm and feminine victimhood in denouncing Andi's recklessness. The validation that Andi wished to receive for being an independent and rebellious 'laddish' young drinker became framed within discourses of stranger danger and female vulnerability. Andi was positioned as being responsible, because of her 'irresponsibility', for any unwanted sexual attention from the 'predatory' older man. Drawing on Foucault's (1975) concept of the panoptican to understand Andi's treatment by her peers, it seemed that these girls turned their gaze inwards in a self-regulatory framing of their actions and drinking identities within their friendship group.

These fieldwork observations support earlier findings on female friendship groups (Hey 1997; George 2007), and their storytelling practices, which could, at times, be brutal, and were used to 'other' and marginalize girls who did not, or refused to, live up to the conditions of membership. The excessive girl, 'the slag', haunted these girls' actions and social mobility (Lees 1993; Hey 1997; Griffin 2005). For Andi, the fun of boozing, of physical intoxication, and of meeting new people on the riverbank could not be told without her audience recounting the wider pathologizing and pedagogizing discourses of 'youth at risk' (Jeffs and Smith 1999). Indeed, Andi becomes a fallen woman, a pitiful victim, at the very moment she tries to express her exuberant sense of individual agency.

The girls' drinking stories can be understood as devices which produce particular types of hierarchical, idealized, normative (hetero)femininities. Through such stories local gendered drinking cultures were developed within and between girls' friendship groups, which validated the times, places, amount and products that could be consumed legitimately. Girls, such as Andi, who wished to take on temporary, alternative, resistant femininities, spoke with pride of the quantity drunk, and relived repeatedly the spectacular and exuberant excesses of their own drinking sprees. Girls could perform differing forms of femininity simultaneously, by wearing 'girly' make-up and heels, but drinking a 'boyish' quantity of alcohol. Such gendered enactments coexisted in the girls' understandings of their performances, and productions of socializing party girl personas.

However, such approaches to 'doing girl differently' were difficult to sustain over long periods of time for the majority of the participants, especially if girls wanted to retain their popularity within their social network and remain sexually desirable for the young men. Even though all the participants interviewed said that they drank alcohol, many of the girls wished to position themselves in the interviews as a 'reformed moderate drinker'. So although girls could perform a kind of 'laddish' (Jackson 2006) drinking persona, in this research context this identity needed to be bracketed in a newly found, 'mature', sensible-drinking self.

While friends often celebrated together the pleasurable, hedonistic excess of nights out, at other times peers collaborated in shared stories in which they revelled in the less pleasurable aspects of drinking and drug taking. These tales also included the sickness, the hangovers and the drunken fracas, framed within a particular, regulatory moral take on the night's events. For example, I first met another 14-year-old girl, Betty, late one Friday evening after closing the youth club. Betty, intoxicated, lay semi-conscious on the pavement after consuming a large amount of alcohol with a female friend in the local park. In the following extract, Betty and I discuss the night we met.

> *Fin*: Do you remember when we first met?
>
> *Betty*: Oh my God! I think I was puking, paralytic outside. I drank 18 cans of Fosters.[3] My mate had drunk 11 . . . She got quite pissed and I was really, really drunk and I was walking over the bridge to meet my friend and I started feeling really, really ill and I started puking so I sat down to wait for her. Then I lay down and then I started being sick everywhere and I was kinda paralytic and I had to be taken home by the police, which wasn't so good . . .
>
> *Fin*: Where did you get the drink?
>
> *Betty*: The shop next to the park. I used to get served there. I was 13 at the time . . . I dunno they [Shopkeepers] just liked me because I wore a short skirt. Just pervy Indian people. We bought 30 cans of Fosters. It was Fosters because I can drink it easily.
>
> *Fin*: Do you drink this now?
>
> *Betty*: No I hate it. I drink Guinness[4] if someone offers me a pint. It's creamy. I can control my drinking normally now. If I go out for a night and I want to get tipsy, I'll drink shots and it's a lot cheaper and you don't have to drink so much.
>
> (Betty, 14, White British, youth centre)

Whether Betty really drank 18 cans of beer and could remember her night in so much detail is immaterial. What is important is that in remembering her 13-year-old self Betty is keen to frame this experience within a drinking career. The binging on beer in the park with her female friend had been replaced as a 14-year-old with visits to city centre bars, and a quest to get 'tipsy' rather than 'paralytic'. Betty said that at age 13 she used her heterosexual feminine attractiveness to get served by the ethnically 'other', sexually predatory males ('pervy Indians'), at the off-licence. At 14, Betty voices her ability to 'control her drinking normally'; she drinks shots and stout in bars rather than beer in the park, and is eager, in common with many of the other girls, to portray an element of self-control and sophistication. Discourses of sophistication, glamour and respectability appear entwined in Betty's account. Such discourses of sophisticated alcohol consumption reflected an aspirational, desirable version of drinking femininity akin to those portrayed in popular contemporary TV shows such as *Sex and the City*. In such shows sophistication is represented by older female characters sipping cocktails in cosmopolitan, city centre bars, and is far removed from images of girls getting drunk on lager and vodka in local parks.

The discourses in shared drinking stories could appear highly contradictory, with girls wanting to articulate simultaneously a youthful exuberance and mature sophistication, a strong sense of personal autonomy and a loss of control. The fun of an escapade would be often bracketed with caveats and provisos about the contexts in which it was acceptable to enjoy the thrill of these hedonistic sprees. For example, another 13-year-old girl, Tilly, spent an entire interview session downplaying her involvement in 'immature' outside drinking in parks, and stated categorically that she only really drank in sophisticated commercial venues. Yet, conversely, my experiences of Tilly in the youth club suggested that she regularly visited outdoor 'hidden' drinking location such as parks, and drank alcohol there with her friends. Tilly's need to claim a sophisticated edge in the space of the interview produced a particular account that stressed her respectability and maturity. The presentation to me as a researcher (and youth worker) of such censored, and reframed versions of their experiences, could suggest the girls' awareness of a moral imperative of 'harm minimization', which casts teenage drinking as problematic (Blackman 2004).

However, despite such reframing, few participants in either of the fieldwork settings positioned themselves as a current or past 'abstainer' from alcohol. Indeed, a period of 'excess' as a narrative trope cropped up in many of the girls' tales, and was perceived as a necessary step into an imagined clean-living, relatively 'sober' adulthood. Such narratives mirror media depictions of '(ex)ladettes' such as the former BBC Radio One DJ Zoe Ball's redemption into a sober, clean-living motherhood (Jackson and Tinkler 2007). However, while Zoe Ball's public transformation into sobriety occurred in her late 20s on the eve of motherhood, these younger girls' narratives of redemption were concertinaed into their early teens. Sade illustrates this in her narrative of accelerated transition from initial 'straightedge' abstainer, to drunk teen, finally progressing to reformed moderate drinker – all by the age of 16:

> *Sade*: I was straightedge[5] until I was 15 and then I started drinking and then I thought 'no it's really gay'[6] and so I stopped. I drink now but I don't get drunk…
> *Fin*: Why did you drink back then?
> *Sade*: Because I was bored and thirsty (Laughs).
> *Fin*: What made the difference?
> *Sade*: I hate conforming to the norm … and now everyone is trying to be different now but everyone is exactly the same 'cos they're all trying to be different. You just can't win can you?…Oh most people just drink to get drunk. I dunno, I drank because I liked to, not just for the sake of getting drunk. I never actually purposefully got drunk.
>
> (Sade, 16, Black African, college)

Sade asserts the tensions between attempts to 'do girl' differently, and conform to wider norms of what it means to be a legible and desirable girl within her social circle. Such tensions meant that while girls needed to prove their autonomy, and to drink to have fun, becoming 'paralytic' opened them up to censure and marginalization by others. These discourses of success, or in Sade's words, trying to 'win', mobilizes notions of individualism *and* conformity. There are multiple discourses in operation here: Sade articulates her need to perform an independent and 'active' girl power, while also dismissing 'excessive' female peers as out-of-control, and not sufficiently individualistic. Purposefully getting drunk to stand out, yet be one of the crowd, highlights the girls' navigation of slippery and complex social drinking scapes.

Pleasure and Peril: Concluding Thoughts

This chapter has outlined some of the tensions and contradictions for girls wishing to perform young drinking femininities. Girls negotiated highly regulated social landscapes, and they attempted to have fun by drinking to excess, yet remaining in control, striving to differentiate themselves from their parents and other girls, whilst needing to conform to be 'cool'. There were many continuities between this study's findings and those of earlier feminist ethnographies on schoolgirl friendships (Hey 1997; Reay 2001; George 2007). For example, the enduring concerns around 'reputation' and 'respectability'; the centrality of girls' friendship groups as spaces where collective identity was upheld through drinking stories, going out and having fun, but also via the subordination of 'othered', overly excessive girls (Hey 1997; Mikel Brown and Chesney-Lind 2005).

Girls' accounts of teenage drinking cultures mirrored wider societal concerns about alcohol use, particularly in relation to how much, when and why it might be consumed legitimately. In line with the older young people in Szmigin et al.'s (2007) study, these younger girls tried to balance the 'physical risk of drinking' with the 'social and cultural credibility of losing control' (2007: 365). There remains much psychic and emotional work for these girls in their highly regulated presentation of 'cool', drinking femininities, meaning that even in these moments of leisure, they must 'try hard' to 'let go' appropriately.

This study has implications regarding the ongoing pedagogic, welfare and popular discourses around teenage drinking. The messages in alcohol health campaigns in English schools remain framed around discourses of harm, rarely acknowledging the pleasures of 'excess' and instead framing interventions in relation to discourses of vulnerable femininity. These discourses stress the risks of sexual violence, premature ageing, liver damage and declining (hetero)sexual attractiveness. Unlike representations of brawling, boozing 'ladettes' of recent media panics, the girls' drinking cultures in this study reflected contingent, regulated, purposeful drunkenness, and varied depending on context, location and time. Such findings problematize some of the dominant discourses evident in much school-based alcohol education and policy, which demote notions of pleasure and female collectivity through alcohol use, and instead construct young female drinkers as amoral hedonists who risk sexual assault and are oblivious to the perils of the 'demon drink'.

Acknowledgements

I would like to thank all the young women who contributed to this study, and the Drug and Alcohol Service for London and TWBA\London for permission to reproduce Figure 13.1. Special thanks are also due to my youth work colleagues, and Rosalyn George, Carrie Paechter, Simon Bradford and Carolyn Jackson for comments on earlier versions of this chapter.

Notes

1. In the UK it is generally illegal for retail or commercial venues to sell alcohol to people under 18-years-old. However, the current laws on alcohol are complicated, and children may drink alcohol legally within the family home from the age of 5.

2. As a spirit, vodka was especially prized because many brands were relatively inexpensive, mixed well in soda, and so could be carried around mixed in bottles of Coca Cola to avoid detection. Vodka was also imagined not to be easily 'smelt' on drinkers' breath, yet was seen as a highly efficient intoxicant.
3. A brand of lager.
4. A brand of stout.
5. Straightedge is a youth sub-culture that valorizes non-drinking and non-drug taking. For more on the straightedged sub-culture see Blackman (2004).
6. The term 'gay', following casual 'homophobic use', was ubiquitous within the field work settings. The phrase had become synonymous with notions of weakness and inferiority.

References

Aapola, S., Gonick, M. and Harris, A. (2005) *Young Femininity: Girlhood, Power and Social Change*. New York: Palgrave.
Blackman, S. (1998) 'Poxy Cupid': an ethnographic and feminist account of a resistant female youth culture – the New Wave Girls, in T. Skelton and G. Valentine (eds) *Cool Places: Geographies of Youth Cultures*. London: RoutledgeFalmer.
Blackman, S. (2004) *Chilling Out: The Cultural Politics of Substance Consumption, Youth and Drug Policy*. Maidenhead: Open University Press.
Brain, K. (2000) Youth, alcohol and the emergence of the post-modern alcohol order, Institute of Alcohol Studies. Available at: http://www.ias.org.uk/resources/papers/occasional/brainpaper.pdf (accessed 9 July 2008).
British Medical Association (BMA) (2008) *Alcohol Misuse: Tacking the UK Epidemic*. London: British Medical Association.
Children and Young People Now (2008) Police to target underage drinkers, 6 February, p. 1.
Coleman, L. and Cater, S. (2005) *Underage 'Risky' Drinking, Motivations and Outcomes*. York: Joseph Rowntree Foundation.
Connell, R.W. (1987) *Gender and Power*. London: Routledge.
Cullen, F. (2007) Why stop having fun? Drinking and smoking as ways of doing girl. Unpublished PhD thesis, Goldsmiths College, University of London.
Foucault, M. (1975) *Discipline and Punish: The Birth of the Prison*. New York: Random House.
George, R. (2007) *Girls in a Goldfish Bowl, Moral Regulation, Ritual and the Use of Power Amongst Inner City Girls*. Amsterdam: Sense.

Griffin, C. (2004) Good girls, bad girls: anglocentrism and diversity in the constitution of contemporary girlhood, in A. Harris (ed.), *All About the Girl: Culture, Power and Identity*. London: Routledge Falmer.

Griffin, C. (2005) Impossible spaces? Femininity as an empty category. Paper presented at the ESRC Seminar Series *New Femininities, Consuming New Femininities*, University of East London, 9 December.

Hey, V. (1997) *The Company She Keeps: An Ethnography of Girls' Friendship*. Buckingham: Open University Press.

H.M. Government (2007) *Safe. Sensible. Social. The Next Steps in the National Alcohol Strategy*. London: Crown Copyright.

H.M. Government (2008) *Youth Alcohol Action Plan*. London: Crown Copyright.

Jackson, C. (2006) *Lads and Ladettes in School: Gender and a Fear of Failure*. Maidenhead: Open University Press.

Jackson, C. and Tinkler, P. (2007) 'Ladettes' and 'Modern Girls': 'troublesome' young femininities, *The Sociological Review*, 55(2): 251–72.

Jeffs, T. and Smith, M.K. (1999) The problem of 'youth' for youth work, *Youth and Policy*, 62: 45–66.

Lees, S. (1993) *Sugar and Spice: Sexuality and Teenage Girls*. London: Penguin.

Measham, F. (2002) 'Doing gender' – 'doing drugs': conceptualizing the gendering of drugs cultures, *Contemporary Drug Problems*, 29: 335–73.

Measham, F. (2004) The decline of ecstasy, the rise of 'binge' drinking and the persistence of pleasure, *Probation Journal The Journal of Community and Criminal Justice*, 51(4): 309–26.

Mikel Brown, L. and Chesney-Lind, M. (2005) Growing up mean: covert aggression and the policing of girlhood, in G. Lloyd (ed.), *Problem Girls: Understanding and Supporting Troubled and Troublesome Girls and Young Women*. London: RoutledgeFalmer.

The Observer (2008) Parents to face court over young drinkers, 1 June, p. 5.

Plant, M. and Plant, M. (2006) *Binge Britain: Alcohol and the National Response*. Oxford: Oxford University Press.

Reay, D. (2001) 'Spice Girls', 'Nice Girls', 'Girlies', and 'Tomboys': gender discourses, girls' cultures and femininities in the primary classroom, *Gender and Education*, 13(2): 153–66.

Renold, E. (2005) *Girls, Boys and Junior Sexualities: Exploring Children's Gender and Sexual Relations in the Primary School*. London: RoutledgeFalmer.

Ringrose, J. (2006) A new universal mean girl: examining the discursive construction and social regulation of a new feminine pathology, *Feminism and Psychology*, 16(4): 405–24.

Skeggs, B. (1997) *Becoming Respectable: Formations of Class and Gender*. London: Sage.

Smith, M.K. (2004) Extended schooling: some issues for informal and community education, *The Encyclopedia of Informal Education*. Available at: www.infed.org/schooling/extended_schooling.htm (accessed 19/09/08).

Sweeting, H. and West, P. (2003) Young people's leisure and risk-taking behaviours: changes in gender patterning in the West of Scotland during the 1990s, *Journal of Youth Studies*, 6(4): 391–412.

Szmigin, I., Griffin, C., Mistral, W., Bengry-Howell, A., Weale, L. and Hackley, C. (2007) Re-framing 'binge drinking' as calculated hedonism: empirical evidence from the UK, *International Journal of Drug Policy*, 19: 359–66.

Ward, J.V. and Cooper Benjamin, B. (2004) Women, girls, and the unfinished work of connection, a critical review of American girls' studies, in A. Harris (ed.), *All About the Girl, Culture, Power and Identity*. London: Routledge Falmer.

Watts, G. (2002) Connexions: the role of a personal advisor in schools, *Pastoral Care in Education*, 19(4): 16–20.

14 New literacies, old identities: young girls' experiences of digital literacy at home and school

Jackie Marsh

Introduction

In this chapter, issues relating to the digital literacy practices of girls aged from three to eight in both home and school contexts are explored. Since the late 1990s, there have been persistent concerns about boys' achievement in literacy. Here, I argue that these concerns have overshadowed matters that should be considered by educationalists who are committed to gender equity in their classrooms. In this first section of the chapter, the nature of the anxieties expressed about boys and literacy are investigated before data from a number of projects that have focused on children's use of new technologies and related literacy practices are discussed. Three key issues are the focus for reflection. First, I suggest that girls' experiences of literacy across homes and early years settings are not as seamless as is often assumed and that girls as well as boys experience dissonance across these domains. Second, I suggest that there is a need to pay attention to the reductive gendered discourses that are embedded in many of the home literacy practices of girls in order to inform the development of critical literacy curricula. Finally, I consider the way in which initiatives designed to motivate boys through the incorporation of popular culture into the literacy curriculum can reinforce gendered stereotypes and marginalize the out-of-school experiences of girls. This discussion is undertaken within a context in which it is acknowledged that there is a need to move beyond a simplistic binary which fuels the see-sawing debate regarding the achievements of one gender at the expense of the other (Jackson 1998). I would suggest, as do many others, that such a position is an over-simplification of the issues and that we should address the needs of all pupils (Skelton and Francis 2003). However, in this chapter I have chosen to focus on an investigation into the experiences of young girls in the early years because this is where it is often erroneously assumed that literacy transitions from home to school are relatively seamless.

Literacy, Gender and Attainment

Concerns about boys' literacy skills in England have been linked to outcomes of national literacy tests, in which girls consistently outperform boys.[1] These results are replicated in international comparisons of reading scores, such as those undertaken in the Programme for International Assessment (PISA 2006). This masks complexities in the situation, however, as 'race' and class impact upon attainment, which means that some groups of girls attain lower results than some groups of boys (Gillborn and Mirza 2000). In 2007, the Department for Education and Skills (DfES) published a report in which it was accepted that 'gender is not the strongest predictor of attainment' (DfES 2007: 4), pointing out that while the gender gap is evident across different social class groups, the social class attainment gap at Key Stage 4 is three times as wide as the gender gap.

However, despite these cautionary warnings, some educationalists have seized on the 'underachievement of boys in literacy' issue with gusto. This 'backlash blockbuster' (Mills 2000) has led to an increased focus on intervention projects in which emphasis has been placed on boys' experiences of literacy. An analysis of the website of the National Literacy Trust, a key source of information on literacy for many schools and teachers, indicates the extent of the problem. On the page dedicated to providing links to resources concerning gender and literacy, 47 references relate to projects focusing on boys and literacy and only one pertains to girls and literacy.[2] A further example is the School Library Association's initiative 'Boys into Books',[3] which was sponsored by the Department for Children, Schools and Families (DCSF). An assumption in much of this work is that girls' experiences of the communication, language and literacy curriculum in the early years are unproblematic. In this chapter, I want to suggest that the discontinuities that exist for some boys across home and school literacy practices also exist for many girls, but this is often overlooked in the current emphasis on boys' underachievement in literacy.

In order to inform my analysis, I draw on data arising from a number of studies conducted over the past four years in which young children's (aged from birth to eight) use of popular culture, media and new technologies in homes and early years settings and schools has been traced (Marsh 2004, 2006, 2008; Marsh et al. 2005). Some of these studies have been large scale in nature. For example, the *Digital Beginnings*[4] project involved a survey of 1852 parents of 0–6-year-olds in ten local authorities in England, along with a survey of 524 early years practitioners who worked in the early years settings these children attended. This study also involved interviews with 60 parents and carers and 12 practitioners (for full details of methodology, see Marsh et al. 2005). Other studies have focused in finer detail on the practices of a small number of children, such as recent work on children's use of virtual worlds, which has involved interviews and observations (Marsh 2008). The studies have focused on the practices of children from a diverse group of families in relation to socio-economic status, 'race', language and geographical location.

New Literacies, Old Identities

Young children are now engaged in a range of practices outside of schools which can be characterized by the phrase 'digital literacy', which signals those reading, writing and multimodal authoring practices that are mediated by new technologies. Girls' engagement in a range of digital literacy practices from birth means that many of them are already competent digital readers and authors by the time they attend pre-school settings, able to orchestrate and remake resources in the production of multi-media, multimodal texts. The data from the 'Digital Beginnings' Project indicate that many girls were creating texts using print and images on their computers and producing still and moving images on mobile telephones in their homes from a young age. For example, the mother of 4-year-old Emma reported that her daughter used a computer at home about four times a week, developing quite independent skills in using the internet and playing games. She was also developing competence with a mobile phone:

> *Mother*: . . . she's got, like, my old phone.
> *Interviewer*: . . . So what sort of things does she do with that, then?
> *Mother*: Oh, she spends ages playing. She'll put the different tunes on and pretend to ring people and pretend that people are ringing her. I mean she takes it everywhere with her. When we go out she'll put it on the table.
> *Interviewer*: . . . And is she aware of text messaging at all?
> *Mother*: Yeah . . . I mean sometimes I put a little bit of money on it just for her to play with her friend because she goes away to the caravan with my mum, her grandma, sometimes on a weekend so she will text little pictures to us and things.

However, when Emma attended her nursery class, she had little access to computers or other ICTs, as the interview with the Head of the nursery she attended indicated:

> *Teacher*: The computer that nursery uses is a very, very old computer, we are not networked and we have no internet access in this building, but we do have computer suites over in the main school.
> *Interviewer*: So you go over there to do it?
> *Teacher*: Well, nursery don't because of the time slot at the moment...

This was also the case with Tanya, whose mother outlined how her daughter used the computer at home independently to play games and access websites, but suggested that this was not the case in the early years setting she attended:

> *Interviewer*: Is she quite independent on the computer?
> *Mother*: She's quite good, yeah, she knows how to use the mouse, she can sit and move that around and sort of see what she's got to do.
> *Interviewer*: And does she use one anywhere else?
> *Mother*: No not yet. I think they are getting one at play school, but they don't use it there yet.

Their experiences were not isolated. In the 'Digital Beginnings' study, 53 per cent of children were reported as having used a computer at home in the week prior to the survey, while only 46 per cent of early years practitioners stated that they had used a computer in their setting with children in that period. In addition, 29 per cent of early years settings reported not having computers at all. Socio-economic status impacted upon children's use of technology in the home. Families with high income and greater degrees of cultural capital (for example, levels of education) were more likely to own more books and have access to the internet than other families, whereas lower-income families with less cultural capital were more likely to demonstrate higher levels of ownership of screen entertainment media. This is a pattern identified in previous studies of the use of media by older children and young people (Livingstone and Bovill 1999).

The social nature of girls' media use was emphasized by parents and carers. For example, for four-year-old Sameena, watching Hindi films and Indian television programmes on a satellite channel was a way of participating in established family rituals, distinct from her time watching children's programming, as indicated by Sameena's mother, who said: 'in the daytime she watch most of the CBeebies or programmes like that and after that 'Spider-man' and evening times she watches our Indian programmes with me and her family'. These ritualized acts often served the purpose of both maintaining family relationships and, in the case of children from Black and Minority Ethnic families, celebrating the cultural heritage of the family, made possible in many homes by the use of satellite television (Kenner 2005). In addition, young children were frequently engaged in media use with younger and older siblings. However, these social and cultural uses of media were not widely reflected in the technological practices reported by early years settings, which primarily consisted of individuals' use of single computers and the predominant use of English language programs.

The lack of use of computers as reported in early years settings in Marsh et al. (2005) may relate to lack of resources, but it was clear from the interviews with practitioners that attitudes also played a part, with low expectations of young children. On practitioner commented: 'some of them do have some computer experience, but they are so very young at three that you don't expect them to be'.

Use of other technologies, such as digital and video cameras, was even less frequent (74 per cent of practitioners stated that they never used digital still cameras with children; 81 per cent stated that they never used video cameras with children). This lack of attention to media production and analysis is not always a deliberate strategy by early years practitioners, as many in the study stated that they would like more training in this area. However, there were early years educators who suggested that they did think that work with both still and digital video cameras was age-inappropriate. For example, one said: 'Personally, I think our children are too young for that. I mean, I have seen the junior school making films and I know the children absolutely adored being able to take part in it, but I think it's just a bit beyond our age group'.

The overall picture is one in which there is still a predominant focus in early years settings on traditional print practices, reading storybooks and writing which involves pencils and paper. The data outlined here focus on the situation in England, but research in Scotland presents a similar pattern (Plowman et al. 2007). The differences between literacy as it is experienced in many homes and early years settings and schools is summarized in Table 14.1.

Inevitably, the picture is complex and these experiences are not universal. Some children lack access to a wide range of technologies in the home and a number of early years settings and schools demonstrate excellent practice in relation to digital literacy (see e.g. Marsh and Bearne 2008). Nevertheless, here I wish to argue that for many girls, the transition between home and school literacy practices is more problematic than is often assumed; it is not only boys that experience textual dislocation across domains.

Table 14.1   Literacy in homes and early years settings/schools

Literacy as experienced in many homes	Literacy as experienced in many early years settings and schools
• On-screen reading extensive	• On-screen reading minimal
• Multimodal	• Focused on written word and image
• Non-linear reading pathways	• Linear reading pathways
• Fluidity/crossing of boundaries	• Limited to written page
• Multiple authorship/unknown authorship	• Known, primarily single authorship
• Always linked to production	• Analysis and production separate
• Embedded in communities of practice/affinity groups	• Individualistic
• Shaped by mediascapes	• Little reference to mediascapes
• Child constituted as social reader	• Child constituted as individual reader
• Reading integral part of identity construction/ performance	• Reading constructs school reader identities (successful or unsuccessful in relation to school practices)

There are additional concerns in relation to girls and their experiences with digital literacy which need to be considered by early years educators. In the next section of the chapter, I move on to analyse the way in which digital literacy practices in the home are often shaped by reductive discourses in relation to constructions of femininities.

Pink Technologies

While many girls use a range of technologies in the home, some of these are located in discourses that perpetuate stereotypical accounts of girls' interests. For example, many of the girls in the studies outlined above used toy computers, laptops and PDAs that were linked to the popular character, *Barbie*™. These artefacts are often pink and feature icons such as flowers and hearts (see Martin's chapter, this volume, for further reflections on the significance of the colour pink in constructions of gender in the early years). These 'pink technologies' sometimes offer more limited features than similar hardware aimed at young boys and they shape the construction of technological competence in particular ways. This is also the case in relation to young girls' increasing use of social networking sites, including virtual worlds. Research in this area so far has tended to focus on teenagers' use of social networking sites such as MySpace and Bebo (Dowdall 2008), but there is evidence that young children from the age of three are using websites that incorporate opportunities for social networking, sites such as virtual worlds. In this chapter, I will focus on the virtual world *Barbie Girls*™.

Barbie Girls™ was developed by Mattel Inc. and launched in 2007. It currently has approximately 17 million registered users.[5] *Barbie Girls*™ enables children to create and dress up an avatar, decorate their avatars' homes, buy and look after pets, send messages to friends and play games in order to earn money to purchase items for their avatars and homes. 'Barbie bucks' are easy to earn in a range of games which include painting nails and giving Ken a make-over. Throughout this heteronormative world, the 'heterosexual matrix' (Butler 1990) is writ large. Ken, for example, is described as 'totally crush-worthy'. Representations of femininity are very limited and stereotypical in nature. The range of skin colours that users can choose for their avatars is restricted and largely pale, and the range of hairstyles appears to be most appropriate for White avatars. The predominant colour used throughout the world is pink and there is a prevalence of pastel shades. The landscape of *Barbie Girls*™ is that of a shopping mall, with a single park that enables avatars to mingle. The discourse here is similar to that surrounding numerous texts and artefacts aimed at young girls, as Carrington (2003) has outlined in her analysis of Bratz™ dolls.

The main in-world activity appears to be shopping. In a recent study of the use of virtual worlds by children in a primary school in the north of England (Marsh 2008), 52 per cent ($n = 91$) of children in a sample of 175 from Foundation Stage to Year 6 stated that they used virtual worlds, 53 per cent ($n = 49$) of whom were girls. Thirteen out of 38 children in Foundation Stage and Key Stage 1 classes identified themselves as users of virtual worlds in the survey (34 per cent). Five out of the six girls in this age category stated that they used *Barbie Girls*. When asked about what they liked about the site, the girls identified shopping as a key attraction:

> It's fun and activities and I like going shopping for the shoes.
>
> (Charlene, aged 6)

> You get to see a lot of the Barbie things. You get to buy handbags and umbrellas what's got Barbie on.
>
> (Judy, aged 5)

The merchandise on offer largely consists of clothes, handbags and shoes. In addition, in-world shopping is related to the Mattel Inc. offline commercial empire. Buying an MP3 player in the 'real' world enables users to access a greater range of items to purchase for their avatars. It would appear that just as forms of capital (Bourdieu 1980/1990) operate in virtual worlds inhabited by adults, such as *Second Life*, the child-orientated worlds are also shaped by social, economic and cultural capital. Sites such as *Barbie Girls*™ are located within a nexus of commercialized practices that operate across online and offline worlds (Grimes 2008).

In *Barbie Girls*™ we can see, as Miller and Rose (1997: 1) suggest, the child constructed as the '"subject of consumption", the individual who is imagined and acted upon by the imperative to consume'. Girls do not, of course, passively digest the discourses on offer; there is a range of research which outlines the ways in which girls do transgress such discourses and forge identities in which they are agentive in relation to a range of technological activities, such as computer gaming (Beavis and Charles 2007). However, as Davies and Saltmarsh (2007: 6) suggest, 'Educational practices, and literacy practices in particular, can be said to produce the constraints through which we "improvise" ourselves as gendered subjects.' Therefore this cursory examination of one popular website for girls indicates that there is a need for practitioners to engage critically with popular cultural sites in order that they can develop appropriate critical pedagogy and curricula that are based on a sound understanding of their affordances.

Unfortunately, evidence of critical literacy practices in the early years of schooling is currently limited, apart from exemplary case studies of practice in Australia and the USA (Comber and Simpson 2001; Vasquez 2004). In England, data from the 'Digital Beginnings' study indicated that attempts to incorporate popular culture in early years settings and classrooms, rather than providing opportunities for critical practice, further replicated reductive discourses about femininities and masculinities, which I will now move on to discuss.

Privileging Boys' Practices

While the overall picture outlined thus far does indicate a lack of attention to the way in which literacy is changing rapidly in the 21st century, some early years settings have attempted to use ICTs more widely in the communication, language and literacy curriculum. However, a close analysis of the data relating to this development indicates that, when this does occur, it is often boys' uses of and interests in digital technologies that are privileged.

Beavis (2005: 3) has suggested, in an analysis of teenage girls' computer-game playing, that 'gendered identities do not simply pre-exist the act and location of game play. Rather, they are actively formed and constituted through particular instances of game play in particular contexts'. This resonates with young girls' use of new technologies. In much of the data from studies of the new literacy practices of 0–6-year-olds (Marsh 2004, 2006, 2008; Marsh et al. 2005), girls could be seen to be forming and performing aspects of their identities in ways that reinforced gendered communities of practice (Paechter 2003). While there were no significant differences in the average daily amount of screen use by boys and girls in the 'Digital Beginnings' study, the texts they were engaged with and the activities undertaken were often very different. However, in their use of popular culture, media and new technologies to promote engagement in schooled literacy practices, practitioners often draw on boys' interests.

In the 'Digital Beginnings' project, practitioners were asked what internet sites they directed children to, if any. The most popular site used by early years settings was *CBeebies*, popular with both boys and girls, but the second most popular site was *Bob the Builder*,[6] which did not appear on *any* of the girls' lists of favourite websites, television programmes or popular characters. Despite this, the *Bob the Builder* narrative was predominant in many of the accounts of how settings had used children's interests in popular culture, media and new technologies to promote learning.

The *Bob the Builder* narrative is saturated with stereotypical representations of gender. The website, used extensively by many of the early years practitioners who had access to the internet in their setting, demonstrates this. The *Bob the Builder* site introduces the show's characters. Bob the Builder is depicted on an introductory screen in a kitchen. This is a high-tech environment in which, if children click on the television and telephone, electronic sounds are emitted. In addition, Bob is portrayed holding his clipboard, obviously ready to start work. Wendy appears in a different room holding a bunch of flowers. In addition, the objects children can click on in Wendy's room are not technological, like those in Bob's domain, and instead feature a teddy-bear, cushion and bird. There is also a kettle that does whistle when clicked on, but it is assumed that this electronic gadget enables Wendy to make tea for the team in addition to organizing their tools (on her profile page it states that 'Wendy's real strength is organization'). This brief analysis of one typical site used by many early years settings suggests that not only are girls being offered access to websites which do not correspond to their own stated interests and preferences, but that some of the sites accessed do little to challenge stereotypical representations of gender.

This emphasis on the practices and preferences of boys is also the case in relation to other initiatives in which early years settings and schools attempt to draw on children's technological interests. There has been much interest in the role that popular computer games can play in the curriculum (McFarlane et al. 2002). However, data from the 'Digital Beginnings' study indicate that 0–6-year-old girls were significantly less likely to play with console games than boys and significantly more likely than boys to use technologies such as dance mats. In some of the interviews, the mothers of girls outlined their children's interest in karaoke machines.

Nevertheless, these items rarely feature in curriculum innovations that aim to respond to children's out-of-school practices, yet they do have potential to stimulate literacy activities, such as the writing of song lyrics. This is not to suggest that young girls do not play computer games, nor to suggest that work on popular computer games cannot lead to a range of exciting and innovative literacy activities in schools, but does indicate that some technologies and digital literacy practices that are adopted primarily by girls are not considered by educators when curriculum planning.

Conclusion

In this chapter, I have suggested that the transition from home to school literacy practices for many young girls is not as straightforward as is often assumed. Girls aged from 0–6 do spend more time engaging in traditional print-based literacy practices in the home than boys (Marsh et al. 2005) and these practices are reflected in early years settings. In that sense, it could be argued that the transition to schooled literacy practices is easier for girls than boys and this may explain many boys' disengagement with the literacy curriculum. However, the situation is more complex than this, because many of the home literacy practices of young girls are also located in new technologies. There is, at present, limited recognition of these digital literacy practices in early years settings and schools, which means that girls have restricted opportunities to develop confidence and expertise in ICTs and this may be one of the reasons for girls' less extensive use of computers than boys in the later years (Valentine et al. 2005).

This is not to suggest that the simple adoption of girls' out-of-school digital literacy practices will offer a panacea. While work involving dance mats and karaoke machines might offer some recognition of girls' preferred practices, this work needs to be embedded in a critical literacy agenda in which issues of identities and agency are explored. Young girls need opportunities to engage reflexively with technologies in early years settings in order to challenge traditional constructions of gender. This work could be undertaken in ways which do not undermine children's pleasurable engagements with such texts, but which enable them to engage in complex, multi-layered readings of popular culture (Alvermann et al. 1999).

However, perhaps a more pressing concern is the proliferation of intervention programmes targeted at promoting boys' achievement in literacy which celebrate uncritically the texts, artefacts and icons related to hegemonic masculinities. Simply regurgitating popular narratives in which stereotypical masculinist discourses are privileged in order to enhance engagement with schooled literacy practices may help to raise boys' attainment in literacy, but will do little to ensure that girls are adequately equipped for the challenges of living in societies in which girls and women still suffer extensive discrimination.

Notes

1. See: DCSF: Foundation Stage Profile Results in England, 2007/08 and DCSF: National Curriculum Assessments at Key Stages 1 and 2 in England, 2008 (Provisional), http://www.dcsf.gov.uk/rsgateway/DB/SFR/ (accessed 01/09).
2. http://www.literacytrust.org.uk/Database/boys/Boysres.html (accessed 08/07).
3. http://www.boysintobooks.co.uk/
4. This study was funded by BBC Worldwide and The Esmée Fairbairn Foundation. See http://www.digtialbeginnings.shef.ac.uk.
5. Data from KZero: http://www.kzero.co.uk/blog/ (accessed 02/09).
6. http://www.bobthebuilder.com/uk/index.html (accessed 03/06).

References

Alvermann, D., Moon, J.S. and Hagood, M.C. (1999) *Popular Culture in the Classroom: Teaching and Researching Critical Media Literacy*. Newark, DE: IRA/NRC.

Beavis, C. (2005) Pretty good for a girl: gender, identity and computer games. Paper presented at the 'Changing Views: Worlds in Play Conference, Vancouver, April. Available at: http://www.gamesconference.org/digra2005/viewabstract.php?id=368, (accessed 03.06).

Beavis, C. and Charles, C. (2007) Would the 'real' girl gamer please stand up? Gender, LAN cafés and the reformulation of the 'girl' gamer, *Gender and Education*, 19(6): 691–705.

Bourdieu, P. (1980/1990) *The Logic of Practice*. Cambridge: Polity Press.

Butler, J. (1990) *Gender Trouble: Feminism and the Subversion of Identity*. London: Routledge.

Carrington, V. (2003) 'I'm in a bad mood. Let's go shopping': Interactive dolls, consumer culture and a 'glocalized' model of literacy, *Journal of Early Childhood Literacy*, 3(1): 83–98.

Comber, B. and Simpson, A. (eds) (2001) *Negotiating Critical Literacies in Classrooms*. Mahwah, NJ: Erlbaum.

Davies, B. and Saltmarsh, S. (2007) Gender economies: literacy and the gendered production of neoliberal subjectivities, *Gender and Education*, 19(1): 1–20.

Department for Education and Skills (2007) *Gender and Education: The Evidence on Pupils in England.* London: HMSO.

Dowdall, C. (2008) The texts of me and the texts of us: improvisation and polished performance in social networking sites, in R. Willett, M. Robinson and J. Marsh (eds), *Play, Creativities and Digital Cultures.* New York: Routledge.

Gillborn, D. and Mirza, H.S. (2000) *Educational Inequality: Mapping Race, Class and Gender.* London: HMSO.

Grimes, S.M. (2008) Saturday morning cartoons go MMOG. *Media International Australia,* Special Issue: Beyond Broadcasting: TV for the Twenty-first Century, 126: 120–31.

Jackson, D. (1998) Breaking out of the binary trap: boys' underachievement, schooling and gender relations, in D. Epstein, J. Elwood, V. Hey and J. Maw (eds), *Failing Boys? Issues in Gender and Achievement.* Buckingham: Open University Press.

Kenner, C. (2005) Bilingual children's uses of popular culture in text-making, in J. Marsh (ed.), *Popular Culture, New Media and Digital Technology in Early Childhood.* London: RoutledgeFalmer.

Livingstone, S. and Bovill, M. (1999) *Young People, New Media: Report of the Research Project: Children, Young People and the Changing Media Environment.* London: London School of Economics and Political Science.

McFarlane, A., Sparrowhawk, A. and Heald, Y. (2002) *Report on the Educational Use of Games.* TEEM (Teachers Evaluating Educational Multimedia): www.teem.org.uk/

Marsh, J. (2004) The techno-literacy practices of young children, *Journal of Early Childhood Research,* 2(1): 51–66.

Marsh, J. (2006) Emergent media literacy: digital animation in early childhood, *Language and Education,* 20(6): 493–506.

Marsh, J. (2008) Out-of-school play in online virtual worlds and the implications for literacy learning. Paper presented at the TACTYC Research Symposium on Play, Leeds Metropolitan University, April.

Marsh, J. and Bearne, E. (2008) *Moving Literacy On: Evaluation of the BFI Lead Practitioner Scheme for Moving Image Education.* Leicester: United Kingdom Literacy Association (UKLA).

Marsh, J., Brooks, G., Hughes, J., Ritchie, L. and Roberts, S. (2005) *Digital Beginnings: Young Children's Use of Popular Culture, Media and New Technologies.* Sheffield: University of Sheffield. Available at: http://www.digitalbeginings.shef.ac.uk/

Miller, P. and Rose, N. (1997) Mobilising the consumer: assembling the subject of consumption, *Theory, Culture and Society,* 14(1): 1–36.

Mills, M. (2000) Shaping the boys' agenda: the backlash blockbusters. Paper presented at ECER Annual Conference, Edinburgh, September.

Paechter, C.F. (2003) Masculinities and femininities as communities of practice, *Women's Studies International Forum*, 26(1): 69–77.

PISA (2006) *Science Competencies for Tomorrow's World.* Available at: http://www.pisa.oecd.org/document/2/0,3343,en_32252351_32236191_39718850_1_1_1_1,00.html (accessed 08/08).

Plowman, L., McPake, J. and Stephen, C. (2007) Supporting young children's learning with technology at home and in preschool. Paper presented at the American Educational Research Association Conference, Chicago, April.

Skelton, C. and Francis, B. (2003) *Boys and Girls in the Primary Classroom.* Buckingham: Open University Press.

Valentine, G., Marsh, J. and Pattie, C. (2005) *Children and Young People's Home Use of ICT for Educational Purposes: The Impact on Attainment at Key Stages 1–4.* London: HMSO.

Vasquez, V. (2004) *Negotiating Critical Literacies with Young Children.* Mahwah, NJ: Erlbaum.

15 Framing girls in girlhood studies: gender/class/ifications in contemporary feminist representations

Valerie Hey

Introduction: The Field of Girlhood Studies

Recent feminist texts on girls/girlhoods (Harris 2004; Aapola et al. 2005; Lloyd 2005), while recognizing the considerable gains made by (some) girls and young women, suggest that social transformation has reworked social relations, among them gender, in uneven and contradictory ways. The proliferation of debates and texts evidences a resilient new confidence in the academic field of girlhood studies, most notably marked in the arrival of the *International Journal of Girlhood Studies*, which formalizes the break from sub-cultural studies – a domain long governed by 'the lads' (McRobbie 1980).

The focus of this chapter is to consider how the knowledge claims of girlhood studies are made and the significance of the different conceptual capital supplied by cultural studies, gender and education and sociology to this.

Feminist Authority and Reflexivity in Girlhood Studies

The following is shaped around a discussion of Angela McRobbie's recent influential book *The Aftermath of Feminism: Gender, Culture and Social Change* (2009) (hereafter cited as *Aftermath*), in order first, to consider its substantive argument and second, to assert the political importance of how we source feminist authority and authorship. I am alternately inspired and disconcerted by this text, and I use other inspirational literature (Walkerdine et al. 2001; Lucey et al. 2003) to think why this is so.

All texts (seek to) secure knowledge/power effects and perhaps none more so than those which contest normative ideas about femininity, class, sexuality and gender. The naming of the 'heterosexual matrix' (Butler 1990) has had an especially creative intellectual and methodological effect. My reading of *Aftermath*'s analysis of the creation of the cultural politics of post-feminism, leads me to wonder if there is not an equivalent 'bourgeois matrix' at work? By analogy, I speculate about the operation of symbolic and unconscious forces (as Butler and Bourdieu assert) working under cover of its author's ostensible social critique, to craft a specifically invested version of the feminist 'real'? Put more starkly, is there a natural tendency to make the girls we study in girlhood studies into an imaginary of ourselves? If so, how do we ensure that our strong decentring of gender is applied also to class, and for that matter to all such other relevant differences? There are some strong precedents of decentring in the domain of gender and education discourse which offer a dual, if difficult, commitment both to record the persistence, as well as the necessary undoing, of norms (Walkerdine et al. 2001; Lucey et al. 2003; Rasmussen 2006; Youdell 2006). Paechter's (2003, 2006) work on the body for example, stipulates the material as well as ideological circumstances needed for non-normative performances in classrooms and playgrounds. This complicated double move retains the exciting focus on agency in cultural studies approaches, but remains aware of structural constraints.

The Discourse of Reflexive Modernity

Western femininities are, as *Aftermath* describes, produced in a new global order so that girls and young women may be simultaneously spatially and culturally remote but intimately tied together through the economic relations of the consumer market in cultural commodities. One dominant vocabulary has theorized these transformative processes using concepts such as reflexive modernization, risk and the project of the self (Beck et al. 1994) to reflect how these global economic, technological, cultural and social forces shape the social and cultural realities of the everyday.

Different national regimes respond to these changed post-industrial circumstances, by shaping and resourcing how populations, for our focus, girls and young women, are addressed in policy and practice. In Anglophone countries, influenced by the ideas of neo-liberalism and the dynamics of a globalized market economy, the narrative of aspiration and choice is dominant. Indeed, within the political regime of New Labour,[1] the aspirational girl serves as an exemplary political subject. This is not accidental (Bradford and Hey 2007), since this recalibration sought to distance the party from its trade union, largely male, militant, working-class legacy.

Beck's (1994) notion of 'detraditionalization' accounts for how class as a collective basis for identity has (allegedly) given way to the 'project of the self', an idea that is ideologically aligned with a focus on 'homo economicus,' the entrepreneurial figure viewed as central to recent UK government policy making. According to Beck and Beck-Gernsheim (2002: 42) the contemporary is therefore the site for the emergence of risk and precariousness structured by 'the compulsion and the pleasure of leading an insecure life of one's own [that demands] co-ordinating it with the distinctive lives of other people'.

There are 'wise' and 'unwise' choosers in the risky deciding of a life course. The wise are those committed to succeeding in higher education and advanced training so as to be fit for the ever-changing employment market. The unwise are those displaying insufficient fortitude and moral purpose (Sayer 2005). Class in this discourse is seen as a 'zombic category' (Beck 1999). Yet, while acknowledging that the opening-up of educational and employment opportunities to girls and young women has been a considerable success (Arnot et al. 1999), feminist authors also illustrate the 'messier' affective aspects, even of successful transformation (Walkerdine 2003; Lucey et al. 2003). They cast a more equivocal light on late modernity by gendering the analysis and acknowledging girls' and young women's conflicted circumstances, not least their having to confront less transformed spaces such as the more intractable (hetero) sexual division of labour.

Below, I describe one key feature of McRobbie's argument – what she calls 'the post-feminist masquerade' – since this acts as an important and sustained gendered analysis, rewriting the cultural sociology of late modernity, along similar critical lines, not least in unearthing the psycho-social contradictions which emerge when young women 'succeed'. I look *at*, rather than *through*, her 'optic[s] of power' (Ball 2008: 651). To do so, I line up research framed by gender and education discourses against it, to suggest some methodological penalties of how and where she places 'successful' subjects in the frame of certain arguments.

Top Girls in the Spotlight: McRobbie's Post-feminist Masquerade

McRobbie locates her argument in relation to numerous cultural and economic transformations. She cites the specific importance of New Labour's discourse of meritocracy in that it simultaneously brings forth girls and women but only by ensuring that feminism 'fades away'. Thus female subjects are made visible through their successful transit (or not) into the education and the labour market. She uses the Deleuzian appropriation of the concept of 'luminosity' to present four specific *forms of attention* (2009: 58–9) through which girls are now routinely made legible and hence governed. These she argues are first, 'the fashion and beauty complex' from 'within which emerges a post-feminist masquerade' (2009: 59) this refers to a specific consumerist shaping of feminine agency to form the terms of a 'new sexual contract' (2009: 9). Second, there is the luminous space of education 'within which is the figure of the working girl' (2009: 59); third, there is the space of sexuality, fertility and reproduction from which emerges the 'phallic girl' (2009: 7). Fourth, is the space of globalization and 'the production of commercial femininities in the developing world' (2009: 59).

This is clearly a hermeneutic, rather than empirical, exercise. Yet, her discourse engages the sociological imagination precisely because it can be so theoretically expansive, by not being weighed down with the minutiae of empirical data. Having said this, tensions remain in working with this level of abstraction, even if, in this case, they are minted by feminism. I turn my own critical light on the *post-feminist masquerade* (McRobbie 2009: 7) not only because it is so central to her thesis but because it also condenses a form of argument *about* the fate of feminism and has implications within, as well as beyond, the field of girlhood studies.

Trading Places: The Mask of Femininity for Feminism Undone?

McRobbie is extremely percipient in her eclectic analysis of gender, weaving a sophisticated form of psycho-social post-structuralist argument influenced by Lacanian and post-Lacanian concepts. The analytic vocabulary drawn from a Deleuze's retheorization of power as a 'luminosity' (Deleuze 1986), is put in touch with Butler's (1990, 1994) idea of 'the phallic girl' and 'heterosexual melancholia'. It is only possible to hint at the richness of McRobbie's recontextualization of such dense theoretical literature by way of an unavoidably reductive summary.

She regrets that while young women achieve 'success', they only do so by reinvigorating a form of femininity and body stylization that conforms to the strictures of masculine codes of 'hyper-sexy' attractiveness. She suggests that it is the psychic threat of masculine punishment held over all girls who 'want too much', that leads successful girls to collude with their self-presentation in the 'masquerade'. This response endorses the fashion and beauty complex, at the same time it works as a displaced form or 'illegible' rage and aggression. Hence young women's investment in perfectibility carries the psychic charge of a fatal disavowal – of a collective voice – which would have allowed young women to 'fight back'. Their repudiation of feminism entails the unacknowledged but *felt* loss of female-centric love, resistance and sociality. Using Butler's (1997) ideas about an ungrievable loss, premised on the taboo against homosexuality instated prior to the incest taboo (Butler 1990; Hey 2006), a post-feminist melancholia ensues. The cost for succeeding via this route is lived as the reprimand of *self*-punishment. She locates the occurrence of anorexia, alcoholic hedonism and other destructive forms of self-inflicted and self-medicating harms, as a consequential post-feminist psycho-social plaint (see also Rich and Evans 2009).

While recognizing the considerable brilliance and force of this thesis, I am interested here in the ways in which girls and young women are made non-intelligible in the problematic of the post-feminist masquerade. I consider them as literally and metaphorically in the discursive shadows of McRobbie's *Aftermath* problematic. Ironically, they are kept in the dark (and out of feminism?) by the adoption of the Deleuzian idea of 'luminosities'.

Losing the Connection? Girls and Class in Girlhood Studies

Scott Lash also asks about those left outside the new social and economic order defined by the reflexive modernity thesis – who he calls 'the reflexivity losers' (1994: 120). These are those unlikely to be in a position to take advantage of globalization through acquiring the advanced professional or high-tech skills. He refers specifically to those whose unskilled prospects are confined in 'the new post-Fordist creation of junk jobs' by inference the low-paid service sector – the type of work pulled into the deindustrialized geographies outside the metropolitan centres. By analogy do working-class and marginal girls figure in this feminist text? Are they cast as the walk-on parts, the extras in the drama of post-feminism now that feminism is itself thought of as a 'zombie' category?

Reading Against the 'Post-feminist Masquerade'

In a recent book on girls' social worlds, Aapola et al. (2005) noted the prevalence of two popular discourses; 'girl power' and 'girl-crisis' as current attempts to 'fix' feminine identity positions. Such 'sound-bites', like 'the mean girl' discourse commented upon by Ringrose (2006), reflect a process of individualization that displaces a more complex reading of gender and class. Critical feminist accounts like *Aftermath* offer a necessary counter-discourse, one that is supported by other feminist commentaries, pointing up middle-class girls' lack of a sense of control and well-being in their pursuit of perfection and the compulsion to appear as 'girl-powerful' (see Allan, Cullen, Francis, this collection).

But more to the point for my ensuing discussion, the discourse on 'Alpha Girls' leaves in its wake, the many unremarkable young women and girls, who can make *no* claims in the new sexual contact but who enter into an entirely different contract (often with the state), positioned as its 'abject' suspect other (Tyler 2008). Indeed, to be a young White working-class woman defined through the stigmatizing discourses of failure such as 'teenage motherhood' (being unemployed, or out of education), risks social death. In the newly configured post-welfare state, this female subject bears the weight of a moralizing of poverty which renders them as wanton bodies, possessing an inherent 'fecklessness'. This stigma has long worked as an historic signifier of working-class femininity (Skeggs 2004).

Hyper-femininity *used* to be the analytic code which defined an earlier generation of working-class girls who 'went wrong' (McRobbie 1978). Yet the hyper-femininity or immaculately groomed hetero-femininity now remarked upon in *Aftermath*, has become the propertized middle-class cultural and symbolic capital used to mark distinction against the bodies of White working- and lower middle-class women (see McRobbie 2009).

It seems to me, any feminist account treading into this visceral territory of how the social now works as cultural (Skeggs 2004) has to be acutely mindful of the need to keep the material and cultural aspects of differ-ence (class and gender) articulated. Or, put another way, is the emphasis on the middle-class girls of the post-feminist masquerade in danger of over-interpreting a form of psycho-social 'self-beratement' as oppression? Can a stress on the *personal* costs of succeeding in a middle-class gender order obscure what this practice *socially* inflicts on working-class and poor young women who *cannot* secure legitimate recognition in this cultural economy of class? I am not reading McRobbie as saying this post-feminist masquerade functions *only* at the level of individual trauma. On the con-trary, her psycho-social analysis positions successful young women as the bearers of a repudiated feminism – which like them is seen as undone.

From Ethnography to Metaphor as Signifiers of Social Transformation

Crucially, it is because girlhood studies have been built in part on exam-ining girls' lived cultures, that it tells an embodied story about sociality and feminine difference. This is in sharp contrast to the disembodied 'big picture' thinking so often associated with the male-stream sociology briefly referenced previously. This has led some commentators to explore how the affective states of female homo-sociality confront and reshape the new economic order (Hey 2002, 2005; McLeod 2002; Nayak and Kehily 2006). While it is important to consider the affects of a reorganized heterosexuality, some of the most powerful cultural co-ordinates of (female) individualization continue to be lived *between* girls and young women in the forms of feminine forms of friendship and class and gendered antagonism (Hey 2006) and what I have called 'the *sociality* of subjectification'.

One significant danger of reading off the psychic from (and in) the social in conditions of individualization is that a new type of (post-feminist) 'functionalism' is installed, aided and abetted with a proliferation of 'therapeutic' discourses which can universalize the psychological subject. In *Aftermath* the logic of the discussion of the post-feminist masquerade privileges heterosexuality as the signifier of young successful women's bodies as well as serving to signify the site of their defeat. Class becomes signified on White working-class older women's bodies as the site of their shame and their re-education. McRobbie's chapter on the symbolic violence of post-feminism offers a powerful class critique of the way working-class and lower middle-class women are represented on television. Yet, one effect is that social difference is dispersed across rather than intersected *within* sites. Does this division of attention in the text between predominantly young middle-class women as occupants of the post-feminist masquerade and older working-class women as the objects of the 'makeover show' mimic rather than fully confront the individualization thesis? Does it pull apart how gender and class are intersected? Does the focus on the media and consumption in the text, rather than on education, where class work is institutionalized and thus more congealed (as well as crafted in the 'cultural'), close down opportunities for a deeper analysis of state power?

Educational studies have shown in practices such as testing, setting and the parental manipulation of the market, just how relentless the exercise of class power is (Reay and Wiliam 1999; Reay et al. 2005). The masquerade may hold the psychic distress of loss for some privileged young women but what happens to those other losers? While a recognition of the painful contradictions of the apparent 'reflexivity winners' complicates a reading of success, not least by gendering the practices of social mobility, it can also distract us from acknowledging the significant systematic class inequities that remain (Cruddas and Haddock 2001; Walkerdine et al. 2001; Osler and Vincent 2003; Reay 2005). The 'can do girl' focus may then snag the analytic thread of classing femininity and gendering class. What may ensue is a tendency for the analysis to be 'sectional' rather than 'intersectional' and a collapsing *into* the individualization thesis rather providing a critical commentary about it. While McRobbie's insights confirm recent findings about the increasing numbers of middle-class girls presenting with the psycho-pathologies of self-harm (Rich and Evans 2009), this may need putting alongside those 'others/bodies' which, far from being able to somatize their illegible rage, are read in terms of an entirely different code, and pathologized rather than psycho-pathologized.

If *Aftermath* suggests that it is middle-class girls' self-regulation which emerges to reconcile them to the punitive destiny of 'fitting in', in contrast, Jones (2006) argues that working-class and Black girls are subjected to a form of external authority that often sees them as disruptive and disturbing rather than disturbed. In this scenario where bodily performances are disqualified as 'unladylike' and all 'too loud', a form of chastisement reminds working-class and Black girls that *they do not 'fit in'* (Jones 2006). Skeggs (2004) points out that the present conventional cultural devaluation of the working class makes it unnecessary for dominant classes to articulate *conscious* disdain and I would suggest that no matter which cultural circumstance prevails – authoritative rebuke or those of generalized unspoken class contempt, it is as impossible for working-class girls to live without resisting this 'pathology', as it is for middle-class girls to live without consequence in the 'masquerade'. The two groups, however, have different routes to agency, which may be taken as evidence of either 'bad ass attitude', 'disaffection' or 'lack of aspiration' or 'psycho-somatic' disorders – there are any number of classed as well as gendered deficit discourses.

Too Much Front: Working-class Girls as Subjects of Attention

If you reverse the logic of the psycho-social order of *Aftermath*, what you may consider is that subordinated groups, bearing the brunt of a disrespect discourse, might actually be *better* at protecting their mental health by *refusing* to turn in on and govern themselves. This does not mean that being insulted by the affects of cultural disdain is not felt, more that it promotes in some girls an 'anti-social' resistance – one, that if it is not collective, is at least turned outwards towards possibly offending others, rather than inwards and towards berating the self.

Because working-class agency has not been (as) historically aligned with the expression of bourgeois ideals of possessive individualism, it may be less prone to *internalize* rage (Connolly 1998; Reay 2001; Francis 2005; Jones 2006; Evans 2008). Disengagement or dissent may be seen as a serviceable social logic, at least in creating a space for a defensive perilous ambiguous autonomy, one that also might make ground for expressing alternative commitments to family and household (Hollway and Jefferson 2000; Hey 2005; Evans 2008).

Not all girls are moved by the appeals of 'getting on' and 'getting out' (Lucey et al. 2003; Macdonald et al. 2005). Some cannot envisage themselves as doing so and act less in defiance of these regulatory ideals as in pursuit of alternative more realizable ones. They may also be compelled through exclusion to make up an improvised style that is anti-aspiration – a refusal, not 'being bothered' (Harris 2004). This might not be the ground for the type of politics making for the longed-for working-class revolution, but neither is it the same formation as a feminism unravelled on the basis of an individualistic identification with self-advancement.

Coda: Gender, Class and Disappointment – Aspects of the Psychic Economy of Girlhood Studies

Critical feminist discourses of girls and young women are sites that can make certain subjects appear or disappear. They also explicitly and implicitly serve at times as metaphors of our own affective 'passionate attachment' (Butler 1997: 7), in this case about how our ideas work as expressions of ourselves. Do 'reflexivity winners' determined by the pursuit of success in meritocracy attract particular forms of sympathetic feminist identification? I note here how the crafting of an academic (feminist) identity bears an uncanny resemblance to that required by the 'reflexivity winners' (Hey 2003). Here is Mary Evans's (2004: 40) 'psycho-analysis' of academic complicity with audit culture:

> Given that Universities are supposed to contain the most astute and intelligent minds of their generation it is inevitable that questions should be asked about how this situation – of the double achievement of the devaluation and de-democratisation of higher education – should have come about. One awful possibility is that academics, ourselves the products of doing-well-in exams, could not resist the possibility of doing even more exams and tests and thus binding ourselves into an endless sado-masochistic tryst with the QAA, TQA and RAE assessors.

My point in connecting authors to their authority and then their texts is not to rebuke one specific academic feminist for being competitive, middle class or both – strictly speaking – we *all* fail that particular test. It is more to think about what always shadows our work, what Jane Miller (1995) usefully called 'the autobiography of the question'.

We need powerfully reflexive forms of analysis to navigate the past in building future political visions. We might in this process put our own projective fantasies under more pressure through acknowledging our investments in things that we wish feminism to be (again). One consequence of assuming feminism as a legacy (Adkins 2004), then locating an account around its failed reproduction, is that we can overlook what lies in the shadow of our own disappointment. We may write out those 'others' and fail to identify with a subject who never saw herself as 'having it all' in the first place. Does the problematic of *Aftermath* defer our having to re/think feminism itself, not least what might be at stake in holding onto feminism as a propertied reified 'thing', rather than being able to conceive of it anew in terms of a necessarily reformed politics in the new post-structural social (Adkins 2004)?

And finally, at a different level of granularity, but picking up on the more optimistic tone of McRobbie's final chapter, I pose some empirical questions back to girlhood studies scholars and educators:

- How do we as educators create socialities that better prepare all girls and young women for the psychic economy of living individualization?
- Do particular socialities offer better psychological resources for managing both aspiration and its disappointment? Are they good at making for the *shared* conditions of resilience?
- Do they open up discursive agency and make different discourses available that question the prevailing terms of individualization?

In sum, what would it mean as teachers, academics, youth workers to construct a pedagogical discourse capable of respecting the autonomy of girls' and young women's social relations while simultaneously providing resources to think with and against their limits? What form of the discussion of girls and young women would avoid the perhaps too easy temptation to give in to our own version of feminist melancholia – a disappointment, about a 'daughter gone to bad', of a feminism 'betrayed'?

Note

1. This is the newly branded Labour Party that was created to break the political hold of Thatcherism and the Radical Right which had governed Britain 1979–1997. In 1997 New Labour came to power in a landslide victory.

References

Aapola, S., Gonick, M. and Harris, A. (2005) *Young Femininity: Girlhood, Power and Social Change.* Basingstoke: Palgrave Macmillan.
Adkins, L. (2004) Passing on feminism: from consciousness to reflexivity? *European Journal of Women's Studies*, 11(4): 427–44.

Arnot, M., David, M. and Weiner, G. (1999) *Closing the Gap: Postwar Education and Social Change*. Cambridge: Polity Press.

Ball, S.J. (2008) Some sociologies of education: a history of problems and places, and segments and gazes, *The Sociological Review*, 56(4): 650–69.

Beck, U., Giddens, A., and Lash, S. 1994 *Reflexive Modernization: Politics, tradition and aesthetics in the modern social order*. Cambridge: Polity Press.

Beck, U. (1999) *World Risk Society*. Cambridge: Polity Press.

Beck, U. and Beck-Gernsheim, E. (2002) *Individualization: Institutionalized Individualism and its Social and Political Consequences*. London: Sage.

Bradford, S. and Hey, V. (2007) Successful subjectivities? The successification of class, ethnic and gender positions, *Journal of Education Policy*, 22(6): 595–614.

Butler, J. (1990) *Gender Trouble: Feminism and the Subversion of Identity*. London: Routledge.

Butler, J. (1994) Gender as performance: an interview with Judith Butler, by P. Osborne and L. Segal, *Radical Philosophy*, 67: 32–9.

Butler, J. (1997) *The Psychic Life of Power*. Stanford, CA: Stanford University Press.

Connolly, P. (1998) *Racism, Gendered Identity and Young Children*. London: Routledge.

Cruddas, L. and Haddock, L. (2001) *Girls Voices, Are They on the Agenda?* London: Newham Special Needs Service.

Deleuze, G. (1986) *Foucault*. Minneapolis, MN: University of Minneapolis Press.

Evans, M. (2004) *Killing Thinking: The Death of the Universities*. London: Continuum.

Evans, S. (2008) Becoming Somebody: Higher Education and the Aspiration of Working-class Girls. Unpublished PhD thesis, University of Kent.

Francis, B. (2005) Not/knowing their place: girls' classroom behaviour, in G. Lloyd (ed.), *Problem Girls: Understanding and Supporting Troubled and Troublesome Young Women*. London: Routledge.

Harris, A. (2004) *All About the Girl: Culture, Power and Identity*. London: Routledge.

Hey, V. (2002) Horizontal solidarities and molten capitalism: the subject, intersubjectivity and the other of late modernity, *Discourse: Studies in the Cultural Politics of Education*, 23(2): 227–41.

Hey, V. (2003) Joining the Club: academia and working class femininities, *Gender and Education*, 15(2): 319–35.

Hey, V. (2005) The contrasting social logics of sociality and survival: cultures of classed be/longing in late modernity, *Sociology*, 39(5): 855–72.

Hey, V. (2006) The politics of performative resignification: translating Judith Butler's theoretical discourse and its potential for a sociology of education, *British Journal of Sociology of Education*, 27(spl. suppl., 4): 439–57.

Hollway, W. and Jefferson, T. (2000) *Doing Qualitative Research Differently: Free Association, Narrative and the Interview Method.* London: Sage.

Jones, S. (2006) Language with an attitude: white girls performing class, *Language Arts*, 114–23.

Lash, S. (1994) Reflexivity and its doubles; structure, aesthetics, community, in U. Beck, A. Giddens and S. Lash (eds), *Reflexive Modernisation, Politics, Tradition and Aesthetics in the Modern Social Order.* Cambridge: Polity.

Lloyd, G. (ed.) (2005) *Problem Girls Understanding and Supporting Troubled and Troublesome Young Women.* London: Routledge.

Lucey, H., Walkerdine, V. and Melody, J. (2003) Uneasy Hybrids, *Gender and Education*, 15(3): 238–51.

Macdonald, R., Shildrick, T., Webster, C and Simpson, D. (2005) Growing up in poor neighbourhoods: the significance of class and place in the extended transitions of 'Socially Excluded' young adults, *Sociology*, 39(5): 873–91.

McLeod, J. (2002) Working out intimacy: young people and friendship in an age of reflexivity, *Discourse: Studies in the Cultural Politics of Education*, 23(2): 211–26.

McRobbie, A. (1978) Working class girls and the cultures of femininity, in Women's Studies Group (ed.), *Women Take Issue: Aspects of Women's Subordination.* London: Hutchinson.

McRobbie, A. (1980) Settling accounts with subcultures: a feminist critique, *Screen Education*, 34: 37–49.

McRobbie, A. (2009) *The Aftermath of Feminism: Gender, Culture and Social Change.* London: Sage.

Miller, J. (1995) Trick or treat? The autobiography of the question, *English Quarterly*, 27(3): 22–6.

Nayak, A. and Kehily, M. (2006) Gender undone; subversion, regulation and embodiment in the work of Judith Butler, *British Journal of Sociology of Education*, 27(4): 459–72.

Osler, A. and Vincent, K. (2003) *Girls and Exclusion: Rethinking the Agenda.* London: Routledge.

Paechter, C. (2003) Power, bodies and identity: how different forms of physical education construct varying masculinities and femininities in secondary schools, *Sex Education*, 3(1): 47–59.

Paechter, C. (2006) Masculine femininities/female masculinities: power, identities and gender, *Gender and Education*, 18(3): 253–63.

Rasmussen, M. (2006) Play school, melancholia, and the politics of recognition, *British Journal of Sociology of Education*, 27(4): 473–87.

Reay, D. (2001) 'Spice girls', 'nice girls', 'girlies' and 'tomboys' gender discourses, girls cultures and femininities in a primary classroom, *Gender and Education*, 13(2): 153–66.

Reay, D. (2005) Beyond consciousness? The psychic landscape of social class, *Sociology*, (39)5: 911–28.

Reay, D. and Wiliam, D. (1999) 'I'll be a nothing': structure, agency and the construction of identity through assessment, *British Education Research Journal*, 25(3): 343–54.

Reay, D., David, M.E. and Ball, S. (2005) *Degrees of Choice: Social Class, Race and Gender in Higher Education*. Stoke: Trentham Books.

Rich, E. and Evans, J. (2009) Now I am NoBody, see me for who I am: the paradox of performativity, *Gender and Education*, 21(1): 1–16.

Ringrose, J. (2006) A new universal mean girl: examining the discursive construction and social regulation of a new feminine pathology, *Feminism & Psychology*, 16(4): 405–24.

Sayer, A. (2005) *The Moral Significance of Class*. Cambridge: Cambridge University Press.

Skeggs, B. (2004) *Class, Self, Culture*. London: Routledge.

Tyler, I. (2008) Chav mum chav scum, *Feminist Media Studies*, 8(1): 17–34.

Walkerdine, V., Lucey, H. and Melody, J. (2001) *Growing Up Girl: Psychosocial Explorations of Gender and Class*. Basingstoke: Palgrave.

Walkerdine, V. (2003) Reclassifying upward mobility: femininity and the neo-liberal subject, *Gender and Education*, 15(3): 238–48.

Youdell, D. (2006) Subjectivation and performative politics – Butler thinking Althusser and Foucault: intelligibility, agency and the raced-national-religioned subjects of education, *British Journal of Sociology of Education*, Special Issue Troubling identities; reflections on Judith Butler's philosophy for the sociology of education, 27(4): 511–28.

Index

UNDERSTANDING GIRLS' FRIENDSHIPS, FIGHTS AND FEUDS

A Practical Approach to Girls' Bullying

Val Besag

Girls' bullying is more subtle and less physical than that perpetrated by boys; however, it can be just as powerful, and the emotional repercussions of bullying among girls can be more destructive and longer lasting than the effects of more obvious forms of bullying. Teachers report that quarrels between girls are far more time-consuming and difficult to resolve than the disputes of boys, yet not enough information is available to guide them on dealing with girls' fighting and unhappiness caused by their relationships with other girls, many of whom may have been their closest friends.

The book offers detailed practical advice for dealing with girls' bullying, which will help both students and teachers to understand and combat different kinds of bullying, as well as comprehensive guidance for preventing or reducing bullying activities among girls, including:

- Whole school approaches
- Programmes for developing emotional literacy and resilience
- Approaches for dealing with gangs
- Using methods such as art and drama
- Developing conflict resolution skills
- Student – parent programmes
- Peer support programmes

Contents: *Acknowledgements - Preface - Section 1 Exploring the problem - She's my best friend, but I hate her! - The activity club - Section 2 Gender differences in children's social behaviour - The power of the peer group: Affiliation and differentiation - Toys for boys: Gossip for girls? - Girls cooperate - but boys compete? - When things go sour - Bullying - Mirror, mirror on the wall: Cruel comparisons - Section 3 Groups - Cliques, groups and gangs - Dyads, triads and lover's quarrels - Little miss popular - Madam machiavelli - Section 4 The language of conflict - The language of conflict - Grassing - Insult - Gossip and rumour - Section 5 Emotional issues - The more deadly of the species? - The green eyed god - Section 6 Case studies - Case studies - Section 7 Remediation, reparation and resolution - Strategies for supporting individual girls - What can the school do? - References.*

2006   217pp

978-0-335-21982-7 (Paperback)   978-0-335-21983-4 (Hardback)

LADS AND LADETTES IN SCHOOL

Carolyn Jackson

FIRST PRIZE WINNER of the SOCIETY FOR EDUCATIONAL STUDIES book award 2006

"I would [therefore] urge everyone concerned with what is happening in schools to read this book, with its fascinating data and nuanced arguments."
Heather Mendick, London Metropolitan University - Review in British Journal of Educational Studies

This innovative book looks at how and why girls and boys adopt 'laddish' behaviours in schools. It examines the ways in which students negotiate pressures to be popular and 'cool' in school alongside pressures to perform academically. It also deals with the fears of academic and social failure that influence pupils' school lives and experiences.

Drawing extensively on the voices of students in secondary schools, it explores key questions about laddish behaviours, such as:

- Are girls becoming more laddish – and if so, which girls?
- Do boys and girls have distinctive versions of laddishness?
- What motivates laddish behaviours?
- What are the consequences of laddish behaviours for pupils?
- What are the implications for teachers and schools?

This topical book is key reading for students, academics and researchers in education, sociology and psychology, as well as school teachers and education policy maker

Contents: *Introduction - 'Don't revise, and be a bit bad, that's more popular': Social motives for 'laddishness' - 'I don't want them to think I'm thick': Academic motives for 'laddishness' - Combining insights to understand 'laddishness': Integrating theories about social and academic motives - 'I don't like failure. I want to get good levels.' Testing times: Academic pressures and fears in school - 'If you work hard in school you're a geek': Exploring the 'uncool to work' discourse - Fibs and fabrications: Strategies to avoid looking 'stupid' or 'swotty' - Balancing acts: Who can balance the books and a social life, and how? - 'If I knew how to tackle "laddishness" I'd bottle it, sell it, and make a fortune': Implications for teachers, schools and policy makers – Conclusion – Notes – Appendices - References*

2006   186pp

978-0-335-21770-0 (Paperback)   978-0-335-21771-7 (Hardback)